Psychoanalysis and Fiction

PSYCHOANALYSIS AND FICTION

AN EXPLORATION OF LITERARY AND PSYCHOANALYTIC BORDERS

DANIEL GUNN

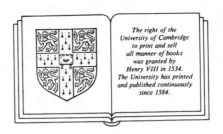

The right of the
University of Cambridge
to print and sell
all manner of books
was granted by
Henry VIII in 1534.
The University has printed
and published continuously
since 1584.

CAMBRIDGE UNIVERSITY PRESS
Cambridge
New York   New Rochelle   Melbourne   Sydney

Published by the Press Syndicate of the University of Cambridge
The Pitt Building, Trumpington Street, Cambridge CB2 1RP
32 East 57th Street, New York, NY 10022, USA
10 Stamford Road, Oakleigh, Melbourne 3166, Australia

First published 1988

Printed in Great Britain at the University Press, Cambridge

British Library cataloguing in publication data
Gunn, Daniel
Psychoanalysis and fiction: an exploration
of literary and psychoanalytic borders.
1. Psychoanalysis and literature
2. Literature – History and criticism
1. Title
801'.92   PN56.P92

Library of Congress cataloguing in publication data
Gunn, Daniel.
Psychoanalysis and fiction.
Bibliography.
Includes index.
1. Psychoanalysis and literature.   1. Title.
PN98.P75G86   1988   809'.93353   87-25589

ISBN 0 521 35068 9

VN

TO MY MOTHER

Contents

Preface

TALK of borders, such as those invoked in my title between psychoanalysis and literature, may tend to suggest something hard-and-fast, firmly demarcated – fences or enclosures. I hope it may also suggest something rather more uncertain, such as the limits or frontiers tentatively drawn at the end of an exploratory journey. For what the present work is largely about is the way in which two areas interact and overlap, and therefore just how fragile and mutable are the borders drawn between them. In the course of this book I shall, like an explorer, be visiting and revisiting the borderland between two terrains, with, I hope, some of the sense of uncertainty and adventure which goes with exploring. By this I do not wish to imply that there is any shortage of books on psychoanalysis and fiction. From Freud's time onwards, the two have of course often been yoked, sometimes forcibly, together. Rather I'd suggest here (and the suggestion is implicit in the rest of the work) that many of these yokings, in seeking boldly to demarcate areas, have covertly – where not explicitly – privileged one area over the other. Psychoanalysis has been revealed as the key to unlock literary secrets; or as having its insights already contained by literature. Behind the attempt to draw borders there has often lurked a rivalry, or indeed a colonising urge.

Quite how I have tried to avoid falling prey to such an urge – my own strategy as an explorer – will only become truly apparent in the detailed workings of my arguments (for such urges cannot be simply wished away). Nevertheless, it may be appropriate here to declare a commitment: to the belief that both areas, both practices, both discourses, literary and psychoanalytic, open possibilities of creativity; open vital, valid, mutually unexclusive ways of finding form for powerful, often troubling need or desire.

If the commitment does not make the task of arguing any easier, it can nonetheless give a lead as to the way my arguments will characteristically be developed and pursued. I shall, I have suggested, be involved more in exploration than in exposition or explanation. Explorers do not always move in straight lines. I shall sometimes, in pursuing a certain writer or text or preoccupation, step off my main track, loop and double back. Each chapter comprises several sub-sections (denoted by the sign §), which are intended to give time to pause. These pauses may also on occasion offer the chance of striking out down a new path. There will be no strict linearity of movement, yet there will be a decided tendency: to move in the direction of example-to-theory, concrete-to-abstract, text-to-idea. While moving in this way, I shall require recognition of many unfamiliar points of similarity and contrast between my two chosen areas. Words and discourses, speakers and writers from different eras, cultures and languages will be juxtaposed and interwoven. Poetry, drama and prose (narrative, descriptive and analytic) will be configured. Writings of great sophistication and beauty will be placed alongside the impetuous utterances of disturbed children and adolescents. The method of procedure will be that which is sometimes called 'eclectic'. By this I want to imply, again, that the boundaries used to divide areas, eras, authors and genres, and hive them off from one other, are not so firm as they are often assumed to be.

One consequence of this eclecticism will be, I suspect, that the reader will sometimes be prompted to ask: if 'X', then why not 'Y'? If Beckett, for example, then why not Joyce? Why Sophocles and not Aeschylus? Why Proust and not Flaubert? Or, in the psychoanalytic domain, if Maud Mannoni then why not her husband Octave? If Winnicott, why not Klein? More generally, if so much French, why not more English, or German – or Japanese for that matter? I have no short answer to these questions. I have an answer which may appear to surrender hostages to fortune, but which at least has the merit of frankness (and may be as true for most works as for this): it is that 'X' seemed interesting, engaging and relevant enough for me not to have a chance to consider 'Y' (if indeed I was aware of his or her or its existence or importance). The present book, to be clear, does not pretend towards inclusiveness or exhaustiveness. It is not a survey. It is a personal attempt to bring together certain writers in such a way as to allow them fruitfully to mingle and interact. Of course it would be disingenuous to claim that these writers do not form or adhere to some sort of a canon. And it is hoped that this canon will include enough familiar figures for most readers to be able to follow the broader arguments without getting lost due to unfamiliarity with the examples. (Where lesser-known writers are discussed, I have tried to provide some background information and summaries of plots, etc.)

This is in fact one of the two other ways in which I could give some indications as to the orientation and procedure of this book – as it were from the (intended) reader's side. If what I say here grows out of overlapping areas, it is, equally, directed at those who presently occupy these areas. I hope this book will be accessible and of use to readers and students of literature, as well as to those working with or in psychoanalysis. Those interested in French will most obviously find work with which they are acquainted (Marcel Proust is a major topic of discussion). But with French as with German (in the cases of Freud or Kafka), Spanish (with J. L. Borges), Italian (with Dante), and Greek (with Homer), I have chosen to use English translations in quotations, and to refer wherever possible to English editions. Where the original seems particularly dense or crucial (most often in the case of poetry) I have included it within square brackets; and where a translation is not readily available, as is often the case with psychoanalytic writings, I have provided my own.

I mentioned *two* other ways in which I could begin to account for the drift of this book. If one was from the possible reader's side, the other would be from the writer's – this writer's, my own. It would be the account of the surges, lurches and sways of my own interests and passions over the last ten years, out of which my work has emerged. Naturally, I do not intend to weigh this book down or burden the reader with such an account. Nonetheless, I do want to request space and patience to thank some of those who have guided my movements over the years, and kept them on some sort of course. I am grateful to friends and teachers at the University of Sussex, to colleagues in the English department at the Ecole Normale Supérieure de Saint-Cloud, and indeed to all those who have befriended and supported me over the years. Among them, for guidance on the present work I particularly wish to thank Malcolm Bowie, Gianni Celati, Bruce Fink, Patrick Guyomard, Merrilyn Julian, Maud Mannoni, Lino Pertile, Jean-Michel Rabaté, Martin Roth and Kevin Taylor. I owe a great deal to Gabriel Josipovici, for his constant encouragement and example. And my greatest debt is to George Craig, for his unfailing ability to turn every movement – even lurching and swaying – into something meaningful and worthwhile.

Introduction

M ost people who have put pen to paper will agree that writing is not always an easy, or in any obvious sense a pleasurable activity. The biographies of the great writers of this century tend to bear this out. The subject matter of these writers' work bears the traces of it too. Everywhere one looks in fiction one seems to encounter forms of negativity, ranging from difficulty, through frustration and fixity, to downright impossibility. Yet the very difficulty of the activity of writing seems to have goaded writers on. This amounts to enough of a conundrum to lead me to suppose that there must be something – beyond what is described and beyond the immediate lack of gratification offered – which writing *permits*, or *enables*. A curiously similar conclusion might be deduced from a cursory look at psychoanalysis. The idea of giving up one's precious time to go to someone's office, and sit or lie, talking, once or several times a week, whether one feels the inclination or not; not just talking, but talking about difficulty, about the unresolved bits of one's self and past; and this to a largely silent listener, whom one has to pay for the privilege! It might be hard to imagine anyone doing this voluntarily.

In fact, in this word 'voluntarily' a question is begged. It may be that one turns to fiction, or to psychoanalysis, not entirely from self-willed motives, and that they may allow a possibility – a field to open, or a mobility to be achieved – which elsewhere in life is unavailable. In his fascinating book, *In Search of a Past*, oral historian Ronald Fraser tells of how he encountered the limits of his own preferred mode of investigation when he had to enquire into his own past. He went back to the manor house where he had been brought up, and interviewed the servants, maids and gardeners; formed a corporate picture of his origins, and of a world of money and privilege which seemed to disappear with the Second World War. But this alone was not enough. Faced with a mental anguish which seemed to have its roots in his childhood, and faced with the responsibility of caring for his moribund father, he found he had to enter psychoanalysis, and there retell his early years. 'I want to be the historian of my own history', he says

I

(p. 114). Psychoanalysis permits him to fill in some of the spaces left by the servants' accounts; fill them in with his own account of a past, based on his memories, but recounted – or discovered or invented – in the 'real' or present time of utterance in analysis. In the end, perhaps even analysis is not enough. For he also writes his book: his book which is both an oral history and a case history; which is, beyond that, a fiction of sorts, which subsumes both 'cases' and 'histories' – public and private – into a narrative to which he can put his name.

Why is this book of note here? The answer is threefold. It allows me to confirm that the reasons for entering the worlds of fiction and psychoanalysis do not always have much to do with choice. It makes clear that what may be 'got out of' them is not restricted to the possible negativity of their content. Finally, it offers an example of what I asserted in my preface – that the relation between psychoanalysis and fiction need not be one of rivalry or exclusiveness.[1]

In the title of the present book, the stressed word is perhaps the 'and'. In the course of my explorations, I shall encounter a broad range of apparent dualities, alternatives, or antinomies which will often turn out to be necessary paradoxes or complements. Psychoanalysis *and* fiction, as I wish my title to read; and as both may be – engrossed in negativity *and yet* dynamically enabling. Moreover, this conjunction is not the only important one in my choice of titles. For chapter 1 proposes 'Fathers and sons' – though this 'and' was a conjunction which was highly problematic for Franz Kafka, on whom this chapter focuses. His relations with his father were highly strained; his confidence in his own ability to become a father was almost non-existent. Where Kafka is concerned, the more appropriate configuration might be 'Fathers *or* sons'. For one could be one or the other; but the movement from one to the other was almost unimaginable. Kafka's work is the very epitome of the immobility and impossibility mentioned above. There are lots of examples of this impossibility; hundreds of ways of detailing and analysing the causes for them. Yet behind them all there lurks a single question – and it is one which has more often been ignored than addressed. It asks: if this is what Kafka's fiction describes, what does it actually achieve? The answer to the question will involve consideration of Kafka, of course. It will also include consideration of the part the reader may play in the processes of his fiction.

Introduction

At the very time Kafka was writing, Sigmund Freud was considering another set of alternatives – that between love and hate. He had already ascertained in his work with dreams that the unconscious bore no allegiance to the principle of selection – either/or – preferring the combination – and . . . and. In working with the 'Rat Man' he confirmed that the principle could also hold sway in the affective life. An individual might be capable of intense love *and* intense hate, directed at a single person or object, without these two affects cancelling each other out. Of course, this complex of feeling, which was termed 'ambivalence', is not the only or necessarily the most important duality in Freud's work. Nor is it necessarily most important in the present work. Where ambivalence is important, however, is in the way it yields a particularly well-focused example of the workings of an apparently non-logical complexity. And in addition to opening a way into an understanding of the structure of such a principle, it also gives some clues as to its genealogy.

It is in childhood, psychoanalysis suggests, that ambivalence is learned. Typically, the complex of feelings which constitute it has been seen to be one directed by children at parents. The two psychoanalysts, Serge Leclaire and Maud Mannoni, whose work I shall look at in some detail (in chapters 2 and 3), have added to this the consideration that parents may introduce their children to ambivalence, by directing its dual beam at them. I have noted that psychoanalysis may deal in negativity – in hate perhaps. In turn, it can also allow its patients to discover the opposite. In the analytic space, sustained by love (or 'transference'), the patient may be able to gain access to words and desires from which he or she had been debarred, and through desire, to desire's prime site, the body. If this is the case for the patient, is it the case for the analyst that the act of writing psychoanalytic texts opens a space which is somehow equivalent?

Through the work – the clinical practice and the writing – of Serge Leclaire and Maud Mannoni I shall try to develop a sense of the psychoanalytic space. I shall also, more indirectly, turn to the ideas of a more famous French analyst, Jacques Lacan. For Leclaire and Maud Mannoni are among the most renowned pupils of Lacan, and are sometime members of Lacan's Ecole freudienne de Paris. Part of their importance derives from the fact that they have revealed certain of the clinical implications of Lacan's work, and so have shown one of the fruitful ways in which the legacy of

Lacan can be picked up and developed.[2] Where the theoretical perspective of Lacan is concerned, the two areas – clinical practice and children – are of special interest and importance. The reason for this has partly to do with the way Lacan's ideas have been diffused and assimilated (particularly in Britain). I believe most readers will have some familiarity with Lacan, if only the name and the reputation. One of the things that is best known about him is that he was particularly concerned with language and its functioning. He is also known for his great fondness for speaking – very abstrusely – to a rarified, intellectually formidable audience. His theories, as a consequence, have often been seen to have more relevance to an elite, quintessentially adult, Parisian milieu (or to academics) than to the milieu more typical of British analysts and their clients. The work of Leclaire and Maud Mannoni helps to redress this tendency. For in it they show how Lacan's theories – his theories of language – can be of vital use when the analyst is confronted by intense need or desperate deprivation – by autistic or psychotic children, for example. They show the radical importance of language and utterance in what Freud's patient 'Anna O.' appropriately called the 'talking cure'.

My enquiry into clinical practice will at times take me some distance from literature. But as my attention will constantly be upon the possibilities language can open, my literary concerns will never disappear. (If from time to time I enlist aid from the work of Roland Barthes, it is partly because few have done more than he to show the ways in which various fields of enquiry overlap, and feed into each other.) In part II of the book, 'Play it again', literature is returned to directly, with the work of Marcel Proust and Samuel Beckett. Both writers seem, like Kafka, to be engrossed in variegations of doubt, immobility and obsessive repetition. Yet both allow a glimpse of the ways in which writing permits the opposite of what it declares. Proust's novel *A la recherche du temps perdu* may be a testament to failure and immobility (as I show in chapter 4). It may, conversely, be a monument of – and to – ambitious achievement. This is not a paradox to which readers will be indifferent. For at one time or another most readers will have felt daunted by the difficulty of Proust and the weight of his achievement. Proust manages to turn such difficulty and doubt into a cornerstone in his work. How exactly does he manage this? The attempt to answer this question will take me again towards a pair of apparent alternatives: between the 'I' which is telling his story, and the 'I' which is told: between the book being written and the one the narrator finds it impossible to write. I shall be led to the idea that these apparent alternatives compel a sort of re-writing, or re-reading, a form of repetition which is at the heart of the novel's structure. It is a repetition very different from the return of the past offered by the famous *madeleine*, or from the 'regaining' of the past which the final book of *A la recherche* proposes.

Repetition and return have been notions to the forefront of modern man's enquiries, as those familiar with Nietzsche or Kierkegaard will know. Freud also shared the preoccupation, and he seems never to have been quite certain if they were beneficent or malignant phenomena. As (in chapter 5) the ramifications of repetition are traced from the structure of Proust's novel through the local details of the narrative, it will be seen that such uncertainty may be appropriate, that apparent alternatives do again mask a latent complementarity. Marcel in love is a thoroughly repetitious business. Yet it is through monotonous repetition that a unique moment or person takes hold of him and the novel. In the case of Beckett, hardly a single of his works does not tell, more or less directly, of some form of insistent repetition. But are the repetitions debilitating or enabling? Is there repetition of that which is identical, or is there rather a highlighting of difference? What is the nature of the temporality involved in repetition? And does repetition point towards some original moment of unity or always towards division and loss?

I should note here that I have not attempted to write a book of theory, be that theory philosophical, literary, or psychoanalytic. Such questions as are asked, even when as general or abstract as those above, are thrown up by the texts themselves, or thrown up, as it may be, by psychoanalysis, with its theory of the repetition compulsion. Despite this, I shall have recourse (in chapter 6 and at other points where the occasion seems to require it) to certain writers who are more adept at abstraction than myself. These writers are among the major spokesmen on such issues as preoccupied Nietzsche and Kierkegaard, and they are the more worth mentioning here as they are not famed for their helpfulness. Of them, Jacques Derrida, to whom I refer, and with whom I briefly take issue, is the best known. Gilles Deleuze and Maurice Blanchot, on whom I lean more heavily, are gradually becoming known to the English-speaking public (the former is a versatile philosopher, the latter a perspicacious literary critic). Though I shall only have a chance to glance at certain of their formulations, it is hoped that this may be enough to indicate, to those who are not already convinced, how valuable the insights of these two writers are.

Yet if I have not written a book of theory it is not solely because of my disinclination to abstraction. It is also because answers will most often be sought in the workings of the texts which have been seen to beg the questions: the texts, for example, of Proust, Beckett, and Freud. In the case of all three I shall try to delve back towards the original moment mentioned above (and implied in the heading to chapter 6). I shall do so because they require it, the repetitions and ambivalence in their work appearing to present the moment as structurally and emotionally crucial. Lived most typically in infancy or childhood, in company with the mother, it is a moment which is so early in the history of the individual as to make itself felt as original (or originating). Its intensity and completeness may suggest that the rest of life and of love is some pale imitation or inadequate repetition of it. Anyone who has ever felt nostalgic will have had intimations of such a moment, such a beginning. Life tends to affirm that nostalgia is always for something that never really existed; that one's intimations are mere fantasy; that all one has ever known is division, ambivalence and repetition. But what of writing? What does literature say? More importantly, what does it *show*? The evidence of Proust, of Beckett, and of Freud will be closely sifted, in the attempt to provide some answers. If this means I end with the notion of beginning, this is not entirely inappropriate, as beginnings and endings constitute a pair of terms whose complementarity will have concerned me throughout.

I suggested at the beginning of this introduction that writing is not always an easy or obviously pleasurable activity. Writers, particularly in this century, have sometimes been seen as taking revenge on their readers by rendering that reading inordinately difficult. Certain of those considered here – Proust, Beckett, Lacan, Blanchot, to name a few – are famed for the problems they pose the reader: not just the ambitious reader who sets out to understand and explicate; but also the more modest reader who wants merely to read, to pass the eyes and attention over the words – beginning to end. However, I also suggested that steps into the worlds of fiction or of psychoanalysis may not necessarily be taken voluntarily. This is another way of saying that need, or urgent desire, has a place in these processes, and must have a place in an understanding of them. With strong desire, forms of resistance and difficulty nearly always go in tow. I hope that the reader will not have too many problems reading my own book – beginning to end. Yet I should not pretend that the obstacles facing the reader of writers such as Proust or Lacan are not real. The obstacles do not simply disappear once they have been addressed. Nevertheless, I hope that by the end of this book it will be clear why the obstacles and difficulties such writers pose may be justified, or even necessary. And I hope a sense will have emerged of how, by attempting to read, and in this way *share* these difficulties, one may in fact be resolving them – as far as is either desirable or possible.

Part I

A family affair

1 · *Fathers and sons*

§ 1.0

WRITING, it should be clear, depends upon a certain mobility: the mobility of the writer, who keeps moving a pen across the page or tapping fingers on the keys. Reading depends upon the corresponding mobility of the reader, who keeps his or her eyes scanning the lines and pages and chapters. As one develops one's sophistication in either of the two related skills one may tend to forget this dependence; indeed it may even be that for the duration of writing or reading one *needs* to forget it (movement, like falling asleep, becomes difficult when one starts to think about it too closely). Yet there are at least three reasons why it is important in the present context to recognise such fundamentals. Firstly, because the writer I wish to discuss in this chapter seems to require such a recognition (as do those I turn to later, in part II). Secondly, because in chapters 2 and 3 I shall be turning to the work of psychoanalysts, which involves many for whom such movements have either become impossible, or have never been possible. And thirdly, because the recognition may encourage more careful consideration of the larger and more accomplished sorts of movement that writing both enacts and enables . . . The hand keeps moving, the eye keeps roving. The form of writing we call 'literature', for its part, may (we say) 'move' us. It moves us not only in ways achieved by other sorts of writing – to sign a petition or join a club, remonstrate or demonstrate – but also in ways less easily translatable into action in the world (unless that action be, perhaps, further writing).

The writers who most 'move' us may often be those who seem most to draw attention to the difficulty, or near impossibility, of primitive, vital forms of movement. I have in mind such writers as Franz Kafka, Samuel Beckett, and Marcel Proust. Consider, for a second, the beetle in *Metamorphosis*, trying unsuccessfully to lever itself off its shell; or Molloy with his crippled leg, trying vainly to cycle home; or Marcel, unable even to get started on his life-work for want of a subject. Consider how the precious lines of Kafka's prose seem to tax the reader's faith in their ability to get to a satisfactory ending (his novels were all 'unfinished'); the huge leap we seem required to make between every word of a late Beckett story ('Ping' or 'Enough', for example); or how often, in the course of reading *A la recherche*, a sentence which has lost us midway makes us wonder if we had not better give up altogether. Or consider, finally, what sort of image might link the three writers: a room, perhaps, a lifetime of work and suffering, played out within the confines of four walls . . . Yet their prose 'moves' us. It seems to achieve something far beyond that which it merely affirms: and far beyond that which may be stated, anecdotally at least, about it or its producers.

All three writers have been childless (as far as is known), and not only that but very self-consciously sterile. Yet all three are peculiarly preoccupied with birth and with the turning of the generations. I wish particularly to look at a form of mobility which centres around the parent–child axis, and to do this I shall turn first to Kafka.

In what way does Kafka's writing allow him to grapple, not with his own father or childhood, so much as with the interconnectedness of his own being-as-a-potential-father and his being-as-a-child? In what way does writing allow him possibilities not open in the rest of his life? In the attempt to develop and answer these questions, I shall call upon the help of other writers from the literary domain, while stepping also into the territory occupied by psychoanalysis, which, almost as much as literature, has addressed itself to the way one generation may hold down or move up against another. But first to Kafka, and to a moment that was to prove crucial in both his life and his work.

§ 1.1

On 2 June 1913 Kafka wrote a letter to Felice Bauer. There was nothing exceptional in this: it was one of several hundred he was to send her between September 1912 and October 1917. He had already been writing to Felice for ten months (letters which fill three hundred pages) when he chose to try to tell her some of what he saw as the significance of his short story 'The Judgement':

Can you discover any meaning in the 'Judgement' – some straightforward, coherent meaning that one could follow? I can't find any, nor can I explain anything in it. But there are a number of strange things about it. Just look at the names! It was written at a time when I had not yet written to you, though I had met you and the world had grown in value owing to your existence.

(*Letters to Felice*, pp. 382–3)

Anyone familiar with Kafka's fiction will, I believe, have been struck by its surface lucidity and its unerring precision. Anyone familiar with his letters or diaries will know that these qualities are to be found reflected there in strict attention to detail, fastidiousness in matters of chronology, clarity of reference, and humility of acknowledgement. Uncharacteristic, then – exceptional even – that he should make a slip, as he does here. And, given the peculiar importance of the moment to which he is referring, doubly strange. In September 1912 Kafka was to start a correspondence, through it a love affair, which was to shape the course of his next five years. He was also to write, in one night-long sitting, 'The Judgement' (the first story with which he was truly satisfied), which was soon followed by 'The Stoker', five new chapters of *America* and, in November to December, *Metamorphosis*. Yet the crucial story, 'The Judgement', achieved as he says in his diaries 'with such a complete opening out of the body and the soul' (p. 213), was not written before he started writing to Felice Bauer – as he claims – but two days *after* the composition of his first letter to her.

Speaking of Kafka's letters in his essay 'Kafka's Other Trial', Elias Canetti goes a long way towards revealing how the exchange of letters gradually came to help Kafka's writing. Yet, for all its talk of establishing 'a connection, a channel of communication' (Canetti, 1978, p. 14), there remains a sense of urgency and release which Canetti's fine essay fails fully to catch. Something in the fact of Felice's presence – Or was it her absence? Or indeed that vacillation of the two which makes of any letter a juggling with the other's nearness and distance? – was profoundly mobilising and dynamically enabling, from the moment of his first writing to her.

Later, in both his diary and his letters, Kafka attempts to chart some of the connections between 'The Judgement' and his new romance – a matter of overlapping names and initials, Frieda and Felice, Bende and Kafka, Georg and Franz (*Diaries*, 11 Feb. 1913, pp. 214–15; letter 2 June 1913, *Letters to Felice*, pp. 382–3). He also dedicates 'The Judgement' 'To Fraülein Felice B.', and admits that he is 'indirectly in her debt for the story' which indeed becomes 'your short story' (Letter 24 Oct. 1912, *Letters to Felice*, pp. 108–10; *Diaries*, 14 Aug. 1913, p. 228; letter 30 Nov. 1912, *Letters to Felice*, p. 186). But no amount of dedication, romantic gesturing, or fiddling with anagrams or homonyms goes far enough. It is to the story itself that one must turn for a clue to the nature of its relation to Felice; a clue to the relation between the life of apparent fixity and the work with its power to move; and perhaps, indirectly, a clue to the little error in Kafka's chronology.

At the centre of 'The Judgement' is a letter. Having set out to write a story about a war, about how 'a young man was to see a vast crowd advancing across the bridge' (letter 2 June 1913, *Letters to Felice*, p. 383), Kafka ends up with a young man defeated, throwing himself off a bridge, perhaps the same one. And when Georg Bendemann jumps, the letter, composed with great care and addressed to a friend in Russia, will not only have failed to reach its destination; it will not even have been sent. The story ends:

He swung himself over, like the distinguished gymnast he had once been in his youth, to his parents' pride. With weakening grip he was still holding on when he spied between the railings a motor-bus coming which would easily cover the noise of his fall, called in a low voice: 'Dear parents, I have always loved you, all the same', and let himself drop.

At this moment an unending stream of traffic was just going over the bridge.
(p. 88)

It is a cruel ending, and all the more cruel for its coming before Georg has really had a chance to begin – begin a life and family of his own. What, or who, is the source of the cruelty? What is it in the letter that provokes such a crisis?

Clearly the letter is a difficult one for Georg to write in the first place, as he sits, wondering what to tell his distant friend, what to omit. He has to decide whether to tell of the upturn in his financial and social fortunes, at the risk of highlighting his friend's contrasting failure to make anything of his life in Russia. The doubts crystallise over whether or not to tell him of his impending marriage, and he goes over a conversation he has had on the subject with his fiancée:

'I don't want to trouble him,' answered Georg, 'don't misunderstand me, he would probably come, at least I think so, but he would feel that his hand had been forced and he would be hurt, perhaps he would envy me and certainly he'd be discontented and without being able to do anything about his discontent he'd have to go away again alone.'
(p. 79)

Georg tries in this way to rationalise his doubts about hesitating to make his friend party to his plans. Yet his explanations to himself strike a hollow note. It is almost as if Georg is seeking to make of his friend's apparent difficulties the cover under which his own real anxiety can hide. Georg's worry seems to be not so much what to say to save his friend from hurt, as whether he can say anything at all. In the first part of 'The Judgement' Georg's anxiety is directed at language itself and at that stylised language-act, the writing of a letter. In his room are being acted out some of the very tensions – between fixity and the ability to get words out – which I have begun to suggest are central to one's experience of Kafka's own writing.[1]

Georg, it becomes clear, is concerned less about his friend's possible hurt than with the possibility of writing a letter which will leave no room for his friend. This would be a letter which would secure the unchanged position of the friend, while unburdening himself of the threat of real exchange (the uncertainty, risk and acceptance upon which friendship is based). Georg's undeclared question is simply: how to write to another without saying anything? Or, how to create himself in a relation of fixity to another – how to write that other as an extension of the self? Deep within Georg's anxiety lies a yearning for a possibility which language seems tantalisingly to offer – the lure of unequivocal selfhood, enshrined in words which would in and of themselves create a plenitude of stable sense. It is a yearning far beyond Georg's capacities to assuage. (His attempt in the past to keep the news on the subject of strangers backfired badly, with the friend starting to become interested in the strangers.)

To declare his impending marriage is, as Georg has it, to 'confess' – to the constraints of society and the positions it allocates. It is also to open a space for the friend's possible response. The friend is no longer written 'into' the letter, but is written *to*; and this is very different to what Georg has been used to allowing, through his presentation of the image of what he thinks his friend wants (or what he wants him to want). Georg's writing has been a sort of amber in which time, desire and friendship have been held suspended. It has perfectly fulfilled in this instance a claim which Alain Buisine (overstating his case) makes in his book *Proust et ses lettres*, concerning all letter-writing:

15

A letter is only ever directed to oneself. There is no literary space more strictly narcissistic than that of letter-writing, where it is above all a matter of giving oneself pleasure, of testing oneself by way of the mediation of the other.

(p. 16)

By writing this letter, Georg is breaking the narcissistic circuit he has created, and opening a space for his friend's response. The letter admits that the friend is ineradicably *other* – is absent indeed, as far away as Russia.

'That's the kind of man I am and he'll have to take me as I am', he said to himself. 'I can't cut myself to another pattern that might make a more suitable friend for him.'

(p. 80)

As he makes this inner declaration, the amber seems to dissolve. Georg seems to stretch his wings and prepare to take off into marriage and adulthood. How is one to know that his father is waiting with scissors to snip those wings off?

One cannot know. Yet a shiver of premonition may run through one as Georg enters his father's room and makes his apparently casual announcement about sending the letter to his distant friend. For something feels not quite right. Whatever the strangeness of the first part of the story, with its complex play of displacement and denial, from the moment Georg makes his announcement to his father, this strangeness is frighteningly intensified.

§ 1.2

Before entering further into this strangeness, it may be appropriate to ask: where does this leave Kafka? I suggested above (§ 1.0) that literary writing does not enjoin any specific action on the reader, unless that action is further writing. I also suggested (§ 1.1) that writing a letter, so long as that letter does not pre-empt the desire of the receiver, can be a way of permitting action – here, the visit from Russia. The two sorts of writing, so similar in many ways, entail crucially different consequences. If one looks at Kafka's letters to Felice, however, the first of which was sent two days before he wrote 'The Judgement', one sees that they often seem (unsuccessfully) to attempt to produce consequences more suitable to the first, the literary mode. It is not only that Kafka employs literary devices or deploys literary effects. Rather, it is as if he tries to write Felice 'into' the letters – to wrap her up in words, contain her with his stifling inquisitiveness and insistence. It is as if he writes in order to keep her at a safe distance – keep her absent – and maintain their situation in a sort of stasis.[2] All he seems to want to enjoin is, precisely, her writing: he is never satisfied with the length or frequency of her replies. Yet for all the letters' attempt not to prompt action – or at least no action that would threaten the epistolary status quo – Kafka's relationship with Felice does develop, with its own expectations. It develops, centrally, with their engagement, and the prospect of marriage and family life this implies. It is as if, in sending his first letter, Kafka opens a channel for communication (as Canetti suggests), but also realises the limits of that communication – limits delineated by the desire of Felice who, however absent, is nonetheless able to make demands and prescribe futures.

To leave Kafka and Felice for the moment and return to 'The Judgement', it may be said that Georg's letter has the function of marriage banns. But it has this function only if it leaves a place for the reality (the reality of the desire) of the friend in Russia. It is this reality which is thrown dramatically into question by Georg's father, when he says:

'You have no friend in St Petersburg. You've always been a leg-puller and you haven't even shrunk from pulling my leg. How can you have a friend out there! I can't believe it.' (p. 83)

I have indicated how 'The Judgement' carries the reader from a distant and supposed difficulty (the friend's possible upset) back to a present, immediate one (how to write?). As Georg faces his father we are forced to make that journey again in our head, to Russia and back. For we must search for a single truth about the 'friend', whose very existence is cast by Georg's father into doubt. If Georg's reminiscences, summoned to persuade his father, seem convincing enough, then we are only beginning to be won over when his father transforms the friend – and in the process, inevitably, the letter – once again:

'But your friend hasn't been betrayed at all!' cried his father, emphasizing the point with stabs of his forefinger. 'I've been representing him here on the spot . . . I've been writing to him, for you forgot to take my writing things away from me. That's why he hasn't been here for years, he knows everything a hundred times better than you do yourself, in his left hand he crumples your letters unopened while in his right hand he holds up my letters to read through!' (pp. 86, 87)

We have had enough doubts already about Georg to be quickly convinced by this dramatic scenario, and Georg's further anecdotal summoning of the friend, though winning enough in its detail, still leaves room for doubt. As we sway this way and that, a question surfaces: who are we to adjudicate between the two versions of the friend? How are we to know? The fact that we are confronted by an intense need to know only intensifies the lack of the authority which would enable knowledge to grow. In the end, how can we be expected to make that distant figure into one single thing when (this the reduplicating of the displacement of worry from 'here' to 'there' and back) we cannot even do as much for Georg's father, who is before us?

We are not, then, faced as readers with a situation in which 'either/or' defines a real choice. Rather, we are trapped within variegated tricks of perspective where there may be, waiting to spring out at us, an enemy within a friend, an old man within a child, an absence within a presence (a pervasive ambiguity which our assumptions about identity barely serve to mask). Georg's father is invalid, unable even to keep his underwear clean. He is the helpless infant being carried to bed, tucked up, reluctant to let go of the gold chain which has caught his eye and which his little fist has clasped. And he is a 'giant of a man', finger on the pulse of business, 'still much the stronger of us two'. It is this fluctuation of his father which hypnotises Georg, and paves the way for his downfall. What chance does he have of sending the letter, of claiming a place as an adult (or the reader of settling into understanding) when that by which he seeks to measure himself is so implacably vacillating, when opposites collide and converge? By way of partial answer I can quote in full a fragment from *Meditation*, the volume Kafka was clutching when he first met Felice Bauer. It is called 'The Trees':

For we are like tree trunks in the snow. In appearance they lie sleekly and a light push should be enough to set them rolling. No, it can't be done, for they are firmly wedded to the ground. But see, even that is only appearance.

In tracing Georg's crisis back to the indeterminacy he calls his father, I am differing from Kafka's own explanation. On 14 August 1913, by which time he had already written a great many letters to Felice, Kafka enters in his diary:

I love her as far as I am capable of it, but the love lies buried to the point of suffocation under fear and self-reproaches.

Conclusion for my case from 'The Judgement'. I am indirectly in her debt for the story. But Georg goes to pieces because of his fiancée.   (p. 228)

In fact, under the discrepancy over the roots of Georg's downfall lies the clue to Georg's letter and his crisis, to Kafka's own first letter to Felice, and his sudden ejaculation of 'The Judgement' as well. For father and fiancée are not discrete entities, from the son's viewpoint, but are inextricably bound one to the other. This is not just any letter Georg is writing, but one which will announce that he intends to marry. He will not just imitate but even replace his father in the cycle of love, family and reproduction. Georg is himself to become a husband and perhaps a father. He is to move the generations, be fertile and reproduce: become an author of sorts, an authority. And this when, in Kafka's life and work, authority – the hierarchy and its minions, the system and its acolytes, the father and his children – is that which is *always already there*.[3]

To the reader of Kafka's *Letter to his Father*, much of this may well be obvious. But one should not forget that as far as is known, the 'letter' was never sent. It is now often collected – correctly I believe – along with his stories. It may now 'move' the reader, but Kafka never sought to make it move its ostensible recipient, in more obvious ways. The insight the 'letter' affords should not blunt the edge of an awareness of the crucial – and in no way predetermined – nexus of struggle: writing letters, getting married, writing fiction; immobility and the power to move; reproducing and producing.

§ 1.3

One can hardly know if Kafka had marriage however distantly in mind when he wrote that first letter to Felice. Nor does this really matter. What does matter is that not only something of the subject of 'The Judgement' may have been suggested to Kafka, but that fiction is invested with a new urgency as a yielder of possibility – or of *mobility*. A channel for words is opened through a letter – and through what a letter, with its incipient fixities of position determined by the other's desire, does *not* permit – to another order of writing which is unavailable to the unfortunate Georg. It is an order in which letters, lovers, parents and marriages may be spoken of without their order being dictated by the necessities of positionality, whether the position be that of father or son, fiancé or celibate,[4] child or ancient, St Petersburg or Prague, Berlin (Felice's home town) or Prague, there or here, absence or presence. It is the order of writing called fiction. It is an order (as has often been taught) over which no one, not even the author, has authority. In it the alternatives – the either/ors which life seems to require – are not all-determining. They need not be resolved and totalised, nor selected and filtered. For narrative, the mainstay of fiction, is able to sustain several – albeit incompatible – strains simultaneously, and tell many stories at once. It is able not merely to pronounce and tell (in the manner of argumentative discourse) but also to enact or perform. Speaking of the function of parables, with one eye on Kafka, Bernard Harrison has this to say of how and why narrative works:

> Narrative offers, in the end, the only way of talking seriously about the moral life. It is serious because it is content to *show* what all other kinds of moral talk attempt, in the face of our condition as beings in a state of becoming, to *say*.
>
> (Harrison, 1981, p. 208)

Kafka sees Georg as 'going to pieces' because of his fiancée, I because of his father. Kafka will himself go to pieces because of the two, and their inextricability. By the time he sends that letter to Felice in which he mistakes the chronology of his first letter and his first wholly successful story, the crisis is already well on its way. Could this indeed be the reason for the slip? Could it be that Kafka wished to separate the story from his own personal history, since the crisis in the story adumbrates the agony in the life? Such speculation, idle though it is, may perhaps be tolerated if it helps clear a space again between areas I have risked blurring: between a faltering letter at the start of a troubled relationship and the writing which was to allow Kafka the night in which he discovered that 'everything can be said, how for everything, for the strangest fancies, there waits a great fire in which they perish and rise up again' (*Diaries*, 23 Sept. 1912, p. 213).

In the end, all Georg's struggle over the letter (and over his friend, his fiancée, and his father) becomes strangely irrelevant. An order is given. A story is told. Irrelevant, then, not because the struggles are anything but paramount or because they do not have consequences (for Kafka as for Georg), but because in the *telling* lies their resolution. It is a resolution which is only ever achieved in movement – the movement of the narrative. And it is a resolution that is one step removed from whatever is told – a step in the reader's direction. When writing of Kafka (in 'Franz Kafka' and 'The Storyteller'), Walter Benjamin does well to free him from those who would variously 'place' him, and to coax him instead towards the one seat which is unreductive, from which the 'storyteller' speaks forth. One may recall in this context that Kafka was rarely happier than when reading aloud his own stories to a captive audience.[5]

'The Judgement' tells of the subjugation of one generation to the order of another. But by the end of the story narrative has itself become the new order to which both son and father are subjected. The narrative's power and freedom lie in its capacity not to render account but simply to tell. A simpler, more lucid and delightfully crushing piece of telling than that of Georg's sentence and drowning would be hard to find. During the course of his story, Kafka obliges his reader to question his or her notions and understanding (or implicit metaphysic) of presence and of identity. He instills a sense of how language may elude the grasp of meaning. By the end of the story enough doubts may have been raised to make one feel that words should no longer be able or allowed to work so simply and innocently as this. 'But see,' Kafka seems to say, 'even that is only appearance.' If one did not know so much about that fateful night of 22–3 September 1912, perhaps one might be forgiven for lapsing momentarily into the thought that, to some extent like the judgement it contains, this story 'The Judgement' has itself always already been there. Where precisely? Here: in that space which one occupies when one sits still and moves, captive to the sound of Kafka's inimitable voice.[6]

§ 1.4

Telling of immobility, and with a peculiar power to 'move'; invoking defeat of a new order, yet itself establishing a new order; built of mutually excluding alternatives, yet a small monument to narrative's power to include – everwhere one looks, in or around Kafka's work, one seems to be drawn in opposite directions, by diverging strains of experience and feeling. In § 1.5 and following,

I shall look further into the two orders highlighted in 'The Judgement': the generations and their opposition. For the moment it may be appropriate to take a broader view of Kafka than that offered by 'The Judgement' alone, to confirm that these strains and oppositions do not disappear in his longer or later work. I hope this will also permit a broader view of the experience of reading Kafka, and how this experience is somehow written 'into' his work (rather as Felice was written 'into' the letters). To be more precise, I shall try to show how central to an understanding of Kafka is one's self-reflexive experience as reader.

In *The Castle* alternatives abound. Jeremiah is a boy if seen with his partner, an old man without. Barnabus's uniform is the essence of smartness until Olga describes it as an inadequate covering shoddily put together in a rush. Frieda is a generous lover to the diffident K., a ravenous megalomaniac to the impotent Olga. Amalia is both traitor and heroine. What of the castle itself, that most intense source of anxiety? It seems to exist solely as the shifting nexus of the villagers' overpoweringly strong fears and expectations. It can, and does, mean anything. Its presence seems to emanate from its bitterly ironic transcendence, from its very absence. No surprise that entering it is an impossible task for one such as K., who is tied down to the earth by his job as a land surveyor.

It is as impossible, one might say, as trying to get to the other side of the shiny, hard, reflective surface of Kafka's own prose in which *The Castle* is told. What should be clear is that within much of Kafka's fiction it is a fullness of presence which is missing (as with the castle). Yet the fiction itself may be the most powerfully insinuating of presences. The tension between that which is told and the prose which is telling it draws the reader into Kafka's work and impels the reading. The tension is not one we merely witness, but one in which we partake in the very act of reading. This is the way we are introduced to the more local tensions and conflicts: by the unflustered rhythm and poise of the writing itself. Away from the nagging worries and obsessions of the fiction, most characteristically at the ends of Kafka's works, we are allowed a perception of the curious *un*importance of the obsessions which have been so motivating us. This is a moment, I suggested in relation to 'The Judgement', when narrative asserts *its* life (which has also been, for the duration of the reading, our life as well).

Fathers and sons

The life of the story, and of narrative in general, depends on the reader's participation. It depends on our initial willingness as readers to suspend not so much our 'disbelief' (as Coleridge has it) as the urgency and impatience of our private desires, and yield to the desires of another – less obvious though these may be. (Sitting still with a blank expression for hours on end, as reading seems to require, involves a great deal of denial, as any baby will testify when obliged to watch its parent read!) Yet the life of narrative equally depends on the premise that when the work is over, our own (non-readerly) desire will reassert itself and we will return to the world. Kafka does not interrupt 'The Judgement' or his other tales to remind us of this, or write an essay 'about' narrative. Yet the tension between what he does write about and the way he writes, added to the way he chooses to stop writing – the way he finishes his tales – may be enough to make us as aware as any essay can of the conditions upon which narrative depends.

In chapter 3 (§ 3.6) I shall have occasion to discuss at greater length this 'venture' which the reader may make into fiction and back; and in chapter 4 (§ 4.4) I shall consider the conditions which render it possible, or the absolute 'conditionality' of its nature. For the moment I wish only to point to the way in which this perception of our readerly participation further heightens the tension engendered by the work – both our anxiety and our sense of release.

I suggested that behind the questions posed in and through Kafka's works – How to send the letter? How to reach the castle? – lurks the suspicion (prompted by the narrative itself, with its ability to move in its measured way, to start and to stop) that the questions are somehow ill-posed, or beside the point. Behind the difficulties of the represented characters, in the gap between what is 'said' and what is 'shown', we momentarily perceive the tension of reading itself. In such moments tension invades us. Obsession and desire leave the 'characters' – Georg or K. – and seem to grab the reader from behind. No writer is more able than Kafka to live close to worry. No writer is so able to suspend that worry for the moment required to let it truly become the reader's own. From behind the preponderant 'How?' which pervades his fictions looms the spectre of the question: 'What if?' Lest I am becoming overly abstract, let me hand over for more concrete evidence to that relentless pursuer of science and truth, Kafka's Investigating Dog.

After he has watched a performance by some musical circus dogs, Investigating Dog reflects:

> As I have already said, this whole episode contains nothing of much note; in the course of a long life one encounters all sorts of things which, taken from their context and seen through the eyes of a child, might well seem far more astonishing. Besides, one may, of course – in the pungent popular phrase – have 'got it all wrong', as well as everything connected with it . . . Or perhaps they did understand him and with great self-control answered his questions, but he, a mere puppy unaccustomed to music, could not distinguish the answer from the music.
>
> ('Investigations of a Dog', pp. 284–5)

To extend the dog's hypothesis, what if, for example, behind the lack of authority, and behind the fear that in the fiction equivalence entails equivocation (or downright negation) Kafka is in fact recounting something very much simpler? What if he is indeed telling what is really the case (when this = this, and that = that) – only we are too inexperienced, or impatient, or full of ourselves to be able to hear him correctly? (Most critics have succumbed to the force of this 'What if?'. Not having the steadfastness of a Benjamin, they have indeed needed to make Kafka tell what is the case – make him into the spokesman of this or that Grand Idea.[7]) I spoke above (§ 1.3) of the step which is taken at the end of 'The Judgement' as being one in the reader's direction. I hope it will now be clear that this step, if it binds us to Kafka's work, can also impress upon us what we may have been missing or denying because of our readerly investment.

I have spoken of the cruel, and cruelly simple ending of 'The Judgement'. Readers of *Metamorphosis* will be unlikely to forget how cruelly that story also ends. When one traces the cruelty back towards its origins, one finds a by now familiar complexity. For a start, only a part of the story's horror originates where one might have expected it to, in the decline and death of Gregor–beetle. A large part of it in fact stems, as Maurice Blanchot suggests (in *La Part du feu*, p. 18), from the story's concluding lines:

> While they were thus conversing, it struck both Mr. and Mrs. Samsa at the same moment, as they became aware of their daughter's increasing vivacity, that in spite of all the sorrow of recent times, which had made her cheeks pale, she had bloomed into a pretty girl with a good figure. They grew quieter and half unconsciously exchanged glances of complete agreement, having come to the conclusion that it would soon be time to find a good husband for her. And it was like a confirmation of their new dreams and excellent intentions that at the end of their journey their daughter sprung to her feet first and stretched her young body.
>
> (p. 139)

Why should this assertion of youth and expectation be so awful? In one obvious sense the youthful stretching of Gregor's sister is not awful at all, a welcome relief in fact after all the agonising and malingering. Yet it is deeply worrying in its ability to give a quite new perspective upon, and distance from, Gregor, with whom we have been so closely suffering. Already the central anguish of the story has in a sense been once displaced (rather as it was in 'The Judgement'), and intensified through displacement. Gregor's problem is not so much that of being a beetle, a problem from whose strangeness we might have drawn some relief. His problem (in which, and from which there's no escape for us) is more that of simply getting on with life. And now, in the end, even that problem seems almost beside the point. We are struck by the sudden realisation of all that has been happening in the meantime, while Gregor has been usurping his family's attention and ours. We are compelled to realise that narrative is not co-terminous with Gregor. Over it, as over his body, he has no absolute right. We are struck by the fact of our own investment in suffering, what we have been missing in the telling of this tale rather than another. If, as the tale seems to persuade, there is really nothing so extraordinary or 'original' in the fact of metamorphosis, then why should there be anything extraordinary about our suffering? The story duly ends, but not, then, before allowing us to glimpse the 'terrible beauty' of all that it *is not*. When I put the book down, what pleasure – what mixed pleasure – I take from rising from the chair in which I have been sitting and myself having a good stretch.

In the ending of *The Trial*, when Joseph K. is led away by his executioners, his worries over Justice and the High Court (which have availed him little, but which have nevertheless given to his life and to our novel their prime driving force) seem to slide away. They cease even to be very relevant as the ceremony of death advances. He dies '"Like a dog"', and 'it was as if he meant the shame of it to outlive him' (p. 251). Death does of course have a way of levelling life's preoccupations. But there is more – or is it less? – than this to Kafka's omission to demonstrate in what way Joseph K.'s death is the fitting conclusion to his novel. Kafka does not explain, he merely 'shows'. Away from Joseph K.'s worries, in 'The End', narrative again imposes *its* life and *its* freedom. The freedom to tell, nothing more; therefore to leave out any legalistic or novelistic hierarchisation of meaning, any justification or declared consequentiality. The reader moves to the tune of this freedom; while Joseph K. dies that most bitterly ironic of deaths – a tangential one.

As he dies, we are again left holding the reins of an experience which is pulling in different directions. One direction is towards relief: we welcome our release from the hold Joseph K. and his obsession were exerting over the story; we are glad to have a bit of realised action at last. Yet even as this is happening, we are pulled in the other direction. For Joseph K. will perhaps not die, but will live on in his blackened reputation. Beyond our shock at the horrible nature of his execution, and beyond a despair (similar to that provoked by *Metamorphosis*) at the peculiar inconsequentiality of all our prior worrying, there is something more intimately troubling about this reminder of Joseph K.'s reputation. The sense of trouble does indeed seem to creep up from behind. For what am I doing now if not endorsing the reminder? Is the present argument not testament to the truth of the prophecy? What if it is *I* who am stirring the ashes of poor Joseph K. into reluctant life and horrible death? The questions – the 'What ifs?' – are not fanciful ones. For I suggested (§ 1.0) that if fictional writing enjoins anything, it enjoins more writing: writing such as this which I am attempting.

The tale finishes. I get up and stretch. I may write of the reading-experience. Joseph K.'s frightening immortality takes root as begin the retrenchments of self, world, reader, writer and work which the novel's conclusion requires. The pull of contradictory feeling is not always a struggle to which I am a witness. It is a struggle in which I am actively involved (for the duration of the reading and beyond). When I finish the novel this struggle may become truly my own. For if I go on to give a version of Joseph K.'s life and death, this will be *my* version – *my* struggle. Georg's death, Gregor's metamorphosis, Joseph K.'s reputation: they are all rooted in the fact that on finishing the novel I do return to my 'self', even if changed and distraught. Joseph K.'s reputation (and Kafka's) grows out of our individuality as readers, out of our ostensible inviolability. We are not innocent. Indeed we are *never* innocent. As I hope will now be clear, by the way he writes and by the way he terminates his writing, Kafka ensures that we can never forget this fact.

§ 1.5

In the course of the present work, I shall return repeatedly to the part we play as readers in the processes of fiction. I have started to indicate how vital this part is. I have suggested, in relation to *The Castle*, *Metamorphosis* and *The Trial*, how fiction may both require and entail a physical and psychic mobility on the part of the reader. And I have tried to show how writing provides Kafka with a range of possibilities which was not available elsewhere in his life. I should like again to broaden the range of my enquiry, in such a way as to include other writers; and in such a way as will also allow a return to the particular sort of movement that was seen to be at the heart of 'The Judgement' – movement between and across the generations.

Two years after writing 'The Judgement', in October 1914, Kafka composed his story 'In the Penal Colony'. The story is not strictly about generations, but it does concern an old order which is under threat from a new one. Again, the story contains a sentence of death. Only this time the judgement is not spoken, but written – with needles upon the flesh of the condemned man:

Many questions were troubling the explorer, but at the sight of the prisoner he asked only: 'Does he know his sentence?' 'No', said the officer, eager to go on with his exposition, but the explorer interrupted him: 'He doesn't know the sentence that has been passed on him?' 'No', said the officer again, pausing a moment as if to let the explorer elaborate his question, and then said: 'There would be no point in telling him. He'll learn it on his body.' (pp. 144–5)

Knowledge of the sentence is gained only after six hours of agony, as the prisoner is approaching unconsciousness, and as the needles which have spelt their message upon his skin move in for the kill. Justice and death: the prisoner is subjected to the first as the second eradicates the very possibility of subjectivity. The machine and method of execution which have long been established in the colony, and which are now being challenged, are nothing if not typical of Kafka. Yet they bring to mind a different writer from a different epoch, whose dramatisation of a legend has in our century helped fire the debate over the conflicts which divide the generations. That writer is Sophocles, and the legend that of Oedipus. It is almost impossible not to think of their names when inter-generational strife is invoked, as our culture is pervaded by the metaphor of Oedipus and his 'complex', in a myriad of ways (as Gilles Deleuze and Félix Guattari have shown in their *Anti-Oedipus*). Though perhaps, where Oedipus is concerned, 'strife' may appear the wrong word. For popular opinion would have it that Oedipus launches a one-sided attack against the old order. Oedipus is the man who kills his father and marries his mother, as everyone knows. This is, after all, what the tragedy is about.

Or is it? Certainly the play is a tragedy. In fact, if for this reason alone, Sophocles (had he wished to) might have had difficulty making Oedipus' slaying of Laius the centrepiece of his play. Not because children do not defy fathers, but because, despite such plays as *Electra* and *King Lear*, this is for the most part the stuff of other sorts of stories, other orders of drama or discourse – the stuff for example of comedy, or more recently of psychoanalysis. I do not wish to suggest that there is anything very comic about psychoanalysis, rather that psychoanalysis shares comedy's preoccupation with a new order's rise against a more established order, and with an ultimate reconciliation of the two. It is a reconciliation rendered possible by initiation into and participation in certain meta-generational rites or symbolic practices: a masque, a dance or a festive marriage ceremony, as it might be in Shakespearean comedy; or language with its 'fiction of the I', as it might be in the recent case of Lacanian psychoanalysis.[8]

Sophocles does *not* attempt to make the murder of the father the centrepiece of his play. As it is, in the Theban legend, Laius dies without the merest intimation of the identity of his slayer. Oedipus kills a stranger, whose death is thus shrouded in unconsciousness. Laius fails to learn the meaning of his death. He is subject to his particular brand of *dike*, his judgement, his infernal machine. His is a death, as it were, like any other. But there is an earlier crime which is just as brutal, and in its way more rich in dramatic significance: that of Laius – committed in full consciousness this time – against his son. As Jocasta recounts:

> Laius,
> It is common knowledge, was killed by outland robbers
> At a place where three roads meet. As for the child,
> It was not yet three days old, when he cast it out
> (By other hands, not his) with riveted ankles
> To perish on the empty mountain-side.

The concentration upon Oedipus which psychoanalysis has helped bring about has tended to obscure all but the passive role of his parents in his life. Yet they were all too frighteningly active.[9] The feeling that Oedipus is 'more sinned against than sinning', that the real criminal of the piece is his father, is borne out by John Munder Ross, in an essay entitled 'Oedipus Revisited: Laius and the "Laius Complex"'. In it he shows that it is indeed remarkable that history has overlooked Laius's crime. He writes:

Yet, in one way or at one time or another, in fact or in fantasy, fathers may be guilty of some variant of psychic infanticide . . . Laius, Oedipus's father, was one of its first would-be perpetrators . . . The myth of Oedipus, the son, is also the story of Laius, the father. Laius is destiny's cruel and indeed capricious human agent. Oedipus, the unwitting patricide, has also narrowly escaped infanticide. If Oedipus forces himself to play out the role of prime actor in his tragedy (and he does so initially for noble reasons, for the general good), he has remained the passive victim not only of some abstract fate, but also of his father.

(Ross, 1982, pp. 171–2)

Sufferers upon the 'apparatus' of Kafka's penal settlement learn corporally the meaning of their wounds. Oedipus' course through the play is towards an understanding of his name and thereby of his body: his swollen foot, his early abandonment, his kinship. When he learns the meaning of his wound, inflicted upon him by his father, it is the need for blindness and exile which overtakes him. Patronymics apart, the 'name of the father' is inscribed notwithstanding, upon Oedipus' very body. The discovering of origins entails a radical loss of positionality (and by this reversal of the processes of rationality the tension which sustains the drama is tightened). Georg's father oscillates from giant to infant, but Oedipus' father slides from murderer to victim and back again, his mother from progenitor to wife and back. This is the paradox: as Oedipus' identity is established it is simultaneously undermined. He grows into the one certainty bequeathed him – his proper name ('Oedipus' means 'swollen foot'). At the heart of his collapse is his father's 'cruel' judgement which, while long since lapsed at the level of the real, returns insistently in plagues, in prophecies, in names, and in the intuited intentions of the gods.

Even the drama which has become the watchword of the revolt of children against adults may in fact be a tale of strife, and of the defeat of this revolt. In 'In the Penal Colony' there is struggle as well, between the new prison methods and the old. The old methods and machine are certainly typical of Kafka. Yet however terribly the prisoners suffer to gain knowledge, the officer who runs the 'apparatus', for his part, ends up with the spike of his machine through his forehead, without even the consolation of his order (to 'BE JUST') being consolidated upon his body. As much as the machine is characteristic, what happens to it, when it falls apart and its engineer dies, appears to be the opposite. The new, more humane order seems to win the day.

This victory is tempered, however, by the fact that the explorer, who is the prophet of the new order, is himself seared by his experience of the machine. The experience takes his initial indifference and turns it into a rapt fascination (the strength and indelibility of his impression is the implicit *raison d'être* of the story). And the victory of 'progress' is provisional. Just before he leaves the island colony, what does the explorer learn but that there is a prophecy which says that after a number of years the old Commandant, instigator of the execution machine, will rise up again with his adherents and recover the colony? The explorer has a final opportunity to prove that he is a harbinger of humanity, when he is offered the chance to free the prisoner and soldier who follow him to the boat. What does he do? He chooses to threaten them with his length of rope, and leave them behind on the island. Even the story which seems to tell of the triumph of the new reveals how the old order leaves its mark – if not in needles or rivets then in ways more subtle – on all it encounters.

§ 1.6

In his diary for 15 September 1912, a week before writing 'The Judgement', Kafka jotted this little poem:

> From the pit
> of exhaustion
> we ascend
> with renewed strength –
> Dark lords
> who wait
> until the children
> exhaust themselves.
>
> [Aus dem Grunde
> der Ermattung
> steigen wir
> mit neuen Kräften,
> Dunkle Herren,
> welche warten,
> bis die Kinder
> sich entkräften.]   (p. 210)

Whatever Kafka's intentions, it remains a rather ambiguous stanza. The ambiguity lies less in either the first section (the first four lines) or the second than in the space between them. It lies in the status of the pause at the end of the fourth line, and the status, therefore, of the 'we'. On first reading 'we' may most obviously be 'Dark lords'. But may 'we' not also be 'children', on a further reading? If as readers we can stay close to the ambiguity, we may regain something: an awareness that we have within us the potential for being 'Dark lords' or 'children', of the order which is being repressed or of the repressors. According to how we speak these words (for in any single reading we must provisionally commit our voice to an approximation of one meaning over another), we may become the one or the other.

Fiction gives Kafka and his readers some choice – or at least the illusion of choice – where the rest of life is more harshly determining. Where Georg is stuck, where the officer in the penal colony is transfixed, and where Oedipus is dually locked, we can learn to change, to move, and to 'turn again'. We can do so along with Kafka and Sophocles – and with Dante and T. S. Eliot too, I want to add. The act of reading may be permeated with an attendant play of contradictory feeling, with tension enforcing readerly vacillation and unrest. Yet at another remove, this very movement may be experienced as more liberating than disturbing. When thinking of reading, one may usefully recall these words of T. S. Eliot's, taken from 'East Coker' v:

> Here or there does not matter
> We must be still and still moving
> Into another intensity
> For a further union, a deeper communion.

The 'further union', I wish to suggest, can be that achieved with writing, and which only reading permits. It is a 'union' to which I shall return later in this book, in the attempt to see more precisely how it is achieved. For now I wish to shift to another era and author, in whose work movement is of crucial importance. I wish to invoke a world in which judgements are unavoidable and justice is paramount – the fictional world of Dante's *Commedia* – and ask: what is it in the agony of *Inferno* that distinguishes Dante the pilgrim from those suffering around him?

The answer is clearly not simply his moral or spiritual superiority. The leopard, the lion and the she-wolf bar Dante's direct path upwards and allow him only the downward route. As in *Inferno* he meets many of his old mentors and guiding lights, one is compelled to wonder: if they, then why not he? There are of course many reasons; but perhaps there is a central one. The inmates of *Inferno* are crushed not only by their need to re-enact the figural fulfilment of their sins, but by the rigour of fixity of their status which is so stringent as to have left them bereft of even the desire for change (left them as uncontrite as they were on earth). They are self-condemned to an eternity of repetition of the same. Dante may falter and hesitate, but if his salvation comes from anything it comes from his ability to keep moving, to turn – *tornare*. He moves from one *bolgia* to the next and with great suffering and effort from one canticle to the next. He is able to move from the position of suppliant to that of initiate, without ever losing the humility proper to the former.[10] Perhaps it is something of such an awareness of the absolute need for mobility that prompts Eliot's enigmatic figure from 'Little Gidding' II (imbued with not a few of Dante's traits) to make the final of his utterances before disappearing:

> From wrong to wrong the exasperated spirit
> Proceeds, unless restored by that refining fire
> Where you must move in measure, like a dancer.

Certainly it is the potency of the possibility of movement that lends to the opening of *Ash Wednesday* so much of its resonance:

> Because I do not hope to turn again
> Because I do not hope
> Because I do not hope to turn.

By the end of *Ash Wednesday*, despite the initial disavowal, a great deal of ground will have been crossed. It is ground made traversible by the possibility of prayer, which transforms that opening 'Because' into an ultimate 'Although' (in section VI).

Returning to Kafka and his brief poem of the 'children' and 'Dark lords', movement is not only declared but demanded of the reader, who is inhabiting the tension of alternating and conflictual readerly possibilities. Conflict is not removed in the movement of writing or reading. It is 'written in', or 'written out'; or 'read through' perhaps, from the reader's side (rather as, in the psychoanalytic context, problems may be 'worked through'). The conflict remains, however, when the poem (or story or novel) is finished. This may equally be the case when one turns from Kafka's texts towards his life.

I suggested (above, § 1.0) that readers of Kafka will, when thinking of his life, tend on the whole to picture the grim sterility, the exhaustion, and the agonised squeezing of stories from a reluctant hand; a life marked by a minimum of events and a maximum of suffering. However, readers of his *Letters to Friends, Family, and Editors* have a surprise in store. After hundreds of pages of letters evincing pain and difficulty (if much else besides), and after the poignant 'Conversation Slips', comes a chronology. What strange reading it makes! One reads of writings and publications, law degrees, meetings with women, engagements, studies, trips to Vienna and Berlin, meetings with Martin Buber and Robert Musil. Is this the same Kafka? One's surprise may partly be reduced by reflection upon the highly conventional, at times arbitrary selection of chronological details. Still, in my mind at least, a doubt lingers. I can barely accept that in Kafka's life so much of a worldly nature does get done. The realisation that it does is both curiously disappointing and powerfully engaging: demystifying (if still mysterious), and humanising (if emphasising still further his singularity).

Nor are the paradoxes less visible in the words Kafka chooses to represent himself and his activity. Few individuals – to repeat – seem more fixed than Kafka: by his chosen job, his perpetual exhaustion, and more than anything by his self-imposed image as one doomed to smallness and sterility. Yet even Kafka, for whom the prospect of moving into marriage and turning the generations was so terrifying, this Kafka seems to himself to give birth when he writes. In his diaries he notes:

> While I read the proofs of 'The Judgement', I'll write down all the relationships which have become clear to me in the story so far as I now remember them. This is necessary because the story came out of me like a real birth, covered with filth and slime, and only I have the hand that can reach to the body itself and the strength of desire to do so. (*Diaries*, 11 Feb. 1913, p. 214)

Of course Kafka would later have had even his most precious progeny disappear. In a letter to Max Brod, discovered posthumously, he writes:

> When I say that these five books and the short story count, I don't mean that I want them to be printed again and handed down to posterity; on the contrary, should they disappear altogether that would be what I want.
>
> (Quoted in 'Epilogue' to *The Trial*, p. 253)

As for his less precious offspring, their fate would have been unequivocal:

> But everything else of mine that I have written . . . without exception . . . is to be burned. ('Epilogue', *The Trial*, pp. 253–4)

Few writers have been drawn so totally into writing; few have mistrusted writing so profoundly. Yet who is to say if Kafka trusted Max Brod, who had done so much to encourage his literary career, to carry out the purge he recommended? Who is to say if Kafka's work had not already come of an age where it too, like any adolescent, was able to claim its independence? It is one of the most cruel of ironies that Kafka's fiction was to survive where so much of his other real-life family was to die in pogroms which even he, with his dark spirit, could hardly have imagined.[11]

Despite his sterility, Kafka gives birth, metaphorically at least. Almost as much as the metaphor of movement, that of birth seems to adhere to literature and literary processes. From the tiniest fictional fragment to the bulkiest epistolary volume, from the work to the life, Kafka catches his reader in a multilateral conflict which is no sooner 'placed' than it proliferates. Holding to the metaphor of movement as one way of exploring the affective range· through which fiction may pull us as readers, this conflict compels a shifting within us and across the space between us and the writer, which is the very prototype of Kafkaesque motion. When we 'turn again' in Kafka's world, we may do so into greater paradox and difficulty. But it is our ability significantly to turn which distinguishes us from the sufferers in the *bolgias* of despair of his fiction. This fiction, engrossed as it is in the lineaments of fear and revulsion, opens up an order of experience quite oppositely charged. When reading his texts, it is not simply one emotional realm or the other we are required to inhabit, but both simultaneously (or at a dizzying rate of intermittence that feels like simultaneity). So long as we can resist the temptation to still dizziness by rendering movement instantly into meaning (so long as we can live with the fears prompted by the aforementioned 'What if?'), we may read, and as we read we may indeed move 'into another intensity / For a further union'. The 'union' will be with writing itself, rather than with the writer. It will nonetheless be achieved *in company with* that paradox of invisible, self-effacing omnipresence – the writer we call Franz Kafka.

2 · Difficult births

THROUGHOUT chapter 1 I have, I hope, been gradually developing a broader vision of the possibilities of creativity, through attention to the work of a small number of writers. It is tempting at this stage to propose that there is something profoundly liberating, even 'comic', about the art of fiction *per se*, whether engaged upon as writer, as reader or as both. Despite all his talk of 'anxiety', it seems to be something of the sort that critic Harold Bloom, himself so concerned with repressive fathers, has been trying to demonstrate. However, before attempting to push this line of enquiry further, through other, more elaborated examples, I should like to backtrack in order to pick up a proposition I made above (§ 1.5) about a configuration of tensions between generations which aligns the preoccupations of comedy with those of psychoanalysis. In this chapter and the following I shall try to improve on such an oversimplification, and to explore further that complex of contradictory feeling which pervades the experience of Kafka so broadly.

In *Beyond the Pleasure Principle*, Freud claims himself to be a dualistic thinker. And Freud's commentators have often laid stress on the apparent dualities in his work, between, for example, *eros* and *thanatos*, the ego and the id, or the life and death instincts. An instance of a related duality which may be of particular use here is that between love and hate, which when combined in certain circumstances came to be called 'ambivalence'. This affective complex can shed light on what has already been said about Kafka; and it will also illuminate my enquiry into what is the prime site of the complex – a site which is already familiar, existing between parents and children.

The focusing within psychoanalysis and the 'Oedipus complex' upon the infant and the child has allowed attention to be paid to infantile aggression and hostility, directed towards parents in particular. Yet this attention has not entirely separated itself from the more important psychoanalytic realisation that in the conflict of the generations, primacy should be given neither to the threatening of sons and daughters nor to that of fathers and mothers, but rather to the rivalry itself (which presupposes two rival sides). Concomitant with this, hostility has never been seen to be the whole story either. It is a force which, though variously and powerfully deployed, is balanced by its opposite force of longing and attraction.

To psychoanalysis, therefore, I shall now turn, in the attempt to explore initially: the nature of ambivalence as a particularly well-focused example of dual, conflictual feeling; and the place this has in parent–child relations. In advancing, I shall be obliged to go back, towards the sort of primitive movements I suggested (§ 1.0) may often be taken for granted, but upon which subsequent, more confident achievements depend. And, equally, my concern about the possibilities opened by writing will not disappear. Indeed, in preparing to turn to psychoanalysis, I may ask that it be borne in mind that psychoanalysis is itself, among other things, a mode of *writing*, which bears certain similarities with (if also some differences from) the writing of a Kafka, a Dante or an Eliot.

§ 2.1

In 1907 a man started treatment with Sigmund Freud who was suffering from a debilitating obsession with a story he had heard, while in the army, of a cruel form of torture said to be employed by the Turks. His was to become, when Freud published in 1909 the paper which told the story, one of the most famous of case histories: 'Notes upon a Case of Obsessional Neurosis'. And he was to be immortalised in the figure of his most acute phobia – the 'Rat Man' (*Standard Edition*, x, 151–249). The charting of the patient's 'Origins of Compulsion and Doubt' obliges Freud to return to the man's early experience. As he delves back, he comes upon a surprising affective configuration wherein positive and negative feelings of great intensity – developing indeed into a 'remarkable relation of love and hatred' – seem to coexist, even when directed at a single object, without cancelling each other out.

The precise relation of the configuration to the 'Rat Man's' neurosis is not my concern here. What concerns me rather is a first charting of an awareness of the configuration as that discrete and identifiable affective complex which comes to be known as ambivalence. In fact, Freud does not use the term 'ambivalence' until his paper of 1912, 'The Dynamics of Transference', where he acknowledges his borrowing of it from E. Bleuler, and where he uses it to account for the coexistence of 'negative' and 'affectionate transference' in the same patient (*Standard Edition*, XII, 106–7). Freud is not, of course, the first writer or thinker to make much of mixed emotions – nor would one so well read as he have claimed any such status. But in uncovering a little the capacity of any individual to contain love and hate which do not cancel each other out, 'the emotional ambivalence which is dominant in the majority of our intimate relations with other people', he drains the complex of some of its mystery and paradox (*Standard Edition*, XVI, 443). In his essay 'Montaigne, Rousseau and Freud', analyst Masud Khan recognises the fundamental and innovatory nature of Freud's discovery, when he writes:

> Freud alone, it seems to me, managed the heroic task of becoming aware of the role of love and hate in his self-experience . . . Human beings, until Freud, had always divided their affections into loving or hating, but never, to my knowledge, loving and hating. And it is precisely the courage to take on this task intra-psychically that made Freud's epistemology of self-experience unique in so far as it became an empirical situation of working through the basic conflicts of love and hate *vis-à-vis* the other as well as oneself. (Khan, 1972, p. 110)

Of course, despite Freud's crucial insight, he had no rights of ownership over the term 'ambivalence', and it has had its meanings multiplied and diffused both within psychoanalytic discourse and within common parlance since his day. Yet if the term is to be useful, it should retain some of the clinical edge which Freud uncovered. In their invaluable volume, *The Language of Psychoanalysis*, J. Laplanche and J.-B. Pontalis express this clearly in the following way:

> If the term is to keep all the descriptive – and even symptomatic – value that it originally possessed, it is advisable to have recourse to it only in the analysis of specific conflicts in which the positive and negative components of the emotional attitude are simultaneously in evidence and inseparable, and where they constitute a non-dialectical opposition which the subject, saying 'yes' and 'no' at the same time, is incapable of transcending. (p. 28)[1]

Following Freud, ambivalence may be taken as characteristic of that phase of psychic development in which the infant is forced to differentiate itself from the world. The infant is caught in a precarious moment in which it is able still to love and hate in equal amounts. (It is able, as more recent Freudians might have it, to consume the mother's otherness – the mother as representative of the Other – and to introject otherness as a necessary but alienating way of coping with the loss of the mother.) The phase will not last, but its influence will. As Freud has it in his study of the 'Rat Man', ambivalence 'has the force of a model to which the rest of his reactions tend to conform' (*Standard Edition*, x, 241).

I should note, however, that in the present context the determining force of ambivalence and the impossibility of trans-cendence of which Laplanche and Pontalis speak may strike a discordant note. For I expressed the hope that my enquiry into ambivalence would, partly, illuminate retrospectively; and in my discussion of Kafka what I began to show was that his writing does indeed offer a provisional release from the obligation of saying 'yes' or 'no'. The notion of transcendence is not an easy one. Nor is it made easier by any association between it and creativity or writing. Yet, in keeping with the present subject, one may want to have one's cake and eat it. One may fall in with the general direction of the clinical formulation of ambivalence; yet demur, place a bracket, where writing and reading are concerned, round the notion of transcendence, and the possibilities it implies. Premature renunciation of the notion might lead to overlooking the importance of the reader's role, and might thereby lead to self-denial. For if some provisional extension, working through, or 'transcendence' of ambivalence is to be found in writing, it intimately involves, and is even dependent upon, the reader. As a reader, then, let me now turn to the work of psychoanalyst Serge Leclaire. What becomes of ambivalence in the analytic situation or in the writing which emerges from it is just one of the things to be explored.

§ 2.2

One work in particular by Serge Leclaire will be considered here. It was published in 1975, with the title *On tue un enfant* ('A Child is Being Killed') and the subtitle *Un essai sur le narcissisme primaire et la pulsion de mort* ('An Essay on Primary Narcissism and the Death Instinct'). It is intended that attention to the detailed workings of this single short text will permit a better understanding of how psychoanalytic texts in general – and thereby psychoanalysis itself – operate. The qualities of Leclaire's work will become apparent in the course of discussion – and the importance to the Lacanian perspective of incorporating clinical work and examples has already been mentioned. It may nonetheless be appropriate to add here a further indication as to why this book in particular has been chosen for close analysis.

The reason again has something to do with how psychoanalysis – especially classical Freudian, and Lacanian analysis – has often been represented, and at times represents itself: as the meeting between a suffering, needy patient and a cool, dispassionate analyst, who is protected by an armchair and by a rigorously applied set of strictures and rules. (It is a stereotype which is little more than a transposed version of the scientist employing the inviolable tools of empiricist methodology.) The image of the analyst, that is to say, often connotes neutrality: both distance and control. I have already hinted at the inappropriateness of such an image in the context of fiction, which may be entered by writer and reader less voluntarily than through need or urgent desire. From the analysand's side similar conditions have been seen to apply. What Serge Leclaire impresses upon his reader is that the fourth party – the analyst – is also driven by equivalent forces, and not dissimilar desires: into encounter with the patient, and into his or her own writing, which emerges out of the encounter. Analysis is no neutral activity, but a passion. As Kafka lets his reader feel that no reading is innocent, so Leclaire makes it clear that no analyst or analytic session is innocent either.

It is to the negative or dark side of such passion that I wish to turn first; but not before noting that an alternative possibility is also evident in the very chapter headings of *On tue un enfant*, which offer 'Béatrice *ou* de l'amour' ('Beatrice *or* About Love') and 'Sygne *ou* de l'amour de transfert' ('Sygne *or* About Transference-Love'). A form of ambivalence is deeply embedded in Leclaire's book. It is an ambivalence whose dual forces beckon and cajole the reader into and through the work. In § 2.3 and following I shall turn to the implications of these headings – to love and its importance for the analyst and patient. First I shall attend to its negative counterpart, and to the relation of adults to children, the potential hostility of which psychoanalysis has not always properly recognised.

In the talk of opposition between children and parents it is easy to lose sight of something that would be striking if a similar intensity of interest were directed at any other sort of competition – the fact that this is a case of mismatch. The degree to which it is a mismatch has been indirectly revealed by psychoanalysis itself, which has insisted upon the 'prematurity' of all births, on the extreme vulnerability – as Freud has it, the 'helplessness' (*Hilflosigkeit*) – of the infant. Against such a creature is pitted the might, weight and determination of the adult. The odds are hardly fair ones. It is something of the shock of this which strikes the reader before even opening *On tue un enfant*. The title, picking up and radicalising the title of Freud's essay 'Ein Kind wird geschlagen', 'On bat un enfant' ('A Child is Being Beaten' – *Standard Edition*, XVII, 175–204), provokes both by the unspecific 'on' ('one'), by which 'I' may be implicated, and by the present tense of the 'tue' ('is killing'), suggesting as it does that the process is a habitual, hence a familiar one. The cover of the book (in the 'Points' edition), which is taken from Duccio's painting of 'The Massacre of the Innocents' and shows a detail of a man plunging a sword deep into a baby's side, while below him lies a pile of murdered infants, confirms the provocative, indeed polemical thrust of the title. What is invoked is cruelty, as it turns out not misleadingly; and specifically that form of cruelty which adults may perpetrate upon the innocent young.

Neither surprise nor shock is likely to be dissipated when one opens Leclaire's book and starts to read its opening lines, which run thus:

Why was it placed on the monumental fireplace? It fell on the stone, in front of the hearth. Fortunately it is only the child of the Virgin, an admirable Roman statue.

(p. 9)

The initial question 'Why?' begs more questions than the one it ostensibly asks. For while we have become used in fiction to first sentences containing an unknowable referent, it retains the power to disturb when a discursive order of writing had been anticipated. As we read on, this referent does not fill out into a knowable 'character' but only into a further strangeness. After a few more lines' description of the broken statue, Leclaire continues:

It's nothing, the torso isn't broken, in fact it's whole, quite whole, I'm sure of it. But it isn't moving. Mummy! That's my child, cold already in front of the fire which has caught light again. It's impossible. And yet I want to cry out.

(p. 9)

40

We encounter the same problem with 'I' that we had with 'it'. What is clear is that there is some sliding of sense from an inanimate thing to an inanimate person, lying before a fire. But what about that 'Mummy!'? Is this a fragment of a case history, a recounted nightmare, a hallucination, a prose poem, a psychoanalytic speculation intended to recall Freud's '"A Child is Being Beaten"'? Is it any or all of these? As the text announces, it is indeed impossible to place, to know, or to understand, because the co-ordinates are withheld which might allow us to place *from where* this text is being spoken (or written). As (or if) we continue, despite such impossibility, we are offered two fathers who may be unable to see or hear the pleas of their children. Rather in the manner of Kafka's puppy, they seem unable to distinguish the question – not the answer this time – from their own preoccupations. If they, then, the suspicion tingles, why not we? The plea goes out: 'Don't you see? Don't you hear?' And the answer comes back: 'No, it's impossible. The death of the child is intolerable' (p. 10).

What does one hope to gain when one opens a psychoanalytic work? New understanding? Fresh knowledge? Insight? 'Inscape' even? What would such an understanding, or intimation of such an understanding imply about our distance from the work? Leclaire impresses such questions upon his reader, and in his own way hints at answers. A text offering gratification of the longing for understanding might perhaps do so by occluding the fact of longing through presentation of a seductive version of what is already known. It might reproduce the reader's assumptions in such a way as to minimise threat and strangeness (and if this recalls the letters Kafka's Georg is accustomed to send to his friend in Russia, it is no coincidence). The reader's essentially narcissistic longing would thus be masked behind a guise of certainty. In this way might be confirmed not only one's rightness and impartiality, but also one's unboundedness and one's potential for multiplication where multiplication (unlike the reproduction considered in relation to Kafka and Georg) does not involve risk or challenge.[2] To open *On tue un enfant* is to be faced with a glimpse of one's overdetermining desire. It is to find one's longing for infinite potentiality revealed as such.

This may seem a lot to draw from a few obscure lines or pages. But Leclaire guides his reader in an understanding of his or her reaction to the text. He guides implicitly, through the central notion which, having first disarmed us (by revealing us as armed), he wishes to have us consider. His notion is that the parents in the text cannot hear the children because of the intensity of their own wishes. He leaves us to draw our conclusion that if we found reading hard it was partly because of the strength of our own latent desire. Why is the aforementioned death of the child intolerable? It is intolerable precisely because 'it is a realisation of our most secret and profound wish' (p. 10). We may be familiar with the idea of a 'death wish', but surely not one of this kind. What a dense and troubling notion this is: that the deepest wish of adults may be the death of children; and that they may be unreceptive to their children's real suffering because of the preponderance of this wish.

To begin to understand the nature of such a wish one has to go back a little, and try to get a picture of what psychoanalysts mean by wishing, which may not match exactly with everyday assumptions. For Leclaire, wishing – or 'desire' as wishing is usually termed – is what Lacan (following Spinoza) calls the 'central function of human experience' (Lacan, 1978, p. 261). In this phrase the emphasis should perhaps be on the *human*. For desire is uniquely human, and it depends upon the infant's purely instinctual demands not being totally satisfied. It is not part of what Freud calls the 'primary process', and is dependent upon the breaking of the primary narcissism through which the infant is appropriating the world into its undifferentiated self. Desire thus presupposes division, of subject and object, desirer and object of desire.

The opening of Leclaire's book makes the reader aware of his or her desire for a particular sort of self-dissemination (and confirmation) in the text. In psychoanalytic terms, this desire is, however, strictly beyond (or before) desire. It is narcissistic. Rather as in 'The Judgement' Georg has to face up to the way desire allots positions, in order to write his letter to his friend, so to read Leclaire's text the reader must face his or her own hidden wishes. By failing to offer immediate narcissistic gratification, Leclaire's text institutes desire as such; and not only institutes it but makes the reader aware of it; makes him or her not only aware of it, but also, through his argument about children, aware of the potentially debilitating consequences of *not* recognising it (consequences which for the reader might entail abandoning his work).

The death of the child as envisaged by Leclaire spells the end of the primary narcissistic possibility which the idea or promise of a child has brought to life. Just what sort of a child can he be thinking of? What sort of narcissism? One may reasonably look to Freud for some clues, but Freud himself has difficulty describing what primary narcissism consists of, and says in his article 'On Narcissism: An Introduction' that it is 'less easy to grasp by direct observation than to confirm by inference from elsewhere' (*Standard Edition*, XIV, 90).[3] On the same page Freud does give some leads, however, when he says that parents' attitudes to their children are 'a revival and reproduction of their own narcissism, which they have long ago abandoned', and that parents 'are under a compulsion to ascribe every perfection to the child – which sober observation would find no occasion to do – and to conceal and forget all his shortcomings'. One may acknowledge that the death of *such a child* (or such a narcissistic fantasy) might give rise to the sort of child everyone recognises: limited, faltering, blemished and needy. The death of the fantasy-child may represent for a parent the most profound desire because, precisely, it represents the death by which this parent's own desire was born (it represents the parent's original and originating desire). The fracturing of parental narcissism leaves a crack through which the real child may push, to find a place for its own desire. What should by now be clear is that it is a particular child of which Leclaire is speaking:

The marvellous child is a primordial unconscious representation where, more than anywhere else, everyone's wishes, nostalgia and hope are bound together. What the transparent reality of the child almost entirely unveils, and renders visible, is the reality of all our desires. It fascinates us, and we are no more able to turn away from it than we are to grasp it. (p. 12)

For Leclaire, the 'marvellous child' encompasses that state anterior to being – the '*infans*' he calls it – which represents most completely primary narcissism in a form available to the undifferentiated unconscious energies of the adult. This child is what he terms an 'unconscious representative' ('représentant inconscient') or a 'primordial signifier'. Because of its nature as a signifier (and source of unconscious energy) it is strictly unnamable as such – 'it doesn't speak nor will it ever speak' (p. 22).

Everyone will be able to bring to mind versions of this 'marvellous child' – this 'child-king', 'His Majesty the Baby' – in recollections, or in myth or imagination. Yet Leclaire's argument may nonetheless remain rather theoretical and even perhaps ironic (therefore implying distance). Talk of 'signifiers' tends to summon the knottier and less graspable parts of Lacan's work; and the idea that all adults may have to sacrifice fantasy-children aligns the reader through irony with the murderer in Duccio's painting on the cover of *On tue un enfant*. Even if the processes of the text can be seen to be tied in an almost mimetic way to its argument, this is still a far cry from the clinical edge which I proposed to uncover through *On tue un enfant*. Yet one more step into the book, and this edge will be seen glimmering, and held against the throat of Leclaire's patients.

The clinical edge of Leclaire's formulations is exposed by the overlapping of the fantasy-child with the better-known biological child. By failing to kill the one, parents may in reality be torturing and slowly killing the other. Maud Mannoni, in chapter 3, will offer several examples of this killing. For Leclaire's part, he introduces a certain 'Pierre-Marie' who has been driven to analysis by his acute distress at the insistent memory he has of his father drowning a puppy, and by his murderous wishes which are directed first at his parents, then at his wife and family, finally at himself. Through the long slow processes of analysis what emerges is that Pierre-Marie had an elder brother, called Pierre, who died in infancy; and that Pierre-Marie was brought into the world by his mother to be an immortal replacement for the insufficiently mourned brother. Like Oedipus, Pierre also bears the parental stigma in his name. Pierre-Marie is the living representative of the 'marvellous child' – born of another's untimely death. He leads a life 'haunted by the paralysing presence of death; he barely tastes, barely brushes with his lips the joys of his family, limiting his passions and his desire to the dimness of uncertain shadows' (p. 22). He dreams of breaking down walls and discovering tombs. He is in search of his dead brother whom he must kill again, once and for all. In order to find his own place and his own desire Pierre-Marie has to kill the child of his mother's unconscious need, and so stop being another's 'child-king', pre-empted in his own desire by the force of his mother's primary narcissism. Only, since his brother is already dead, logically the child he has to kill is the one he is – or contains within – himself. The analytic process will enable a sort of suicide which will also be a murder of the 'marvellous child' that Pierre-Marie represents for his mother's unconscious. And this will amount to a miraculous release: from the 'murderous' way in which his mother's failure to mourn her first son has forced him to take this dead son's place.

There are more subtle and more sinister ways of killing a child than by the sword. One form of killing may be necessary – a real killing of a fantasy-child. Failure to attempt this killing can have hateful consequences. For as Leclaire shows, a second form of killing arises out of the failure: this time an unconscious killing (through fantasy) of a real child. There are more subtle, and also *more pervasive* ways of killing . . . Nor does Leclaire allow his reader to imagine that all this business of murdering and narcissism is one to which he or she is merely a witness. Everyone has a child within. Indeed one has not so much a single child as several children: the child one once was; the child one was – and even more the 'marvellous child' one *was not* – for one's parents; the child one might want to have; and the child one is still, every day, when one thinks of what one might have been and done. Leclaire writes:

For everyone there is always a child to kill, a representation of plenitude and immobile ecstasy [jouissance immobile] to mourn and mourn repeatedly. There is a light which has to be doused so that it can shine out and fade away against a background of darkness. (p. 12)[4]

At its crudest, what Leclaire seems to be saying is that one must renounce the lure of infinite potentiality and of identity with the variegation of another's fantasies, and accept the terrible but compelling singleness of choice and purpose. Yet one must not forget infinity. He goes on:

Whoever does not mourn and mourn repeatedly the marvellous child that he would have been, remains in limbo, in a milky light shed by a hopeless state of waiting which casts no shadow. But whoever believes he has settled his account once and for all with the figure of the tyrant, is exiling himself from the sources of his genius, and is taking himself to be strong-minded in the face of the reign of ecstasy [le règne de la jouissance]. (p. 12)

The 'marvellous child' inhabits the familiar terrain of a many-faceted ambivalence. It is both necessary, to be welcomed as a source of energy and excitement; *and* debilitating, to be killed as a necessary first step on the road through language to desire ('"I" begins at that moment in time', Leclaire writes (p. 13)).

Just how familiar the terrain is becomes clear if I return for a second to the opening of Leclaire's book. For what I failed to bring out is the way in which the trauma of the broken figurine and the cries for help may not only make the reader aware of his or her narcissistic yearnings, but may also represent the fracturing of parallel yearnings on the part of the analyst–writer. In chapter 4 I shall have occasion to look further at the way in which beginnings in general may somehow be traumatic. Here it is perhaps enough to say that by committing himself to an unashamedly idiosyncratic prose, Leclaire also breaks the fantasy-figurine: the fantasy that he might be able to write a totally satisfying text – a text which, through some dreamed neutrality, would be available to the universality of readers. The nature of the fantasy encountered in the first chapter of *On tue un enfant*, and the risk involved in murdering it, are perhaps already familiar under another form. The production of a story or a book may at times be described as a birth. A book – it is only logical – may therefore be a child. A 'marvellous child'? I believe so.

When I spoke in my introduction of the frustration most writers feel with writing, I may without realising it have been referring to such a 'marvellous child'. This child is a book that would end all books and have the final word. It is a book that would say what the writer really meant, and be universally addressed yet wholly personal. It is a book that is inevitably betrayed by the words committed to the page. For to write is to be obliged to abandon such a book (abandon Rimbaud's dream of private language) and commit oneself to the public domain of choice and risk. It is to confront the impossibility of the 'representation of plenitude' which Leclaire mentioned above. Through the adult's willingness to kill (and re-kill) the 'fantasy-child', his or her real child may find a place for its own desire. Only in the acceptance of the partiality and awful finality of words, and from the ashes of the narcissistic fantasy of universality, can writing emerge which will leave a place not for all readers but for any single reader, and this individual reader's unique desire.

§ 2.3

For Leclaire, psychoanalysis can never be a neutral activity, and the analyst can never truly be dispassionate or innocent. The analyst does not merely encourage the patient to murder a 'marvellous child', but must also do the same for his own corresponding fantasy, when analysing as when writing (ambivalence cannot be avoided but must be taken on board and worked through). The text which emerges from the analyst's pen may bear the traces of this murder. This may be characterised as the darker side of the passion of analysis. It is now time to flip the coin of ambivalence and turn to the brighter, though in the end scarcely less threatening side of Leclaire's analytic and writerly activities. This is the side which opens not upon killing but upon loving. Without first identifying them, let me quote two passages, from different books and different writers. Here is the first:

(Desire is everywhere, but in the amorous state it becomes something very special: languor.)
'and you tell me my other self will you answer me at last I am tired of you I want you I dream of you for you against you answer me your name is a perfume about me your color bursts among the thorns bring back my heart with cool wine make me a coverlet of the morning I suffocate beneath this mask withered shrunken skin nothing exists save desire'.

And now the second:

When, in a moment of grace, it happens that I say to a woman, 'I love you', something flashes within me and I am reborn. Her *beauty* releases this marvel, her beauty which gives off a flash that fascinates me, a light I bathe in, and which gives to every part of her body an attraction that nothing can belie – to her scent, her voice, her skin and her words. I lose myself in her ears, her mouth, her hair and her loins. For I am suddenly assured of something whose strength is the measure of my torment and my peace – that she loves me. And I fear, without believing it, that this time of grace may disappear. But in fact she is waiting for me, and I desire her. When we embrace it is an absolute certainty that each of us has together found the source: of earth, water and fire; a moment of truth which comes well before death.

What can be said about these two decontextualised passages?

As they stand, both may be said to take certain risks. The first, with its abandonment of punctuation encouraging a breathlessness and a blurring of edges between the 'me' and the 'you', does so in ways that are perhaps more striking. But the second takes risks of its own. It indulges in a particularised and eroticised evocation of 'a woman'. Yet it has shifted from the dedicatory mode of the first passage, with its 'you' and 'your', to the more impersonal celebration of 'she' and 'her'. In fact, as the initial 'when' announces, this celebration is also an exposition, part of a larger argument about something as abstract as 'truth'. These two passages have been snatched from their contexts not only to allow some of their similarities to emerge through juxtaposition, but also to allow the quality of the passages to shine free of expectations: as words scorched by exposure to desire and desire's potential for ecstasy (for *jouissance*). It is time now to place the passages. The first comes from Roland Barthes's *A Lover's Discourse: Fragments* and is composed largely of a quotation from *Paradis* by the novelist Philippe Sollers (p. 155). The second forms the opening of the second chapter of *On tue un enfant*, entitled 'Béatrice *ou* de l'amour' (p. 31).

In this chapter, Leclaire sets out to show that the 'marvellous child' is not the sole 'unconscious signifier' with the power to represent itself to consciousness in forms both liberating and destructive. The 'phallus' is another such signifier. Leclaire's argument is a complex and dense one, as it charts the way the phallus is represented by the body and by male and female anatomy, and as it charts the pathogenic potential of these representations. I have neither the space nor the analytic experience to comment in detail upon the steps of the argument, which links the signifier to the penis and its lack (the threat of castration), and thus to fundamental notions of sexuality and gender. Yet I do intend to discuss the importance of the phallus for Leclaire; and to help me do this I shall call upon certain elements of Jacques Lacan's formulations, upon which Leclaire's argument leans.

Few concepts are more central and pervading in Lacan's work than that of the phallus. Yet few concepts are more ungraspable (the essay 'La signification du phallus' – 'The Meaning of the Phallus' – remains one of the most difficult in the *Ecrits*).[5] Certain indications can nonetheless be given, which may help in subsequent dealings with Leclaire. For Lacan, the phallus is not the penis itself but rather a signifier – the supreme signifier – of desire. The phallus may be thought of at its most general as functioning in much the way that language does for anthropologist Claude Lévi-Strauss: it effects a primordial division (of the child from the mother, of the sexes, of the signifier from the signified) and later offers the possibility of a new unity, achievable at a different level (the level one may usefully associate with Freud's notion of sublimation). The phallus divides, and thus inaugurates lack (or 'lack-of-being'). To simplify, one may say that the child has to pass from a stage of 'being' the phallus (for the mother) to 'having' it (or not). Either alternative is premised on division and suffused with lack. In turn, such lack is at the heart of all desire, as it is of language itself. The phallus thus stands at the crossroads of language, as Lacan suggests in 'The Meaning of the Phallus' when he says that 'The phallus is the privileged signifier of that mark where the share of the logos is wedded to the advent of desire' (Mitchell and Rose, 1982, p. 82).

Even from this precariously brief sketch the crucial role of the phallus in Lacanian doctrine may be apparent; though, as it turns out, what is important here is less the notion of the phallus (and its promotion or demotion), than the way the topic of the phallus impinges – and opens doors – on to areas of experience which may concern everyone (if psychoanalysts most of all). By recognising the phallus as only one among several privileged primordial signifiers, Leclaire unquestionably deviates from Lacanian doctrine; and it is a deviation which later leads him (under pressure from feminist critiques of phallocentrism in Lacan's work) to reject the notion of the phallus altogether.[6] Despite this, the phallus is important in his work, because it allows him not so much to illustrate or argue a case as to move, by way of a well-worn theoretical road, deep into common areas of existence, and to emerge with a unique way of describing them. The point Leclaire wishes to make is subservient to a broader experiential account which he wishes somehow to render. This is so when the experience (as may be clear from the brief exposition of the notion of the phallus) is generative of language, but at the same time not immediately accessible to language.

Like the 'marvellous child', the phallus is topologically in the 'beyond'. It is a pure signifier, only partly available through the metonymies of a discourse over which theory (implying as it does both distance and some degree of control) has no dominance. From within the armoury of Lacan's own discourse, such a disavowal of control can at times seem disingenuous. But Leclaire takes the insight to heart. And the metaphor is a strong one. For if the phallus is 'beyond', it is negotiable only through certain heightened experiences. One does not have to look far to know what sort of experiences – only back to the opening of the second chapter of *On tue un enfant*, which was quoted above. As Leclaire explains a little further on:

> The phallus is a referent in the order of the unconscious, and so it cannot be grasped within any concept. Like a prime number whose figure it would be

impossible to divide, it escapes inscription by the way its one-ness is cut. This means that there exists no picture or text of the phallus. It can only be encountered in the ecstasy experienced by bodies in the risk of love. (pp. 32–3)

This disavowal of control and of the empire of theory does not imply, however, that psychoanalysis is not concerned with truth. Far from it. It is truth Leclaire hopes to discover, with and for his patients. Only, this truth is the truth of the unconscious, which is never commensurate with knowledge.[7] The 'moment of truth' of which Leclaire writes is no generality or abstractable equation, but is a lover's moment of absolute particularity. 'If truth speaks', he says, 'it is with the voice of the unconscious; and at the heart of what makes truth talk, there is no more certain mouth for telling it than the ecstasy of lovers' (pp. 31–2).

This formulation gives some sense of the psychoanalytic practice Leclaire envisages, and a sense of his writing, and the risks he takes in the way he writes. In an essay entitled 'Les contrebandiers de l'écriture' ('The Writing Smugglers'), critic Bernard Pingaud has some trenchant things to say about psychoanalysts' incursions into the literary domain – 'psycholiterature', as he rather disdainfully calls it (Pingaud, 1979).[8] He even mentions Serge Leclaire as an extreme example of his worry about the blurring of boundaries of discourse. What his talk of mastery and of the psychoanalysts' necessary grounding in the primacy of the conceptual tends to ignore is the way psychoanalysis reveals the illusory nature of all aspirations to neutrality in language. For patient as for analyst, language is necessarily symptomatic (especially language which establishes certainties and erects hierarchies). When the analyst tries to speak of the 'primordial signifiers' (the 'marvellous child' or the 'phallus') the very words he uses – indeed the fact of using words – bear witness to his ineluctable removedness from that towards which he or she is gesturing. It is a perception of something similar that 'The lunatic, the lover, and the poet' who 'Are of imagination all compact' (as Theseus has it in *A Midsummer Night's Dream*, v, 1) have kept alive. Yet it is a perception whose range has not always been recognised.

The psychoanalyst may try to help the patient to encounter the phallus, but still has no monopoly over the language of desire and love. The phallus inhabits the unconscious; and the unconscious is 'another scene' (as Leclaire calls it in an article significantly entitled 'Fragments de langue d'avant Babel' – 'Fragments of Language from before Babel').[9] This 'other scene' is both intimately familiar and worryingly strange. In it the drama of desire is played out, 'with all the parts of our body – our fingers, our eyes, our skin and our mouth – which are stripped of any imaginary clothing, and speak among themselves the forgotten language of love where it is *words of desire* that are conjugated and arranged' (Leclaire, 1981, p. 88). For as long as the analyst stays in contact with the 'other scene' and its erotic particularity, his or her own language will be under the severest of pressures. This will be the case in the analytic session, of course; and, in so far as the writing which emerges from it is not serving merely as a disguise or defence, it will be the case in the analytic text as well. The assumption of an article such as that by Bernard Pingaud, that genre or degree of literariness is subject to the analyst–writer's choice, overlooks the force of such pressure. Words, tracking love, may have to unwork themselves, point to possibilities rather than boldly demarcate territories. Indeed, if Leclaire is suggesting that love is the royal road towards a relation with the unconscious which is fundamentally constitutive of the self, then it is so paradoxically – or ambivalently perhaps. For it constitutes the self through loss of that very self, in its merging with the loved one. There are no linguistic short-cuts on this royal road. Travel down it is premised upon a degree of letting go, not just by the patient, but by the analyst and analytic writer as well. Leclaire acknowledges this in *On tue un enfant*, when he says of his own writing:

I must come back to my psychoanalyst's armchair (which is the same one in which I write) in order to reflect again, as my patients do, upon this experience of truth. I must do this above all in order not to go in for any easy renunciation of the experience on the grounds that it might be difficult for a psychoanalyst, or unworthy of his state, to love. I must be able to write what it means to love, and what contributes to love's marvels, its impasses and its defeats.   (p. 41)

Perhaps there is a final dimension to the juxtaposition of Serge Leclaire with Roland Barthes. For what is *A Lover's Discourse: Fragments* if not an attempt to unravel the significance of the confidently announced yet formidably overdetermined remark with which Barthes introduces his book: '*So it is a lover who speaks and who says*' (p. 9)? Leclaire might almost have said the same. In the following two sections (§ 2.4, 2.5) I shall have further occasion to juxtapose the two writers and show just how close they are. The overlap between them should not obscure their differences, however. For where Barthes can give some freedom of rein to his speculations, where there are only inner pressures determining his exploration, Leclaire has bearing upon him the weight of his patients' need (of psychoanalysis as a received practice). The need is for linguistic repair of a love which cannot find its relation through the body to the phallus and the unconscious sources of energy. The impasses and blocks which love encounters are legion. Leclaire implies that it is the duty of psychoanalysis to minimise them. This is a duty the analyst pursues at his peril.

§ 2.4

It is time to draw a more precise picture of the love which Leclaire situates at the centre of his practice, and to see its relation to the concepts of desire and language which psychoanalytic texts more frequently canvass. It has already been seen that Freud talks of love when he discusses ambivalence; and soon I shall show (in § 2.5) just how important a role he confers upon love in his analytic practice. Yet the emphasis I am giving could be misleading. For most readers of Freud will agree that love as an idea in his work tends to be submerged under the surge of the instincts or drives, or exiled by the urgency of the libido. Variants of desire are everywhere in Freud; but love is a more precarious notion altogether.

In the introduction to his book *Freud, Proust and Lacan*, Malcolm Bowie speaks of the traditions of 'high' and 'low' desire. He locates part of the importance of Freud and psychoanalysis in the fact that they belong to both the 'high' tradition ('Hegel through Kierkegaard, Darwin and Nietzsche to Sartre, Foucault and Deleuze/Guattari') and the 'low' ('from Sade through Krafft-Ebing, Havelock Ellis and Weininger to Kinsey and Masters/Johnson') (pp. 2–3). He suggests that psychoanalysis helps usher in the Era of Desire, as 'the cosmological principle of our secular age' (p. 3). To the very extent that one may agree with this, it is important to see that what Serge Leclaire is attempting to articulate is slightly unorthodox – it is tempting to say almost old-fashioned – and that this constitutes a part of the peril of his venture. Not that for him, Lacanian as he is (or was), desire is not central; but that the divisions implicit in desire may ultimately be tempered and eroded by the 'moment of truth' which love can usher in. Such a moment may be strictly unnamable in language, which always betokens division; yet the mere intimation of it takes him some way from Lacan himself, for whom love, if possible at all, is often equivalent to a form of suicide.[10] In this sense Leclaire is indeed closer to Barthes who, in his *The Pleasure of the Text*, goes so far as to complain about the preponderance of talk about desire, which he sees as going on at the expense of talk about pleasure.

What of the relation of love to the desire which psychoanalysis privileges? This is a question which again summons the pervasive field of ambivalence. For the closer desire is inspected, the more its underlying dynamic starts to resemble something approaching the hate which was characterised as attendant on the moment of the child's differentiation of self and world, subject and object. To be less paradoxical: desire (of which Lacan suggests the phallus is the supreme signifier) is born of division, the rupture of primordial unity or primary narcissism. This is the primitive or originating context. As for adult desire, it is at times devastating in its force and hateful in its mechanics (as there will be ample chance to confirm in the work of Proust). Lacanian desire inhabits a post-lapsarian world, and is token of its inevitable insatiability. Yet this picture of insatiability is not the whole story either. For if the phallus is the principle of division, then, like language, it may also (for example through sublimation) permit a new form of unity on a different level or register. The phallus yields desire. This in turn offers the road down which, in the adult context, the individual must pass towards any possible 'truth' of love. This is perhaps a common-sensical idea; but familiarity with it should not lead one to overlook the stress Leclaire puts on what is at the end of the road. Nor should one overlook the cutting edge of his observation that even if the 'truth' of love is found, it will not be namable (in the way, say, that an object of desire is namable) since it is a truth of the unconscious.

Where love boldly declares, or 'knows' itself, it may not be original or 'truthful' in Leclaire's sense, but already a fabric of interlacing conflicts and tensions into whose threads and fibres it threatens to decompose. An example drawn from literature can help make this more concrete, and serve as a route back to Leclaire's way of helping his patients. It is an example again drawn from T. S. Eliot. I have already cited some lines from *Ash Wednesday*, where the importance of 'turning' was seen to be paramount. In the lines I now wish to cite (from part II), a collection of 'dissembled' bones pray thus to a 'Lady of silences':

> The single Rose
> Is now the Garden
> Where all loves end
> Terminate torment
> Of love unsatisfied
> The greater torment
> Of love satisfied.

Such love as can be named here, and which craves satisfaction, is in a way less than adequate to itself (or is greater than any of its objects). This is what the lines seem to assert. Yet even while this most awful and 'adult' of conclusions is being asserted, the poetry is allowing a more subtle possibility to emerge. These lines form part of a prayer; and oxymoron, paradox and conflict may to an extent be resolved through the very special listener that prayer implies. This glimmering possibility is bodied forth in the subsequent lines, which run:

> Under a juniper-tree the bones sang, scattered and shining
> We are glad to be scattered, we did little good to each other,
> Under a tree in the cool of the day, with the blessing of sand,
> Forgetting themselves and each other, united
> In the quiet of the desert. This is the land which ye
> Shall divide by lot. And neither division nor unity
> Matters. This is the land. We have our inheritance.

As in Ezekiel's vision in the Bible, the bones are scattered, and they forget themselves. In this very moment of unconsciousness and dispersal, through 'the blessing of sand', they seem truly to unite and take possession. They take possession of a lover's ideal place, where 'neither division nor unity / Matters', and where belonging is permanently protected by right: 'This is the land. We have our inheritance.'

Serge Leclaire attempts to allow his patients to speak the words which open love's possibilities, and he describes this in the chapter entitled 'Béatrice *ou* de l'amour'. Ideally, he suggests, in the one she loves, a woman should find herself as woman, as 'Beatrice. By whom the ways are opened.' In a world less than ideal, the analyst tries to become that 'Beatrice' (for woman or for man). And as he does so, the case history of 'Beatrice' slides into invention and literary allusion. For one cannot read this name without thinking of Dante. The ways Dante's Beatrice opens to the pilgrim, through Virgil, are not easy ones. Scarcely easier, Leclaire implies, will be the ways of psychoanalysis. Yet it is through Beatrice and his love for her that Dante comes from despair to experience *Paradiso*. Many readers will encounter increasing difficulty, the higher they mount into *Paradiso*; and of course there is only silence in face of the supreme light and love. Yet even those readers who prefer the *bolgias* of *Inferno* cannot doubt that the entire journey and *Comedy* are utterly dependent upon the hope and need for what is beyond and above. Leclaire's patients' overriding need has been mentioned, and so it would be wrong to forget Dante's. After all, there are few needs greater than his, in *Canto* I of *Inferno*, after he has failed to mount directly to the stars and has 'ruined' down to the 'place below . . . where the sun is silent'.

However, lest Leclaire's claims for psychoanalysis should start to seem grandiose, it is worth remembering the nature of the love which it hopes to make available, which will never free itself from the body in the way that Eliot's or Dante's aspires to. If, through analysis, the sufferer is able provisionally to come to terms with narcissism, with the phallus and the threat of castration, an opening may be gained into realms of a 'lover's discourse'. This will be a mixed blessing, owing to the object-less nature of the discourse (Barthes's own 'lover's discourse' is suffused with anxiety and melancholy). But the necessary pull of such mixed feelings should by now be familiar. When prayer is not viable, when the analysand's Beatrice is restrained by the working out of the counter-transference, what will be opened up is a body in its unfulfilled erotogenic potential. This constitutes one further layer to the peril of Leclaire's analytic practice and writing. For of all things the body is most particular and available, and yet general and unknowable. The body is that through which all is comprehended, yet is itself comprehended by nothing. The experience towards which the analyst eases his patients by way of language appears again to be unmappable by language.

Nor does the analyst's problem stop there. For if his attempt to open his patients to an erotic potentiality is dependent upon a certain experience of loss, then, as suggested above, the transformation of this potential into reality (the achievement of erotic fulfilment) is to be achieved only through yet further loss. For the body must go out of itself, and 'lose' itself in union with another.

Jouissance beckons the body. But it threatens to be as hard to find as a pot of gold, for as long as words and language are the colours of the rainbow. In his book *Roland Barthes by Roland Barthes*, the author speaks tantalisingly of the 'sensual delight' of the possibility of being able 'to discourse and make love', of the 'simultaneous use of speech and the kiss: to speak while kissing, to kiss while speaking'.[11] But he does so in the realisation that the 'sensual delight' is imaginary, the vision of simultaneity a fulfilment of wishes alone. The mouth can be used for kissing or for talking, but not for both at once!

The transforming into words of something of *jouissance* which is at love's heart is for Leclaire a necessary, but formidable task. Barthes helps again with an indication of why, when he writes:

> The asocial character of bliss [jouissance]: it is the abrupt loss of sociality, and yet there follows no recurrence to the subject (subjectivity), the person, solitude: *everything* is lost, integrally. Extremity of the clandestine, darkness of the motion-picture theater.   (Barthes, 1976, p. 39)

Of course Barthes is talking here, in *The Pleasure of the Text*, of a possible relation between a person and a literary text rather than of a relation between two bodies. Then again, herein lies the crucial project of *The Pleasure of the Text*, which is to do for the literary text what Serge Leclaire is trying to do for the body physical: restore to it the fullness of its erotic range. (Read alongside Leclaire's book, this most elusive of Barthes's works becomes significantly more persuasive – as well as shedding light sideways on to *On tue un enfant*.) The literary text may indeed be a body, Barthes suggests. Nor is he alone in his conviction. In the conclusion to the first chapter of his *Writing and the Body*, Gabriel Josipovici suggests that 'in the right hands' the novel *'as it is read'* may become 'a living body' (p. 33). Psychoanalyst Didier Anzieu chooses for his weighty enquiry into literary creativity the title *Le Corps de l'oeuvre* ('The Body of the Work'). It is no coincidence that the word 'corpus' has come to designate the totality of a writer's work. Yet if for Barthes the text is a body, it is not just any body. 'Does the text have human form, is it a figure, an anagram of the body? Yes, but of our erotic body' (Barthes, 1976, p. 17).

I have already discussed the metaphor of movement. I have brushed, and will further engage with that of birth. The power of metaphor is daunting indeed. The assimilation of a text into a body may be metaphoric. Given what has been said about the unmappable scope of the body, it may seem to imply that the text is strictly unmappable as well. There is some truth in this implication, no doubt; but one need not be reduced to silence by this part-truth. For perhaps the metaphor works both ways. The very notion of a body, when viewed psychoanalytically at least, is itself first and foremost a metaphoric, or textual construction.[12] The body itself is a sort of fiction – and this is one of the implications of the notion of the phallus, and of the primordial division which it is designated as effecting. For when the infant returns from its confrontation with the lack of the phallus, it is to a body which has been refracted through desire and language (through the mediation of the signifier).

There will be occasion to look closer at the role of language in the infant's experience of its body in relation to the work of Maud Mannoni. For now, this part of the discussion of love in Leclaire's work may perhaps be concluded with the observation that while the body – signally the body in love – may not be totally available to language, this does not imply that there is any alternative road towards it. Kissing and speaking may be mutually exclusive activities. But it is usually the case in adult life that the former becomes possible only because of the latter. Of the several bodies which Barthes suggests one inhabits – that of the physiologists, the scientists, or the grammarians – it is the 'body of bliss consisting solely of erotic relations' which most interests him (Barthes, 1976, p. 16). This is a body to which access *can* be facilitated by the appropriate words. In *The Pleasure of the Text* Barthes seeks to free this text-body from the tyranny of ideology, of 'doxa', of scientificity and of common sense. He cannot name it, as it consists of 'the open list of the fires of language'. What he can do is point his reader towards it.

Leclaire cannot hope within the analytic setting to name his patients' love, and so hand it to them, as it were on a plate. He can, nonetheless, open a space through words in which they may discover it for themselves. Or so he claims. The status of his account as claim highlights another difference between the two writers, Leclaire and Barthes. For Barthes can return his reader to the familiar texts to which he refers, with eyes opened, whereas for Leclaire the equivalent 'text' of his patients' love does not pre-exist his attempt to put it into words. (His reader is not familiar with his patients, as only in the process of reading is he or she getting to know them.) For Leclaire's claim to be anything more than just that, he must communicate something of the analytic space and love's 'moments of truth' – not to his patients now but to his reader. How does he attempt to achieve this? In what further difficulties does it involve him? These are, broadly, the questions which lie behind the various discussions in the remainder of this chapter.

§ 2.5

In the present argument there has been much talk of learning how to love. What has so far been withheld is the term under which this love is often ranged within the psychoanalytic field – the term 'transference'. The analysand does not do all his or her learning in a void or in an unconducive world, but in the chair or on the couch, in the analytic session. From the analyst's side, with transference goes counter-transference in tandem. One of the dangers grappled with in 'Béatrice *ou* de l'amour' and in the final chapter of *On tue un enfant*, 'Sygne *ou* de l'amour de transfert', is that of what happens when the clinical veneer comes off these two terms 'transference' and 'counter-transference'.

Just how extreme is the danger can be gathered again from Barthes's *The Pleasure of the Text*. Speaking of his project with the literary text, in a terribly dense and suggestive sentence, Barthes proposes: 'However, if one were to manage it, the very utterance of drifting would today be a suicidal discourse' (p. 19) ['Cependant, si l'on y parvenait, dire la dérive serait aujourd'hui un discours suicidaire' (p. 33)]. Some of what Barthes means should already be apparent: try to chart the margins of experience ('la dérive') which *jouissance* inhabits, and silence is lurking there, waiting to net the explorer. For Barthes the writer such silence may amount to suicide. For Leclaire the psychoanalyst, attempting to 'dire la dérive' may also entail the risk of professional suicide. When the clinical veneer disappears, does Leclaire drift ineluctably into the realm of 'la dérive'? In all the talk of love, bodies and *jouissance*, where is the analyst? Still seated some distance from the analytic couch, listening Zen-like to the elaboration of the patient's lover's discourse? By admitting to the urgent reality of a patient's transference-love (in this case that of Sygne), and by trying to articulate his own responding love, is Leclaire eroding the distance which distinguishes a psychoanalyst from any other sort of listener? Is he, to put it crudely, washing his dirty linen in public? At a simple level the answer must be 'no'. He is not advocating or admitting to a passage from some form of recognition to 'an act of the flesh'. But this hardly resolves the deeper question of what he *is* advocating.

The problem of just what a psychoanalyst can allow him- or herself is one which still divides camps. In her book *Psychoanalysis: The Impossible Profession*, Janet Malcolm suggests that America is split between those analysts who remain quite impassive and those who express some sympathy when their patient announces the death of their father; between those who look only to the patient's reaction and those who apologise when they arrive late to a session. Such intense conflicts can seem a little unreal to the lay European. Yet the underlying issues are real enough. It is worth remembering, as Leclaire recalls, that the confrontation with transference-love became rather too much for Freud's early associate Joseph Breuer, who sought escape in travel and marriage. Sandor Ferenczi also seems to have walked the counter-transferential tightrope rather dangerously – so much so that Freud saw fit to rebuke him for his wavering.[13]

What of Freud's own reaction to transference-love? To try to understand the context of Leclaire's psychoanalytic practice and writing, one may usefully turn to Freud, to see how he proposed to withstand the force of transference-love, and how he attempted at the same time to express this force in his writing. Close attention to certain passages from his work in fact reveals that the relation between these two procedures – the withstanding and the writing – is more intimate than might be imagined.

In his essay 'Observations on Transference-Love' (1915) and in his 'Introductory Lectures on Psychoanalysis' delivered two years later, Freud broaches the question of transference. He writes (in the lectures):

It may still pass muster if a woman who is unhappy in her marriage appears to be seized with a serious passion for a doctor who is still unattached, if she is ready to seek a divorce in order to be his, or if, where there are social obstacles, she even expresses no hesitation about entering into a secret *liaison* with him. Such things come about even outside psychoanalysis. But in these circumstances we are astonished to hear declarations by married women and girls which bear witness to a quite particular attitude to the therapeutic problem: they had always known, they say, that they could only be cured by love.

(Standard Edition, XVI, 441)

The love for an analyst is real, Freud suggests, and should be accepted as therapeutic.[14] Indeed it is only to be bothered over when it starts to decay or be resisted. Yet even while he is insisting on the reality of the patient's transference-love, Freud also affirms that it must be shelved in favour of higher ideals. He continues:

We overcome the transference by pointing out to the patient that his feelings do not arise from the present situation and do not apply to the person of the doctor, but that they are repeating something that happened to him earlier. In this way we oblige him to transfer his repetition into a memory.

(Standard Edition, XVI, 443–4)

In chapter 6 (§ 6.4) I shall have occasion to look at the relation of transference to repetition. For the moment it may be enough to say that what Freud suggests is not as easy as it sounds. This is the case not only because of the resistance on the part of the patient to being so summarily dealt with, but because the analyst is human too. Freud has already admitted something of this in the earlier essay on the subject, where he writes:

Sexual love is undoubtedly one of the chief things in life, and the union of mental and bodily satisfaction in the enjoyment of love is one of its culminating peaks. Apart from a few queer fanatics, all the world knows this and conducts its life accordingly; science alone is too delicate to admit it. When a woman sues for love, to reject and refuse is a distressing part for a man to play; and, in spite of neurosis and resistance, there is an incomparable fascination in a woman of high principles who confesses her passion. *(Standard Edition*, XII, 169–70)

Such fascination must, nonetheless, be roundly overcome for the greater good of the patient and for the ideal of psychoanalysis:

I have already let it be understood that analytic technique requires of the physician that he should deny to the patient who is craving for love the satisfaction she demands. The treatment must be carried out in abstinence . . . For the doctor, ethical motives unite with the technical ones to restrain him from giving the patient his love. *(Standard Edition*, XII, 165, 169)

Lest one remain in any doubt over the plausibility of such mutual deferment of gratification for the higher and more distant ideals of mental health and analytic rigour, Freud draws towards the end of his 'Observations on Transference-Love' with a little moral tale:

He [the analyst] must not stage the scene of a dog-race in which the prize was to be a garland of sausages but which some humorist spoilt by throwing a single sausage on to the track. The result was, of course, that the dogs threw themselves upon it and forgot all about the race and about the garland that was luring them to victory in the far distance. (*Standard Edition*, XII, 169)

Freud confronts the issue of transference head on. Or he seems to take it in his strong, manly grasp, and put it firmly behind him. Reading his papers – and I imagine this would be even more the case had I heard his lecture – I am inclined to put aside my doubts and join in the pursuit of that victory (forget my single Freudian sausage and go for the garland!), which is strange, as elsewhere I would not accept so easily, or expect him to have me accept, the transformation of libidinal impulses of unimaginable intensity into the beneficent workings of a rational scheme. Of course Freud makes a theoretical point, one upon which he will elaborate, one formally consistent with his theories of neurosis and the psychoanalytic process. But this is scarcely enough to carry the day, or to account for the ease with which I am persuaded.

The longer one looks at such passages the clearer it becomes that one is not being won over by anything that is being said. One is won because, as Roland Barthes has it in *The Pleasure of the Text*, 'The text chooses me, by a whole disposition of invisible screens [and] selective baffles' (p. 27). One is seduced, but less by an argument working either on the side of the conscientious analyst or on that of the diffident analysand than by an alignment with the Freud – now neither analyst nor patient but *writer* or *speaker* – who is artfully deploying argument, anecdote and authority to one's own quite immediate *readerly* gratification. One is seduced by the man's *inimitable personal style*. His style is no superimposed gloss, but is of the essence. Through it Freud bodies himself forth. Jean-Louis Baudry is perhaps correct to insist throughout his book *Proust, Freud et l'autre* that Freud is first and foremost a writer. He is a writer, according to Baudry, who recognises 'what is most singular in us – vocabulary, rhythm, syntax – in short the style which defines us but which we learn to be also the most faithful expression of a stranger within us over whom we have no power' (p. 84). If such an argument seems to imply that Freud is concerned with the very same matter as that of novelists, then this is indeed the conclusion that Baudry wishes to draw: 'The psychoanalyst and the novelist, each with his own paths and methods, were devoting themselves despite it all to the same object, the same activity' (pp. 56–7).

This is not an appropriate place to examine at length the components of Freud's style.[15] It varied in any case over time and according to the degree of certainty or conviction his subject matter allowed him – to the point where it might be truer to speak of Freud's 'styles'. (In his *Freud, Proust and Lacan*, Malcolm Bowie shows several different Freud personas, including Freud-the-archaeologist and Freud-the-conquistador.) Suffice perhaps to say that while it would take a sensitive and penetrating mind to describe the various styles, in the extracts quoted every reader can recognise a particular Freud style, and is likely to be wooed by it. If his writing allows his patients' transference-love to become real for the reader, this reality is subservient to the stronger feeling of his ability to cope with that love. At such moments it is almost as if Freud were really the figure often found in Ernest Jones's biography. It is Freud the confident, modest, understanding, committed, married, paternal head of an established movement who finds representation in this polished prose which tells the case histories of nervous, claustral, intelligent, strait-laced, middle-class Viennese ladies. What fine histories – love stories indeed – he writes. However, like all good stories, whether of love or of hate, his are winning because so rooted in their historical moment. Freud allows his reader to feel the pulse of love and sexuality in the early twentieth century while he is in the very process of reconstructing the arteries down which that love flows.

Freud's withstanding of the force of transference-love, and his expression of this necessary force in his writing are therefore not entirely discrete achievements. Both are sustained by his personal analytic and writerly style (when these two are barely distinguishable). Serge Leclaire follows in the footsteps of Freud, and he passes down certain familiar theoretical paths. But if his own stories are to be *telling*, they have to allow him to write down different, more nearly contemporary alleyways. After Freud, Lawrence, and Henry Miller, after Joyce and de Beauvoir, not to mention the advent of modern feminism, sexology, cinema and video (the list is indeed rather arbitrary), a love story of today must needs be differently told, even when it is told within a tradition whose lineage goes directly to Freud. Styles not only do, but *must* change; and this is quite as true for psychoanalytic style as for literary.[16] The force of the imperative is not to be underestimated, especially if one goes any way towards endorsing the claim made by psychoanalyst François Roustang, that 'It is the style of the analysis which, in the cure, produces analysis' (Roustang, 1977, p. 95).[17] However infuriating at times may be the knowingness and recondite gamesmanship of Jacques Lacan's enormously influential work, there seems little point in making a direct adverse contrast between this and Freud's lucidity (as it may be tempting to do) on the basis that the one is telling a tale obscurely, the other clearly. Not when so much of the tale is in the telling; not when Lacan is known to have been fond of Buffon's maxim 'le style est l'homme même' ('style makes the man');[18] and not when the conditions determining the style of telling have altered so dramatically. It would be almost as misleading to hold up the blithe and covert eroticism one finds in a Walter Scott romance as a model to the impossible yearning found in the novels of Marguerite Duras; or to claim priority for the hysteria compellingly told in Mary Shelley's *Frankenstein* over the convolutions and obtrusive mannerisms of the early sections of D. M. Thomas's *The White Hotel*. Which is not to say that one must wholeheartedly condone Lacan's self-consciously rebarbative prose. Freud's writing cast a long shadow forward in time. Yet where Freud's writing is wonderfully alive, it is often the case that post-Freudian analysts, working as it were in this shadow, end up being leaden and repetitive.[19] Freud's style, palely re-presented now, does not tell the same story. Lacan and his followers, of whom Leclaire was one, are to be congratulated for realising this.

When attempting to express the force of transference and counter-transference, and his response to them, Leclaire leaves the shelter of Freud's protection. He commits himself to his own personal style: of analysis and of writing. I shall soon turn back to Leclaire to try (in § 2.7) to give a clearer picture of what this style comprises. But to provide a further context – certain pointers to the manner in which writers in the latter half of this century have faced the need for innovation – I wish to invoke another example from poetry. The poem I shall discuss will offer the chance to characterise the psychoanalytic procedure as it is promoted by Leclaire, and will in addition provide a more eloquent introduction to Leclaire's avowal of love than I could possibly achieve alone.

§ 2.6

The poet I wish to call on for assistance wrote under the name of Paul Celan (his original name was Paul Antschel). He is still relatively little known to the British poetry-reading public, but his reputation is nonetheless growing as one of the major post-war European poets, and one of the most important writers in German this century. The poem I wish to cite is from his collection of 1952, *Mohn und Gedächtnis*, and is entitled 'Crystal' (in Michael Hamburger's translation). It runs thus:

> Not on my lips look for your mouth,
> not in front of the gate for the stranger,
> not in the eye for the tear,
>
> Seven nights higher red makes for red,
> seven hearts deeper the hand knocks on the gate,
> seven roses later plashes the fountain.
>
> [Kristall
>
> Nict an meinen Lippen suche deinen Mund,
> nict vorm Tor den Fremdling,
> nicht im Aug die Träne.
>
> Sieben Nächte höher wandert Rot zu Rot,
> sieben Herzen tiefer pocht die Hand ans Tor,
> sieben Rosen später rauscht der Brunnen.]
>
> (Celan, 1980, pp. 58, 59)[20]

Even in his early poetry, of which this is an example, Celan is not easy; though the difficulties he poses – of gaps between words and lines, of elusive yet specific references, of indeterminate tone – are ones with which one may be familiar, through being reared on a diet of the modern. A single feature is clear, however, and even on a preliminary reading it reaches out and seizes the reader: there is a stark contrast between the fixity of the first verse of the poem and the surging openness of the second.

By the time the poem starts, love has dried up. The possibility of discovering oneself in another, even if that other is the loved one, has given way to the hardened surfaces of discrete bodies. Expectation, even of the unexpected, is to be forgone. Even compassion, in or for this breakdown of the chance of relation, is precluded. The first three lines do not describe suffering. Rather suffering is where the words emerge from and where they return to after faltering through three inconsequentialities whose only point of binding is negation (the word 'not'). Talk of movement, even from suffering to suffering, is perhaps misleading. The first stanza testifies to cessation, disappearance and stasis: the cruelty of crystal. Of course this poem, as is typical of those in Celan's early collections, is distinctly located, in the space between an 'I' (of 'my') and a 'you' (of 'your'). Yet the withdrawal of the 'me' seems to merge with the withdrawal of the speaker–poet, in something like a nightmare version of the Mallarméan dream of the 'disappearance of the poet as speaker' ['disparition élocutoire du poëte'] (Mallarmé, 1945, p. 366). The 'you' emerges deprived not only of love and expectation, but almost of the means (the words) with which expecting or wanting might become possible. More than any poem whose centre is the suffering 'I' (where deprivation will be measured against the lyrical plenitude of the first person pronoun), this poem allows the reader to experience suffering by so nearly removing it altogether.

I have already pointed to a not dissimilar suffering in Kafka's work, where the fictional characters are beset with incapacities. There are, however, important differences between Kafka and Celan, and of these one is worth mentioning here. I suggested that for the reader the exemplary clarity of Kafka's prose cuts across the characters' incapacities. The prose disables them, but still renders them 'characters'. Despite their inadequacy and distance from the grace of Kafka's telling, Georg and Gregor, the penal colony's officer and Joseph K. do offer the reader a semblance of 'character'. If they do not have a fullness of being, at least they are struggling towards such fullness. Celan's verse is very different. In it the syntax and often the words themselves are menaced and broken. Even the hope of fullness seems largely to have vanished. Celan's poetry – the sheer fact of it – is witness of course to an achieving. Yet one of its strengths is its ability to allow the reader so far into a world in which a notion like achievement is unimaginably distant. This is a world in which wanting, hoping, expecting – being indeed, being a character – seem to have vanished. In his later poetry these blocks and droughts often quite overtake the verse, rendering it extremely difficult and ineradicably strange: 'Illegibility / of this world', as one title announces it.[21] But at the time of 'Crystal' the stops upon being are still to some extent absorbed by the poems' sparse pronouns and occasional proper names – even if these do point more towards an absence than a presence.

I said I wish to call on Celan partly because he can offer a context typical of stylistic innovation in the latter half of this century. Some of the features of this innovation are becoming apparent. Yet there is a sense in which nothing is ever 'typical' about poetic genius. By a similar paradox, when one tries to penetrate the causes for the distressing feel of Celan's poetry one comes up against the general condition of this century and at the same time the peculiar awfulness with which Celan endured it. The world against which the poetry is pushing has contained the 'impossible possibility' which 'Death Fugue' (one of Celan's most famous poems) describes, in which 'death death is a master from Germany'. When this is so, it is not only those most directly subjugated, who are sustained by the 'Black milk of daybreak', who find themselves exiled from life and its mainstay, desire.[22] The brief facts of Celan's biography might be enough to account for the exile which is implicit throughout his verse. For Celan was born a Jew in 1920 in Czernowitz, Bukovina (in what was part of the Austrian Empire and is now in the Soviet Union). In 1942 his parents were deported and murdered in a concentration camp, while he was sent to a forced labour camp. He survived the war, and from 1948 lived in Paris, writing in and translating into German, till his suicide by drowning in the Seine in 1970.

These barest of facts might account for the immanence of appalled silence in Celan's poems: for the snow, the stone, the 'crystal dressed in the style of your silence', and the eyes uncomprehending, their irises lost.[23] As Michael Hamburger points out in the introduction to his translation of the poems, the reality of Celan's survival of the Holocaust may belie the inner wound suffered. Perhaps any biography – the facts of the twentieth century – might almost be enough to account for anyone's inability or reluctance to live and want in a world which has given full rein to the destruction to which Celan's verse obliquely testifies. One hardly needs the reminders of an Adorno or a George Steiner to perceive that desire – including the desire to create – is less than ever innocent in the world of those who survived the Holocaust (on *Mr Sammler's Planet*, as Saul Bellow has it in his poignant fictive account of what it means to survive).

Yet the very readiness with which this account of the difficulty of Celan's poetry presents itself should prompt caution. For, as I said, however common his fate, Celan lived it with a peculiar intensity. Others who survived bore their wound less deeply. Few could transform their wound into a poetry which kept the wound so open. If the Holocaust offers itself as one way of understanding the sense of exile or impossibility – that state somewhere beyond or before desire – in Celan's poetry, the experience of psychoanalysis offers itself as another. For the patients of psychoanalysis may often be living a proximate exile. In their case too, desire has often ceased, and the road is blocked into the personal pronoun with which language would open its gates to the formation of a human (desiring) subject. It is from such an exile that Leclaire and his colleagues are trying to guide their patients. Strictly and rationally, words always belong to a time after – a time of partial presence, of desiring, and of a symbolic reciprocity squeezed out of the world. It is one of the wonders of Celan, and of poetry, that they can together unwork the benevolent tyranny of such 'strict rationality'. In the short poem 'Crystal', and in his poetry more generally, Celan offers a glimpse of what it would be like to be exiled into the desireless ground of unbeing which psychoanalysts explore.

§ 2.7

In the following chapter the work of Maud Mannoni will offer a chance to explore further the exile that psychoanalytic patients may experience. First, returning a final time to Serge Leclaire, one may keep this suffering and the first stanza of 'Crystal' in mind, while following what becomes of them. I suggested there is no mistaking the fact that there is a gap between the two stanzas of the poem, and that the second stanza is surging and open. The reciprocity which was blocked is regained, the lost expectation refound, and the tears which were invisible become a fountain in the sixth line. The look which was forgone is functioning again, and it is this which seems to reopen all the possibilities, and allow love tentatively to re-emerge. Celan's poem was invoked partly as an introduction to Leclaire's discussion of transference and counter-transference. I left Leclaire faced with the need to carve out his own style, and avow his love when unprotected by the Freudian shelter. To see how he goes about this I shall now quote certain passages from his writing (as I did for Freud). From these, and from the discussion which surrounds them, something more may emerge of how Leclaire proceeds as both a psychoanalyst and a writer.

In the final chapter of *On tue un enfant*, 'Sygne *ou* de l'amour de transfert', Leclaire cites the instance of Freud and gestures towards the heroic steadfastness he showed where others (such as Breuer) feared to stray. He speaks with respect of 'Freud's fearlessness in front of the desires of women' (p. 102). But still he must find his own way of expressing his reaction to his patients and to the power of their transference-love. How problematic this may be can be gathered from certain comments made by Masud Khan (a psychoanalyst working within an Anglo-Saxon tradition) in a paper entitled '"To Hear with Eyes": Clinical Notes on Body as Subject and Object'. The importance of the look in Celan's poem has already been noted. What can now be added is that one of the prime ways in which the analyst is able to express his or her feelings is through the look – exchanged with the patient, and later transmitted in words to the reader. Yet according to Khan, 'Looking can be either affectionate and empathic or hostile and rejective. It cannot be neutral' (Khan, 1974, p. 246). Khan claims that this loss of neutrality is one reason why the look has been ignored in psychoanalytic literature. The other reason he offers is that '*Looking at* a patient, when translated into language, travesties and misrepresents the experience. It is in fact a contradiction of it' (p. 246). If one bears these suggestions in mind, and bears in mind the second stanza of Celan's poem, one can see the scope of Leclaire's ambition, when he speaks of Sygne and attempts to allow her transference into words:

Through this smile, whether it lights up her eyes or her voice, a new ear opens where what can finally be told, without pathos and in a truthful voice, is the misfortune of being nothing, of being born only out of nothing. In the end, that which does not say a word and is an *infans* more than an adorable cherub, makes a place between two breaths and two words for what could not be said. This is where the transference binds itself. Sygne says it in figurative terms: your smile on your face, my pain on your face, your pain on my face, my smile on my face.

(pp. 96–7)

This writing qualifies the general truth of Masud Khan's second assertion. It might almost be thought of as a sort of prose coda to Celan's poem. In a discussion of Leclaire's description of Sygne, the poet Michel Deguy expresses this succinctly when he writes 'Here the art of the portrait is consummate' (Deguy, 1977, p. 216). If the poem 'Crystal' is to help characterise the psychoanalytic procedure as promoted by Leclaire, perhaps it is not too fanciful to imagine psychoanalysis as occupying the space between the two stanzas of Celan's poem. Psychoanalysis thus returns expectation, recognition and the possibility of love. The imagining may not in fact be as fanciful as it seems. Leclaire, for one, would perhaps not reject it, for of his role as analyst he writes:

I remain an analyst only in so far as I listen to the analysand from this opening, across which the words and space of desire are ceaselessly being born and reborn. It is only in this place that the syncopated voice of the subject can make itself heard and the singularity of the analysand's 'primal scene' can be recounted.

(p. 99)

Leclaire listens attentively for the words which will breathe life into desire and desire into life.

What it is that effects the transition between the two stanzas of Celan's poem is deeply mysterious, yet full of romance – nights, hearts, roses, seven of each. Beyond the mystery, the reader can share the benefits as a kiss is sealed, the unexpected arrives, and water flows. In the end the process called psychoanalysis is not very much less mysterious. It is to such mystery that Leclaire is committed, despite his theoretical expositions. He writes that 'there should remain a free place for the omphalos of dreams, and the doors of night should stay open' (p. 101). The same mystery holds true of love, of the language which may first (in the primitive context) cause division and so make it necessary; and which then goes so far (in the adult context) towards provisionally mending that division. Psychoanalysis is broaching that mystery; and so is writing – here, psychoanalytic writing.

Leclaire allows his reader to feel Sygne's nervous passion. Through the interstices in a theory one feels her unfulfilled presence. Yet if Leclaire's attitude to transference-love is partly contained in his account's power to engage, he yet yields more than this. Does he 'drift' or 'dire la dérive'? Perhaps he does. Within the constraints laid down by Freud in his 'Observations on Transference-Love', certainly he does. Yet Leclaire's account feels neither irresponsible nor suicidal. By allowing his reader to feel the spur of his own desire, as an analyst and as a man, Leclaire makes clear where it ends and another's desire begins; beyond this, where two desires might meet. He writes:

I would now be in very bad faith if I claimed that Sygne – to speak only of her – left me quite cold. In this business of love it is my entire life which reverberates harmonically: not only my loves, the words (and silences) of women which are imprinted on my body, and the children, but also my concern for psychoanalysis, my research into the origins of speech, my work on the discourse of repression, my quest for half the universe. Is this as much as to say that I love her? No: that is, not 'really'. But outside analysis it might, or might have been able to come about.

(p. 109)

Leclaire exposes his reader to – and himself through – his own unabashed personal style. If he is a 'smuggler', as Bernard Pingaud suggests, then the merchandise he is illegally importing into his writing is this particular and personal sense of himself as *embodied* in his style. The 'contraband' is the very sense of his living body. Again, as with Freud, it would take a penetrating analysis to describe the style; again, in these extracts (in so far as my translations are not a betrayal), it is there for his reader to recognise.

The 'beyond', where analyst and analysand may meet as lovers of sorts, is not a moment in which the body takes over. It is not a lover's silence. If one still has Celan's poem in mind, this fact should not be surprising, however. For the movement between the two stanzas is in one sense less towards than away from carnal immediacies. (The lips that move in 'red makes for red' are the reader's own; the hand which moves the pages, and knocks at the gate of the poem is also the reader's; the fountain, if it suggests tears, also has its own autonomy – so much so as to plash in the title of a later, still more elliptical poem.[24]) Yet the force and the release involved in the movement are not in the least reduced by this fact. For Leclaire and his patients, the 'beyond' is constituted of words. These are words which open on to the 'moments of truth' of the unconscious. They are words shared in the unknown, 'as in love, certainly, but with naked words and muzzled bodies' (p. 110). As Leclaire has already affirmed, and as he reaffirms here, in this 'beyond' a new and difficult birth may take place:

Each face has its promise of truth: as alive as it was at the time of the invention of psychoanalysis, this is always the hope of *an utterance which may be released* [*parole à naître*]. More hazardous to engender than a child, this utterance can only be conceived in a meeting with another utterance which is being born. This is what psychoanalytic manuals indicate as 'interpretation of transference'. (p. 113)

This is not the first instance in the present argument of the metaphor of birth – nor will it be the last. Here the relation between the creation of words and the other process of creation one is more used to calling birth seems to reach through the metaphoric towards what it is tempting to call the 'symbiotic'. Such a birth may indeed be the only kind that one can experience at first hand if one is a man.[25] Words – Sygne's word, Leclaire's word – may reach out from voices and give birth: to her and to him. Birth may always be 'difficult' (as my chapter heading suggests). This at least is the claim made by Vladimir, in Beckett's *Waiting for Godot*, from whom I borrow this heading. Towards the end of the play, in one of the most poignant speeches in modern drama, he bemoans to his companion Estragon: 'Astride of a grave and a difficult birth. Down in the hole, lingeringly, the grave-digger puts on the forceps. We have time to grow old. The air is full of our cries' (pp. 90–1). Birth carries antithesis and ambivalence in tow. Within Leclaire's understanding, birth and death, living and killing, are soul mates. Such antithesis and ambivalence, though formidable, may be one's necessary dwelling. That the stakes are of the highest should no longer be alarming. Analysand, analyst, psychoanalytic writer, novelist, 'crritic' (to borrow a term of abuse from Estragon) – one's words may have an ambivalent status. But the very fact of being able to use words may afford some freedom from ambivalence's more brutal edge. Even Vladimir derives some comfort from his talking, if only the comfort of passing a little more time while waiting for Godot.

For Leclaire, the writing of his book may be the final seal on his relation with his patients. However, it also offers new possibilities of relation and experience, with and to his readers. In my discussion of forms of ambivalence in his work (narcissism and desire, murder and love) there has been little of theoretical weight not already to be found in the work of Freud or Lacan. This absence is not debilitating, however. For his re-telling – or *relating* – is crucial. It opens the prospect of a readerly engagement which may be quite as important as any new, more obviously theoretical understanding; and important in ways which are quite consistent with the theory he is exploiting. Nor does Leclaire the psycho-analyst and writer remain confined to his chamber. Like his patient Sygne, he leaves his room and leaves his text. For Sygne, the birth of which Leclaire talks is naturally only a beginning. There is a further dimension to any resolving to be done, and it will take her outside the analyst's double chamber, of room and book. There she may, alone or with another, re-inhabit her body (the new

71

body to which psychoanalysis has given rise). Leclaire will also leave his room and his text, and he will do so not as an example of any one thing – psychoanalysis, L'Ecole freudienne de Paris, a theory of desire, this or that branch of epistemology, or whatever. He will leave them as that which is called a human being: that is a desiring and (if the conditions are right) a *loving* being. Leclaire concludes *On tue un enfant* on a site for which he has long been laying the foundation, one which bears the mark of paradox and ambivalence which has characterised his work. His closing statement catches up many of the strains he has been developing. But if his conclusion does much that is well grounded, it also forms a plea, the broadening of a theory and a strain of emotion that allows through a quite unjustified hope. This is a hope which reaches out from his text and across to the reader. It is a humanistic hope that is all the more powerful for its lack of justificatory armour. With words about a possible future, Leclaire concludes:

Floating like the spirit above the waters, the attention of the psychoanalyst is first of all a faculty of listening [écoute] which is open to the transparency of words: to their shadowy roots as well as their fruits of light. The unfolding of history will reveal what price psychoanalysts are paying today for the sacrilegious obstinacy which pushes them to usurp the place of the Holy Spirit, and if they will be able to leave their armchairs and live with their bodies naked and their words veiled. It is not that they will invent among themselves 'some new way of making love'.[26] But it can be hoped that, upholding to the end the excess of their unreasonable passion, they will finally know a time for loving. It can be hoped that *she*, recognising on the Tree of Science the fruit that makes her a woman, will know how to nourish man with her light, like a new Eve who takes her body from words rather than from his bones; and that perhaps *he*, taking his eyes off the clock which measures his listening, will finally realise that he will not be able to love and give to each day its dawn unless, like Chronos, he devours his children.

(pp. 113–14)

3 · Mother tongues

I N chapter 2 I have given some indication as to the direction I shall be taking in turning to the work of psychoanalyst Maud Mannoni (not a single work this time, but the œuvre of a prolific writer). I shall, among other things, explore further the role which language and the 'I' play in the development of subjectivity, desire, and a sense of the body; and indicate the place this development may have in parent–child relations. While attending to this, however, I shall also have in view the way in which Maud Mannoni represents her patients and their needs, and how this may bring her writing more or less in line with writing that is called 'literary'.

So much for what will be the general drift of the argument. A more dynamic sense of its movement may be offered by the notion of ambivalence, which was introduced with Freud (in § 2.1), and which appeared and reappeared in the work of Serge Leclaire. Within the psychoanalytic tradition it has been the infant's ambivalent relation to one or both parents, either in childhood proper or carried unresolved into adulthood, that has received most attention. Freud himself encouraged this by his studies of the 'Rat Man' and of 'Little Hans', in the latter of which the father–son relation was seen to be crucial (*Standard Edition*, x, 41–7). In Freud's later comments on the case of 'Little Hans' in his paper of 1926, 'Inhibitions, Symptoms and Anxiety', ambivalence becomes one of the mainstays of the Oedipal conflict, as he explains:

> He was at the time in the jealous and hostile Oedipus attitude towards his father, whom nevertheless – except in so far as his mother was the cause of estrangement – he clearly loved. Here, then, we have a conflict due to ambivalence: a well-grounded love and a no less justifiable hatred directed towards one and the same person.
> (*Standard Edition*, xx, 101–2)

When rooted in the Oedipal in this way, ambivalence is presented as intractable, something to be assimilated in a child's advance towards acceptance into the adult world of culture. Psychoanalysis has indeed tended to dramatise the problems of children in coming to terms with adult demands. Since the moment when Freud realised the fantasy nature of the scene of primal seduction, these demands have commonly come to be seen as commensurate with culture itself, imbued therefore with necessity and the obligation of civilisation. Freud's one major child analysis, that of 'Little Hans' – 'Analysis of a Phobia in a Five-Year-Old Boy' – was carried out not only at the instigation but also through the mediation of Hans's father. It was carried out, therefore, at one remove. Not surprisingly, child analysis has at times risked being subsumed into a more general process of normalising the child and of rendering him or her adequate to the demands of the parents and the dominant culture.

One thing a reading of Kafka or of Shakespearean comedy – *As You Like It* or *A Midsummer Night's Dream* – should give is the confidence to contend that parental demands need not necessarily be so self-evidently just or so free of the ambivalence with which the child is trying to cope as psychoanalysis has tended to imply. What if parental demands are not inherent and natural, but are rather the recycling of a previous demand which has been inadequately dealt with? What is truly necessary to a child for it to be accepted into civilisation? What, on the other hand, is necessary to a parent for him or her to continue to occupy a place alongside his or her child within that same culture? And what is the relation of these two questions? In the work of Maud Mannoni one may search for answers. For from within a Freudian (and Lacanian) tradition, she has sought to unmask the distorting and limiting pressures which may lurk under the skin of civilisation's acceptable face.

Ambivalence may, then, be a complex of feelings which exists within a child. But for Maud Mannoni, this is not because it has been dreamt up by the child in response to a situation of affective or structural difficulty. Ambivalence, like so much else, including the words which may be used to express it, is learned from parents who are directing its dual beam at the child. An example may help to illustrate this. It is that of Isabelle, a nine-year-old dyslexic child who is suffering personality problems and difficulties over schooling, to whom Maud Mannoni dedicates a chapter of her first book, *L'Enfant arriéré et sa mère* . . . Towards the end of this chapter, as its title 'Effets d'une rééducation chez une enfant névrotique' ('Effects of Re-education in a Neurotic Girl') is beginning to be realised, Maud Mannoni relocates Isabelle's ambivalent attitude to her world. She writes: 'Ambivalence and contradiction existed before the birth. The mother brought Isabelle into the world, at one and the same time rejecting and hoping for this birth' (p. 228). Isabelle is thus the embodiment (in the strongest sense) of her mother's own ambivalence. This being the case, the onus is upon the mother to change the predeterminants upon which her daughter's existence is predicated. Bearing in mind the formulations of Laplanche and Pontalis on the subject who says 'yes' and 'no' at the same time (§ 2.1), one may listen to how Maud Mannoni continues:

> It is mother and daughter who in some sense must be helped to forgo one another, the suffering being much greater for the mother than for the child . . . Isabelle was at origin a boy–girl, yes–no, an echo of the exact situation of the mother. It was necessary that the mother first get out of her own contradiction and into agreement with the universe of the signifier for her daughter then in turn to discover her sex as a signifier. (p. 229)

The shift in emphasis Maud Mannoni carries out here is compatible with Serge Leclaire's formulations on primary narcissism. It is a shift that, in all the inertia it has had to counter and in its own cautious sallies and urgent surges, has been *the* driving force of Maud Mannoni's work. From her first published book of 1964 to her recent book of 1986, the ground of this work has been plain to see. It has unequivocally been that of the infant, the child and the adolescent: the pre-adult.

And it has not just been any children that Maud Mannoni has attended to, but specifically children in crisis. From the start, her work has been deeply embedded in acute forms of difficulty. Mental retardation and its ramifications into dyslexia, learning difficulties and speech defects, even those disabilities termed 'organic' such as 'Down's Syndrome' – children assaulted by these form the substance of *L'Enfant arriéré et sa mère*. The precise difficulty on which her work focuses changes to include psychosis (in *L'Enfant, sa 'maladie' et les autres* and *La Théorie comme fiction*), paranoia and psychopathic perversity (in *Education impossible*), neurosis, autism and hysteria (in *Un lieu pour vivre, D'un impossible à l'autre* and *Un savoir qui ne se sait pas*); but the charge remains constantly and unrelentingly negative. It might of course be thought that it is the duty of psychoanalysis to keep close to difficulty and despair – psychoanalysis as psychopathology. Yet a rapid scan of the work of Freud or Lacan (not to mention Carl Jung) reveals that the writings of psychoanalysts are by no means commensurate with psychopathology. Maud Mannoni has held inordinately close to suffering, and that suffering which has been in the margins of psychoanalysis: psychosis, mutism, autism, and above all the *locus classicus* of these and other problems – children themselves. To read her work is to enter a world in which darkness threatens in multifarious guises. It is to move in close to disorder and to those foundering under its cruel sway; and close also, as I shall show, to unspeakably callous, unforgiving and exploitative sources of power within the family and the state.

For this is the paradox. It is she who has stayed so close to early experience who has helped fill a gap left by psychoanalysis. She has filled it with all that adults are directing at children, whether necessarily or pathologically. It is precisely because Maud Mannoni has never flinched from her commitment to children in trouble that she has revealed so much of adult need. Thinking of the example of Isabelle, it can now be added that what is important in it is not only ambivalence itself, or the particular set of problems and disabilities it focuses. It is rather the particular *relation* of child to parent and analyst which is important, as it typifies Maud Mannoni's brand of psychoanalysis. In her work, ambivalence slides from the level of ostensible preoccupation to that of latent, sustaining energy. Before I can claim meaningfully to have faced this work I shall have to try and come to terms with this energy. For the moment, however, I shall keep to the ostensible.

§ 3.1

If I have given some sense of the range of sufferings and debilities to which Maud Mannoni has attended throughout her career, I should now re-emphasise what I have already hinted, that beyond the fact of their being situated in children, there are two major and interconnecting areas of difficulty which link the various sufferings. These are the body, and the 'I' through which the body attempts to gain access to language and desire; both of which come into existence, for better or for worse, within the context of certain institutions (of which the most important is usually the family). In § 3.3 I shall turn to these institutions (and in § 3.2 to certain examples of names and pronouns in literature). First it is to language itself that I shall address myself, and to the particular instance of language which is often taken for granted but which is always problematic for Maud Mannoni's patients: the 'I', or first person pronoun. Need or urgent desire may be troubling forces, as has already been seen. They have the power to disturb the 'I' with which one tries to articulate them. Psychoanalysis recalls that pain and suffering can be troubling in this sense as well. Or it should perhaps be put the other way round: desire and need, or pain and suffering, may emerge from the instability of the pronoun 'I'.

There are few more striking ways of perceiving this than that offered by Maud Mannoni's patients. Here is part of a dialogue which takes place with a child patient, reported by analyst Françoise Dolto (who was one of Maud Mannoni's mentors) in the preface to Maud Mannoni's *Le Premier rendez-vous avec le psychanalyste*. It leads directly into the troubled heartland of the pronoun.

'I've got a headache', said a single child of three. (He had been brought to me because it was impossible to keep him in infant school where he endlessly complained about his head, and seemed ill, passive and in pain. In addition, he was subject to insomnia, for which his doctor could find no organic cause.) With me he went through the same soliloquy.
'Who is saying that', I asked him.
'I've got a headache', he went on repeating in the same plaintive tone.
'Where? Show me where your head aches.' It was not a question he'd ever been asked.
'There', he said, pointing to his thigh near the groin.
'And whose head's that?'
'It's Mummy's.'
This reply, you can well believe, stupefied both parents who were present.
(p. 15)

Readers of this dialogue may be almost as surprised as the parents. What becomes clear when surprise recedes is that the child patient with the sore head–leg is not speaking of or for himself alone when he says 'I'. This is in fact what his pain seems to be saying, in its own language which the psychoanalyst tries to decipher through everyday language: that the 'I' am is part of the 'he' I am (or is) for my mother. In short, that there is no appropriate division between the various pronouns and names through which 'I', the child, am trying to articulate and place myself.

This child's difficulties are not untypical. Maud Mannoni's work is densely populated with the ghosts of children for whom the act of naming remains an impossibility. (And in the case cited here, in which the patient is able to utter these words that point however erroneously to the hurt, the child has achieved a degree of articulacy greater than many others – the autistic or the psychotic for example – can expect.) In an essay entitled 'The Becoming of a Psychoanalyst', Masud Khan puts the imperative which faces such a child with wonderful succinctness. He writes that 'In order to speak one's mind, one must speak it in one's own person' (Khan, 1974, p. 112). Yet the common-sense force of this should not blind one to what may be the enormous difficulty of 'speaking in one's own person'. Indeed the very directness of Masud Khan's statement begs the question of the significance of the words 'one's own'. What does it mean to say that one's person, or one's 'I' is one's own? In what way is one proprietor of one's self? Or of that which is most intimate to one's self – one's body? These are among the questions which are frequently posed through Maud Mannoni's work, and which lurk behind almost all her case-presentations.

To answer some of them one can best look in the direction characteristically chosen by Maud Mannoni herself – towards the work of Jacques Lacan. The underlying factor linking Maud Mannoni's child-patients is that they are all suffering from a degree of exclusion, which runs from partial to total, from what Lacan calls the realm of the Symbolic. At the risk of over-simplifying grossly, it may be said that where the Symbolic is deficient, the Real, whose prime site is the body, calls on the Imaginary (the third term in the tripartite reality) to make up the deficit. The 'I' is the crucial instance of this Symbolic Order, as Lacan has implied from the time when he elaborated his now famous theory of the 'mirror stage' (1949).[1] The function of the 'I' is ineluctably bound to the need to move beyond the 'fragmented body' ['corps morcelé'] of pure infantile sensation, through 'jubilant assumption of [his] specular image' ['l'assomption jubilatoire de son image spéculaire'], towards a totalised reflexive vision (Lacan, 1966, p. 94; trans. p. 2). The 'I' emerges from and is in hazardous relation to the alienating identification with a totalised image of the self (or ideal-ego) perceived as it were in the mirror. The 'I' allows an identification with an image or 'person' which, in the present context, the subject might at a later stage be said to 'possess'.[2] For the neurotic or hysterical child, such an identification is often inadequately achieved. For the autistic or psychotic child it is blocked altogether (as Lacan has it, 'foreclosed'). Where this is so, the child is unable at a fundamental level to become a body. Hence it suffers within it or through it. For a body as one knows it (one's own) may be tantamount to an image of that body. However 'real' it is, the body will only be realised from within as outside and other than itself. The Symbolic, with its avatar the 'I', is that necessary other, as Lacan affirms when he says that 'the fact is that we have no means of apprehending reality – on all levels, and not only on that of knowing – other than by the intermediary of the Symbolic' (Lacan, 1978, p. 122). The child must move from simply being a body to having a body (even if what count as one's greatest adult experiences will often be those when one is most thoroughly 'inside' one's own body). The idea that one owns one's body is of course a fantasy of sorts, as Lacan points out when he says: 'It is very amusing, it implies a truly strange incoherence, that one says – man *has* a body' (Lacan, 1978, p. 93). But the necessity of living by this fantasy is inescapable.

To illustrate this, I need only return to the boy with the head–leg, or indeed open any one of Maud Mannoni's books. For what one invariably finds is a small body suffering the torments of an unimaginable hell – a hell it is suffering precisely because it is unable to imagine it (unable to symbolise its dilemma). If it is the ambivalent Isabelle who cries out in *L'Enfant arriéré et sa mère*, then in *Le Psychiatre, son 'fou' et la psychanalyse* it is perhaps Sidonie who claims attention most tragically, with her suicidal swallowing of aspirins and vinegar, her course from hospital to home to hospital, to her eventual enactment of a kind of self-destruction. Maud Mannoni reports part of a talk with Sidonie:

Me: What about you – how is it that you don't feel what your body's demanding?
Sidonie: I thought I'd be able to stop death in time. My wishes and what my body wants – it's not the same thing.
Me: And you, what do you want?
Sidonie: I want to die so as to know who I am. (p. 152)

It is as if Sidonie hopes that through death (in negation) she will be able to find the nature of her body's desire: only when 'I' am no longer, will 'I' be 'I' (and by extension 'you' be 'you', 'she' 'she', and so on). For Sidonie language is locked in itself, and the body is mute. As she speaks, her decorporealised body may become a presence for the reader. But it is a presence for reader alone. Maud

Mannoni's task as an analyst (rather than as a writer) is to make it present, and articulate, for Sidonie herself. Or it is to enable Sidonie to talk in such a way that she may say who 'I am', and in this way re-inhabit – or *repossess* – her own 'person' and body.

This possession will only ever be provisional at best, since the body one 'has' is ever ready to be overtaken by the body one 'is' (as the experience of illness and the threat of death remind one). The 'I' the patient will learn to speak with and through will not be an acquisition flying the colours of romantic individualism or self-generating truth. It will remain what the linguists call a 'shifter', taking its meaning from its context, and from intersubjective relations in general. It will be trappable within the alienating net of the ego, and will never be freed of the otherness which marks all dealings with language. Yet to such a necessary 'I' and to such a vital body the analytic process tends.

In § 3.3 I shall try to give a clearer picture of this analytic tendency, and try in the case of Maud Mannoni to see the particular blocks which are impeding it. Before doing this, and before moving briefly into the world of literature (in § 3.2), I can finish this section with one of Lacan's most famous formulations of the goals of analysis. They are goals which summarise well the scope and thrust of Maud Mannoni's psychoanalytic venture. They may not on first reading seem very ambitious; but by now it can be understood just how much is implied in these lines.

I used to say it schematically in the earliest days of these seminars: the subject begins by talking of himself but he doesn't talk to you; then he talks to you but he doesn't talk of himself; when he will have talked to you of himself (who will have changed perceptibly in the interval), we will have arrived at the end of the analysis.   (Lacan, 1981, pp. 181–2)

§ 3.2

I suggested above that the body one 'has' is open to invasion and interference from the body one 'is'. I might add that this body one 'has' is in fact little more or less than the body over which one is so used to exercising some control that one only realises one 'is' it when it is too late, when it has already started to go wrong and disobey. In his book *Différence et répétition*, one of the things Gilles Deleuze does is to question the philosophical implications of this divide between being and having. His conclusion is of some relevance to the present argument, for he writes: 'In the end one is only what one *has*: it is by having that being is formed here, or that the passive self *is*' (p. 107). The direction in which this conclusion leads him is also of relevance, as it leads him towards one of the writers I wish to mention to help amplify what has been said of the importance of names and pronouns, and to show again just how fine the psychoanalytic and literary border can be. Deleuze is led by his argument towards the work of Samuel Beckett. At the risk of pre-empting what I shall say in the second half of this book, I should like to turn to Beckett briefly, along with the figure who will be the other principal focus of part II, Marcel Proust.

Many things – many awful things – happen to the bodies in Beckett's work. But a single word can stand for most of them: decrepitude. It happens more or less quickly, more or less comfortably; but happen it will and does, unfailingly. In chapter 1 (§ 1.0) I mentioned Molloy's difficulties with his leg. His difficulties get worse, to the point where his chronic arthritis forbids him from all but crawling, on his back or front, and managing a mere fifteen paces a day. Thinking ahead in the *Trilogy*, what can be said in this context of Malone? He is confined to his bed, catatonia slowly encroaching, his reach diminishing as he loses his stick with the hook, as his pencil wears down, and as those tending him desert him. As for the Unnamable, his situation is still more severe, for he is reduced to an immobile, ruined carcass. Yet as the range diminishes of what these three (Molloy, Malone and the Unnamable) can be said to 'have', there is a need which ever strengthens: the need to take possession of something – anything, however intangible. Crucially, the need is to make a history or story their own. When this proves difficult or impossible, what subsists is the need to take possession of their names, and thus to 'be', even if being is tantamount to naming, and if such being only becomes truly possible in silence or death.

As the title of the third book of the *Trilogy* announces, even the possibility of naming, by the time it starts, has ceased to be available. The Unnamable is literally that. Murphy, Watt, Mercier, Moran and Molloy all rotate round him; Mahood and Worm are never still. The name is obligatory, object of the Unnamable's absolute need. As he says – 'nothing doing without proper names' (p. 340).[3] But names only amount to seductive lures when they are inevitably the tags of others. The Unnamable tries out various names, but is left with his pronoun, which is precisely what he starts with. On the very first line of the novel, he notes – 'I, say I' (p. 293). But this pronoun offers no escape, for in saying 'I' the Unnamable only ever seems to name another for another with another's word. He goes on: 'I seem to speak, it is not I, about me, it is not about me.' From such an inauspicious beginning, the novel grows into a vast and driving exploration of (among other things) this absolute necessity of the pronoun, and its absolute otherness and insufficiency. As the Unnamable's frustration mounts, and his breathlessness establishes its peculiar urgency, the situation becomes such that he decides to renounce the 'I' altogether. (In aspiring to grow out of his personal pronoun, he takes as it were the reverse course to the patients of psychoanalysis.) He says,

I shall not say I again, ever again, it's too farcical. I shall put in its place, whenever I hear it, the third person, if I think of it. Anything to please them. It will make no difference. Where I am there is no one but me, who am not. So much for that.
(p. 358)

Yet as he already realises when he says it, this renunciation is no solution either. For the Unnamable is no more 'he' than he is 'I'. The one name is just as arbitrary as the other, when reduced to its denominative function. Neither cuts out a pre-ordained space for the speaker. The Unnamable may turn the resources of language against language, but still the words have to be found which will somehow ascribe the name, and so allow the Unnamable's own story to be told.

In chapter 5 (§ 5.4) I shall try to show what this story consists of, and how there are in fact two stories – the one which is told by the Unnamable and the one which in the final pages he aspires to tell. Thinking for now of the names one finds in this novel, there is certainly no shortage of them – only of the ones that seem to matter. And this is not a situation unique to *The Unnamable*. Moving for a moment to Proust's novel, *A la recherche du temps perdu*, names abound there as well. Any reader could come up with scores of them, from every era and embracing every class of society. Why, then, is there an embarrassment when it comes to talking about this novel – an embarrassment which centres on names and naming, and which critics skirt around with greater or lesser agility? The answer seems to lie in the fact that the one who is immeasurably the most important character in the novel is virtually unnamed (and hence unnamable).

Whatever critical book one opens on the subject of Proust, the awkwardness this provokes is evident. By the unsophisticated this most important character is called 'Marcel Proust' (and I hardly need point out why this is unsatisfactory, given the many obvious differences between Proust and his creation). By others he is called 'the narrator' (but this is scarcely adequate, since he is also a character in his own right). By others again (such as myself) he is called 'the most important character' (but this is hardly correct either, since he is also the narrator). Finally, almost in desperation, he is called 'Marcel'. This is as good a name as any. But it is worth noting how hard one has to work to glean it. The reader is well into volume three of the novel, some two thousand pages in, before there is any evidence that such a name might be appropriate. Even then the evidence is slender, as one realises when one recalls the circumstances in which the name is offered. (The narrator thinks of the joy he once experienced in watching Albertine wake up. He remembers the words she used to say to him: '"My – " or "My darling – "', and then adds to these, almost hypothetically, a name. He writes that these possessives were 'followed by my Christian name, which, if we give the narrator the same name as the author of this book, would be "My Marcel" or "My darling Marcel"' (III, 69; III, 75).[4] If this conjectural appearance is the evidence on which we call Marcel 'Marcel', it is not a lot to go on – scarcely a certain identification.)

Since one does still need to call him *something*, one is obliged to ask what else is left? What is left is the single name 'I'. The force of this is considerable: for there is no other way into the novel than through the narrow passageway of the pronoun – and this from the very first sentence. To read Proust's novel is to adopt another's 'I', for hours and, intermittently, months on end. Even when one emerges from the novel it is not easy to shake free of it, for as soon as one tries to speak of it, and finds oneself in the business of naming, one is returned to the only adequate name, which is the same name one uses of oneself. (Such roundabout routes as 'the Proustian "I" is . . .' offer a temporary escape, but an inelegant and quickly tiresome one.) In and around the experience of Proust's novel one may indeed find one's own 'I' to be divided. Nor is this entirely inappropriate, as the Proustian 'I' is already divided, within and at times against itself (the implications of which will be discussed at length in chapter 4). But though one's 'I' may be divided, perhaps fragmented, the banner of the pronoun is nonetheless single, unitary, and monosyllabically simple (in French as in English). From a minimal base it offers maximal opportunities (and therefore maximal risk as well). It does so to Proust, to the reader who is under Proust's spell, and perhaps to others as well . . .

For Roland Barthes would have it that modern fiction can be characterised by its tendency to subvert names and pronouns. He suggests that as far back as Balzac the subversion characteristic of our times had already started. It is one of the central projects of *S/Z*, his lengthy analysis of Balzac's novella *Sarrasine*, to reveal how Balzac unsettles the reader's tacit acceptance of the denotative power of pronouns. In this book, with Proust in mind, Barthes writes:

> All subversion, or all novelistic submission, thus begins with the Proper Name: specific – as well as specified – as is the Proustian narrator's social position, his perilously maintained lack of name creates a serious deflation of the realistic illusion: the Proustian I is not of itself a name (in contrast to the substantive character of the novelistic pronoun . . .), because it is undermined, troubled by the disturbances of age, it loses its biographical tense by a certain blurring. What is obsolescent in today's novel is not the novelistic, it is the character; what can no longer be written is the Proper Name. (p. 102)

One may go along with the drift of what Barthes is saying, yet hold back from his conclusions. The reason for holding back becomes clearer when, on the inside cover of *Roland Barthes by Roland Barthes*, the autobiography (of sorts) which he was to publish within five years of *S/Z*, one reads: 'It must all be considered as if spoken by a character in a novel.' In a single quip, Barthes attempts to explode the autobiographical illusion by which the 'I' invokes a truth free of the strategies which a novelist deploys. There is something too easy about his attempt. While one can accept that autobiography is inevitably not free of novelistic devices, such an explosion of the 'realistic illusion' *a priori* feels like a piece of misplaced gamesmanship. For the pronoun is an area of urgent, primordial *need* – and it is as such that Beckett and Proust allow the reader to experience it. Barthes's discarding of its denominative power in the context of Proust, and even more his shedding of it for the scope of novelistic invention, appear flippant at best. In his formulations on the proper name Barthes fixes on a challenging tendency in modern fiction, no doubt. But he overstates his case, as critics, even the subtlest amongst them, tend to do. The writers I have already looked at confirm this. One of the most forceful and pervasive ways of understanding *A la recherche* (a way that is thrust at the reader by the novel) is precisely *as autobiography*.[5] As I suggested in the case of Kafka, the story 'The Judgement' was written with a grace and poise that the questioning of the 'realistic illusion' of identity in the story might have decreed to be 'obsolescent'. The poem 'Crystal' by Paul Celan was seen to inhabit the tenuous space between pronouns, and Celan's verse might more generally be understood as desperately trying to *create* a 'you' or interlocutor, to whom it might address itself.[6] Writers of fiction and poetry, in short, even those who name their characters Joseph K. or just K., have one foot firmly in what Barthes rather dismissively calls the 'realistic illusion'.

§ 3.3

To know what life might be like without this 'illusion' of which Barthes speaks, one could scarcely do better than return to Maud Mannoni. One can wryly imagine Barthes telling of the freedom to be gained from subversion of the 'illusion' to one of her patients, or to Françoise Dolto's child who is suffering his mother's headaches. The 'realistic illusion' is founded upon a certain identity – of words with their referent, signifier with signified – and it is, according to Lacan, in the 'mirror stage' that this vital identification emerges. (The specular mode of Imaginary identification may be thought of here as the model of the Symbolic Order which partially supersedes it.) By failing to identify himself correctly, the boy with the headache leaves himself open to the invasion of his mother's desire, which results in his experiencing his own body as undifferentiated from that of the mother.

The burden of Maud Mannoni's task has been to show how various institutions, signally the parental institution, can have an investment in keeping children at the level of partial objects, and in reducing them to inadequate bodies unable to express themselves except through the symptom. In Maud Mannoni's work, the child is typically debarred from subjectivity, from an experience of its own body as total and separate, and from the 'I' which hails the presence of desire in language. The precise ways in which this can happen are as complex and variegated as the individuals Maud Mannoni treats and the family structures she confronts. But their underlying dynamic is shared . . . The infant is spoken within the words and desires of its parents when it comes into the world, and in fact its place has long been prepared by the words and expectations which the approach of the baby has provoked. The infant is thus objectivised, as is perhaps inevitable. But if the parents, because of some failed love or uncompleted mourning or unarticulated family instability on their part (because of their own problematic relation to the Symbolic), are experiencing intense frustration and lack in their own lives, they may allow or even oblige the infant to become (and remain) the object which fills this lack, satisfies the frustration, and cauterises the scar of the unsaid.

Examples of parental overdetermination are all too abundant in Maud Mannoni's work. Sidonie, for her mother, is a rapacious need to be satisfied on an instinctual level, and at the same time an invalid to whom the mother can sacrifice herself. For her father she is little more than an interesting 'medical case'. Sidonie's anorexia and her death wish are her sole and self-mutilating means of expressing her desire. For Isabelle, whom I have also presented, the case is a little different. For she must try to remedy the unfulfilment which has permeated her mother's life since the time of this mother's premature adoption of her own mother's role. Isabelle's trouble is thus largely attributable to the mother's ambivalent relation to her own mother, and to this grandmother's untimely death. Isabelle is described (in § 3.0) as 'at origin a boy–girl, yes–no, an echo of the exact situation of the mother'. Her ambivalence, which is directed at her own very being, is thus little more than an attempt to integrate her mother's prior ambivalence.

Ambivalence may indeed be one of the prime forms of parental overdetermination. And if ambivalence is to be characterised as a stage at which the infant has a capacity for union with, and differentiation from, another, then this capacity can now as easily be located in parenthood. In his early paper (of 1938) in the encyclopaedia *La Vie mentale*, in what is as direct a statement as he ever made on the family, Jacques Lacan gives an example which could stand as a model of this reversal of ambivalence. He suggests that for the infant the act of sucking may itself give rise to a form of ambivalence:

The proprioceptive sensations of sucking and prehension clearly form the basis of the ambivalence of what is lived, which emerges from the situation itself: the being that is absorbing is entirely absorbed, and the archaic complex finds a correspondence in the maternal embrace.   (Lacan, 1938, 8, 40–7)

If this is the case from the infant's side, then from the mother's side the act of suckling can in turn provide the chance to relive this ambivalence, this pulsation of fusion and severing. Lacan goes on:

Constituted in this way, the imago of the maternal breast dominates man's entire life. Through its ambivalence, however, it can find the means with which to satiate itself in a reversal of the situation it represents. Strictly, this is realised only in the occasion offered by maternity. In suckling, embracing and contemplating the baby, the mother at one and the same time receives and satisfies the most primitive of all desires.

Whether or not one agrees with Lacan that it is at the breast that the original root and satisfaction of desire are to be located, his model of desire and ambivalence is helpful in the present context, and particularly when its male perspective is modified by the insight that Christiane Olivier brings to bear upon suckling in *Les Enfants de Jocaste*. For what Lacan proposes (and perhaps a little enviously) as a norm, may in fact, Olivier shows, be suffused with malaise (such as that encountered in the case of Isabelle). Olivier suggests that in most cases girl-children are never desired in an absolute (or sexual) sense by their mothers; that they are prematurely weaned; and that they spend a large part of the rest of their lives trying to fill the 'void' which this inadequate loving has engendered.[7] A woman, Olivier suggests, may in certain instances turn to mothering as a final, desperate attempt to find true union with another – her child. Olivier adds to this the contention that boy-children spend their growing lives trying to break the ties of an over-sufficient, absolute love experienced with their mothers, and so in adulthood often shun the risk of true contact with their wives and children. When the implication of this is that the father withholds from the girl-child the chance of experiencing thoroughgoing parental desire, one seems to have the recipe for self-perpetuating misery, tending to disaster.

If Christiane Olivier indicates a merciless side of the 'psychopathology of everyday life', then Maud Mannoni deals with what happens when the family conjunction and history are such that the tendencies latent within the norm come to the surface. A mother, if her 'void' is demanding enough, and her opportunities of assuaging it are unsatisfactory enough (and how shadowy and insubstantial, if not downright absent, most of Maud Mannoni's patients' fathers are), may have her child (to) fill it. Nor need this process of demanding and filling, this frightening reversal of roles, stop at the breast. Born 'prematurely', as psychoanalysts contend, the child is in the first instance utterly dependent on the mother. What is necessary (or 'phase-adequate') in Lacan's model, becomes unquestionably pathological when over-extended in time. Even as it starts to grow and develop biologically, the child may be required to remain in what becomes an increasingly incestuous symbiosis with the mother, being satisfied only at the level of its needs. It may thus be unable to reach into the realm of the other, in and through which it could begin to recognise itself. It may be unable, except through the agency of the symptom, to begin to change the 'he' or 'she' (or indeed 'it') with which it is spoken by others into an 'I' through which to speak 'in its own person'. In such a case, the crucial transition from demand (which seeks satisfaction of the organism's needs) to desire (which cuts out a space between subject and object, child and parent) is blocked by the sentinels of *parental* need.

Maud Mannoni spells out one aspect of the danger when she writes, 'When the mother is over-present and over-concerned to satisfy the child at the level of its needs, it becomes impossible for the child to make itself heard in the register of desire' (M. Mannoni, 1973b, p. 77). The damage caused by such 'over-concern' is all the more sinister in that the parent can be seen (and often claims) to be 'satisfying the child's every need'.[8] In discussing Serge Leclaire, I suggested (§ 2.2) that while some child murders are plain to see, others are more covert. This is confirmed by Maud Mannoni. This particular murder we might almost think of as 'killing with kindness'. Killing is killing just the same. The death is not of the biological child, but is of that which makes this biological child human (which is, to repeat, his or her desire). To become truly human, the child must cease to be a mere biological organism, and start to represent its biology (or body) to itself. This it cannot do if, as in the case of the boy with the head–leg, the body has been pre-emptively appropriated by its mother. As Maud Mannoni puts it, in such a case the Symbolic (of the mother) 'makes a return into the Real, leaving the subject completely unequipped' (M. Mannoni, 1973b, p. 108). The precise nature of the parent's need to restrain the infant is, I suggested, as variable as are individual personal histories. Yet beyond the distinguishing features, something of a pattern of distress should now be emerging in and through Maud Mannoni's work. One statement, which I shall now quote, indicates as clearly as any other the bold outline of this pattern. With exemplary concision Maud Mannoni writes:

To add up to *one* with the other – this is a logical impossibility, since the one requires the *two*. Hence the child can wish to occupy the function of a zero, which means becoming what the other is lacking. (M. Mannoni, 1973b, p. 79)

If this statement contains something of a summary of what has already been seen, by the terms in which it is couched it also emphasises a crucial aspect of Maud Mannoni's work which has been implicit here, but which should now be rendered explicit.

The definition of deprivation which Maud Mannoni offers here does not imply that the child is being deprived of a more or less necessary object – be it food, clothing, shelter, or even affection. (There would, after all, be nothing new in the suggestion that parental negligence can adversely affect a child.) Rather, the child is being deprived of a place within what is an unmistakably *symbolic* (here numerical) chain. What concerns Maud Mannoni is not primarily material deprivation, but deprivation in the Symbolic – lack of words indeed – which will bring about suffering at the level of another's language and another's body (another's Real). From the beginning of her career, Maud Mannoni has fixed her critical gaze less upon the social or material world as such (though her work has important implications for it) than upon this world as it is transformed into meaning, or *as it is represented*.[9] She works upon this representation in order to render articulate certain of its rigid unspoken elements and render mobile and fluent its stagnant underground waters.[10] She listens to the parents' words and tries to understand the situation through what they say, and perhaps even more through what they do *not say*. She listens to the symptom of the child, which is its distorted message, but which may be the only form of articulation available to it. She searches in fact for 'the enigma of the symptom by paying attention to the words of *child and parents* regarded as an entity' (M. Mannoni, 1967, p. 189; trans, p. 199).

Maud Mannoni is not therefore *against* parents, parenthood, or the family, in any obvious way. What she might be said to be against is the family as an institution; or the way in which a family may represent itself – through certain suppressions, silences, lies and sacrifices – as an entity as stable and immobile as an institution. Perhaps one may think of her as engaged upon a project in relation to the family a little similar to that of a poet such as Stéphan Mallarmé in relation to language itself. For Mallarmé seeks to give life and music to the 'universal *reportage*' ['l'universel *reportage*'] by which language had become (in his view) a mere means for transmitting thought, as if it were so much coinage to be exchanged in silence (Mallarmé, 1945, p. 368). Nor is the suggestion as far-fetched as it may seem. For if institutions are tantamount to stable and ossified forms of representation, then language itself can often become the most intractable of such institutions. One instance of this is contained in the notion and term 'illness'. By the time Maud Mannoni gets to see her patients, they will almost invariably have become representative of the meaning attributed to their symptom: by the parents, of course, but aided and abetted by the terms deployed by medical and psychiatric discourse. Of all the representations which Maud Mannoni uncovers, that of the child as embodiment of some illness or other is indeed the one against which she pushes most consistently.

Behind the notion or fact of illness, she suggests, may be a host of more or less hidden desires.[11] Parents may make an investment in the fact of illness, and in the medical words and devices which substantiate (and even protract) it. An ambivalence is thus established which is a later version of the early prototype by which the infant had been nurtured while being debarred from subjectivity. In the case of Sidonie, her principal drama lies in the 'desire of the mother who can accept to lose her (as a subject of desire) only in so far as she recovers her as an object of care' (M. Mannoni, 1970, p. 157). Sidonie's symptom is redoubled by the second 'symptom' of the illness itself, the name of which is the new sign under which Sidonie can be kept as adult escape route. This is the case even when the initial symptom imposes the most intolerable of demands.[12] Frustrated in its attempt at differentiation, the child falls sick. This in turn requires the upholding of the very state which caused the sickness. Increasingly it becomes hard to see just who is destroying whom as the child is reduced (or elevated) to a state of what Masud Khan calls 'symbiotic omnipotence', which he describes as 'this mood of inertia, helpless dependence and coercing' (Khan, 1974, p. 84). Mother and child are caught, like Ugolino feeding off Archbishop Ruggieri in *Cantos* 32 and 33 of Dante's *Inferno*, in a nightmare of parasitic dependency.

Maud Mannoni does not seek to refute the notion of diagnosis, any more than she tries to suggest one might do without the family. But she insists that, if it is to be understood, the child's illness must not be hypostasised or viewed as a self-evident source of suffering. It must be understood rather as a matrix of meaning produced by (and in turn reinforcing) the family and psychiatric institutions. The illness is not a self-substantiating 'reality'. Rather it is a symbolic nexus which, unless viewed and treated as such, will take its toll at the level of the patient's most intimate reality (or Real). Maud Mannoni fights against the covert transforming of desires latent within psychiatry into nosological coins which, once minted, threaten to become permanent. She tries to break the body down into the discourses and desires that are constituting it. As a psychoanalyst she tries to open a space – a symbolic space offered by the third element outside the dual relation of parent and child – from which a question can be launched. She writes: 'The subject is carried by the single question: What does it want of me?' ['Qu'est-ce que ça veut de moi?'] (M. Mannoni, 1970, p. 206). And included in this 'it' ['ça'] are both the desires of the parents and the desires of the psychiatric and medical infrastructures which they may support and be supported by. The 'truth' to which she leads her child-patient is that of a recognition of its place in this circuit of desire: a recognition, through the symptom, of a word which is *not* the child's own. Thus the boy with whom I started might learn to say: 'Do not cease to love me, Mother, do not abandon me; but get your head out of my leg, your tongue out of my mouth.'

Maud Mannoni's vision thus has a deconstructive edge, which shows itself in her clinical practice. It is an edge which flashes in her writing as well – and dangerously. For if language is open to reification and ossification, then there is no reason to suppose that the language with which she writes will be immune from this same danger. How does Maud Mannoni try to counter this danger in her work as a disseminator of ideas and words? This is one of the questions which underlie the discussion of Maud Mannoni's writing which follows, and underlie my attempt in the next section (§ 3.4) to give a short survey of her books, and in the following sections (to the end of the chapter) to give details of how language operates in and through these books (and how this differs from the way language operates in books thought of as 'literary').

§ 3.4

The principal thrust of Maud Mannoni's writing is against a form of 'lie' which the family offers the easiest possibility of perpetrating. But she holds back much of her aggressive energy to direct at broader institutionalisations of the 'lie' – of which language is broadest of all. Here the deconstructive edge of her work at times threatens to become downright destruction. When I looked (in § 3.2) at Beckett's *The Unnamable*, I indicated how language was used against language. Here too, at the heart of Maud Mannoni's project, is the exercising of a precarious freedom, whose first flexings are felt in certain of her books' very titles.[13] Round the 'maladie' ('illness') and round the 'fou' ('lunatic') she puts inverted commas, suggesting that the terms are to be understood as situated within and quoted sceptically from a particular, alien discourse. The word 'impossible' crops up twice. Once it qualifies 'éducation' (and functions almost as an oxymoron). The other time it serves as a barely locatable point of departure for *D'un impossible à l'autre* ('From One Impossible to the Other'). Language worlds are conflated by the 'comme' in the title *La Théorie comme fiction* ('Theory as Fiction'). Two even more obviously incompatible phenomena are juxtaposed by the 'et' in the provocative title *Le Symptôme et le savoir* ('Symptom and Knowledge'). Finally knowledge itself is proposed as a form of ignorance, an incapacity for reflexiveness, in the title *Un Savoir qui ne se sait pas* ('A Knowledge which Knows not Itself'/'A Knowledge which Cannot be Known').

The precarious freedom is exercised and fought for quite as energetically inside Maud Mannoni's books as on their front covers. Most often the fighting takes the form of a spirited defence of the children who are in her charge, against the various discourses which are transforming them into 'sick' or 'mad' objects of study and knowledge. But the fighting also threatens inwards. Since the bodies of her child-patients speak most directly through their symptoms rather than through words, these bodies must be converted into words to be communicated to the reader. The child's unreadability, its sheer corporeality, has to be made readable. Maud Mannoni comes perilously close to repeating the process she is resisting. Language is the great redeemer within her work (and within Lacanian psychoanalysis in general). Yet at the same time it threatens ever to become the cruel despot. The list (in § 3.0) of sufferings Maud Mannoni tries to alleviate is a long one – the autism, psychosis and the rest. And in the list, in the terms themselves, the threat to her psychoanalytic venture is contained. For as her whole œuvre insists, so much of the suffering derives from these very titles which, once ascribed, become 'a verdict with no appeal' (M. Mannoni, 1964, p. 243). Yet no other terms are readily available – and even if they were, it is unlikely they would condemn her patients any the less. Language is the most dangerous because the most potent and ungraspable of systems. It is like the mysterious jar in Wallace Stevens's poem 'Anecdote of the Jar'. This jar, once placed upon a hillside, organises the 'wilderness' around it, and takes 'dominion everywhere'. Language deploys itself multilaterally, and has at times to be countered with such strategies as inverted commas, paradox, litotes, and downright pleading.

To go back to Maud Mannoni's first book, *L'Enfant arriéré et sa mère*, it is, here, the very intensity of the childrens' debility which necessitates their defence. What Maud Mannoni tries to show in this book is that even children who have been organically afflicted will have had their illnesses redistributed as a variable meaning. This meaning tends to be hidden or even erased by the pressure of medical scientificity, with its props of intelligence quotients and diagnostic definitions. An alternative discourse, which would attribute a new significance to the child's debility, and a new place to the child as subject of its wants, has to be won in the movement between patient and analyst, and subsequently between writer and reader. It is the passage of words, the moment of connection, if it is anything. And as this is so, it is perhaps appropriate that this first work finishes on an unanswered question:

> What is a mental defective?
> This book will leave the reader without a reply.
> For that is not what is essential. What matters is the search, beyond what is deficient, for the words which constitute him as a subject prey to desire.
>
> (p. 244)

Maud Mannoni pushes against the urge to define, in the attempt to maintain the possibility of creation which her patient's words open.

The precise focus of Maud Mannoni's struggle changes over the twenty years which separate this early work from her most recent books. But its intensity hardly wavers. I have invoked a notion of 'personal style'. Any picture of Maud Mannoni's 'personal style' would have to figure a fierce resistance to systematisation, while representing around it that undoubted system which is Freudian or neo-Freudian psychoanalysis. It would, as validation of this ambiguity (or ambivalence), be a picture full of children, children in need. Maud Mannoni takes the risk of a writing which shuns totalisation. The fact that her books over the years have been so consistent, coherent, and unswerving in their energy, may be paradoxical proof of this fact. Above all, Maud Mannoni's 'personal style' is an inclusive one. It is one which includes her commitment to her children's individuality, but also her fears and anxieties, her hostility and rage; so that, even if these are not directed at her reader, one may still shelve one's doubts over this or that point in appreciation of words which have allowed one so far into the individual – be it her patient, her patient's parent, or, indeed, herself.

To move on, her works of 1967 and 1970, *L'Enfant, sa 'maladie' et les autres* and *Le Psychiatre, son 'fou' et la psychanalyse*, attack the violence which is executed between these inverted commas. In the first case it is primarily the ratification of the term within the family which concerns her, while in the second it is the reification of the 'lunatic' within psychiatry and its supportive institutions. This is not the place to elaborate upon her precise arguments (which share some ground with R. D. Laing and David Cooper's anti-psychiatry and Michel Foucault's 'archaeology' of the history of madness). What should be noted here, rather, is the direction and vigour of Maud Mannoni's attacks, and the risk she runs of self-destruction. For if it is again the various hypostasisations of language which are unworked, where does this leave psychoanalysis? Not just any psychoanalysis, but one (and here is a contrast to Anglo-Saxon anti-psychiatry with its emphasis on material conditions of existence) which relies so entirely upon language. Rather than give a direct answer perhaps it is enough to present another conclusion offered by Maud Mannoni – the conclusion to *Le*

Psychiatre, son 'fou' et la psychanalyse. Here one finds a little story of a mother who had a certain knowledge of psychoanalysis and whose child became as deranged as the worst of cases. One finds shades of another great parent, D. F. M. Schreber, the disastrous effects of whose popular pedagogical method upon his unfortunate son, Daniel Paul, were charted by Freud in his 'Psychoanalytic Notes on an Autobiographical Account of a Case of Paranoia' (*Standard Edition*, XII, 1–82). Only this time the violence has been exerted not by a grotesquely repressive Victorian morality, but by psycho-analysis itself. Maud Mannoni asks the guilty mother a question. The mother's answer resounds back across the pages of the book the reader has just finished:

'Is it the failure of psychoanalysis that you are seeking to underline?'
'No, its the system. We've all been (against this child) as complicit as cops.'
(p. 232)

The mother's answer resounds not just back but forward too, across Maud Mannoni's books which follow. It is perhaps less than surprising that Maud Mannoni should have devoted her energies long and hard to a place which announces the abandonment of traditional psychoanalysis as such. At Bonneuil, the 'school' which she founded in 1969, and which forms the substance of the two books *Education impossible* and *Un lieu pour vivre* (as well as of the co-authored *Secrète enfance* and the recent *Bonneuil, seize ans après*), it is intended that all institutionalised discourses should be repelled (at least in their most blatant forms). If the most obvious of these are the pedagogical, the pediatric and the psychiatric, then the psychoanalytic is notable for the fact that, ostensibly at least, it has been forgone (at Bonneuil the children do not enter orthodox analyses). Yet forgone it is not, in at least two important senses. It is there in the books which emerge from the experience of Bonneuil, which contain some of Maud Mannoni's most revealing case histories and most penetrating expositions of psychoanalytic theory. And it is there in the very principle of Bonneuil, the 'exploded institution' ['institution éclatée']. One brief example can serve to show this. The adolescents of Bonneuil are strongly encouraged to have periods away from the place, often in the Cévennes mountains or in the Dordogne. This is no holiday camp principle, but an attempt at *embodiment* of the psychoanalytic principle of presence and absence. This principle is as old and well-established as *Beyond the Pleasure Principle*, in which Freud shows how the *fort/da* game offers the child a means of coming to terms with the terrifying absence of the mother (and thereby with suffering as such). Maud Mannoni explains:

> On the occasion of a successful separation, the child becomes a subject in so much as he is an absent object, and he plays on this in the choice or the refusal to return to the former place. This scansion in the alternation of a stay *here* and *there* brings into play something essential in the case of the psychotic, in that the child manages to occupy a place in an imaginary space which up till then has not been inhabited by him.   (M. Mannoni, 1973b, p. 74)

Through such means as the 'stay-away', Bonneuil attempts to reverse the violence of institutionalisation of latent desire by institutionalising a lack of desire or a space *for* desire. In an interview with Guy Seligmann (who made two films on the subject of Bonneuil) the school's medical doctor, Roger Gentis, puts Maud Mannoni's case simply thus: 'One must never desire in the sick person's place' (M. Mannoni, 1973b, p. 50). Like the principle of de-institutionalising discourse, this desire (not to desire) remains strictly unrealised and unrealisable. But this is perhaps not of great importance since there is one thing that Maud Mannoni is emphatic about: that Bonneuil is no realised ideal or model, but is rather a *creative venture*, beset from within and without by all the difficulties and impossibilities such a venture implies.

Since the time of *Un lieu pour vivre*, Maud Mannoni's attention and ambivalence have been turned still more directly upon the process in which she is actively engaged – psychoanalysis itself, and psychoanalytic theory-building.[14] Her subsequent pair of books (and her books do seem to group themselves into pairs), *La Théorie comme fiction* and *D'un impossible à l'autre*, are testaments to her long engagement and gradual disenchantment with Jacques Lacan and the Ecole freudienne de Paris. Her shift, which is in fact less from the ideas of Lacan than from what she sees as the various attempts to inflate and fix these ideas into immutable objects of knowledge supported by institutions, is also borne out in her most recent pair of books, *Un savoir qui ne se sait pas* and *Bonneuil, seize ans après* (which are both largely historical or retrospective in their focus). Her objective in these works may perhaps be summed up in the proposition with which she concludes *Un savoir qui ne se sait pas*. She proposes that when the analyst's desire is to test out and prove a psychoanalytic theory, however sophisticated the theory may be, it is the patient who becomes the sacrifice. This is the case when, she argues, it is the analyst's duty to sacrifice her- or himself – as subject of knowledge – to the cause of the successful analysis.[15]

I suggested above that Maud Mannoni's work shuns the lure of easy totalisation. It is one of the risks of my short survey that I have flattened this work out, making it seem more coherent and consistent than it is or intends to be. There *are* real difficulties and contradictions. (For one thing, Bonneuil *is* an institution, if despite itself, and, as *Bonneuil, seize ans après* shows, it is one which is quite as susceptible to the political winds of change as any other. For another, despite her resistance to formalised knowledge, Maud Mannoni has entered the academic circuit – however challengingly – in submitting her work for the *Doctorat d'Etat*. And thirdly, she is currently at the heart of the Centre de Formation et de Recherches Psychanalytiques, which is among the two or three most important Lacanian training and research centres in France.) Yet if it is worth noting that there are nodes of inconsistency (and there are others) then it should also be noted that certain at least of them are simply points where Maud Mannoni's ambivalence is most apparent. I suggested (§ 3.0) that to face her work I should have to try to come to terms with this ambivalence. Nor would it be fruitful to spend longer on local quibbles. For it has not been Maud Mannoni's precise landing points that I have tried to chart here, so much as her *trajectory*. That remains unwavering: away from the fixity of knowledge and self-adequate theorising, into the heartland of psychoanalysis as, in its practice as in its writing, 'a *passion*, across a quest for being, marked for certain people by the limit of madness and death' (M. Mannoni, 1979, p. 159). It is a passion of which one may partake, as one follows the generous movements of Maud Mannoni's texts. For these texts open on to a possibility of creation and uncertain birth – a possibility which is sustained by ambivalence itself.[16]

§ 3.5

If psychoanalysis and the psychoanalytic text can be described as essentially 'creative', I should try to show how far this creativity is the same as, or different from, that exercised in literary writing. I should try to show, more generally, the opportunities open to language in each instance. Two of Maud Mannoni's cases – those of Jacques and of Guy, both of whom are struggling to make language their own – may help do this.

If many of Maud Mannoni's patients are unforgettable, few leap out of her work with the violence of Jacques – who does so in moments of worrying lucidity and fantasies of Nazism and misogyny, from the pages of *Education impossible* and *Un lieu pour vivre*. Here are a few of his own words:

Jacques: I slept with my mother . . . I'm in despair.
M. M.: Yes, you wrote it to me in Russian. You've no one to help you?
Jacques: I've no one! Before, my mother was that someone. Now she doesn't want to any more. I feel so old, with a fatal illness that'll carry me off . . . I want to be given what's in my demand.
M. M.: What exactly do you want?
Jacques: . . . I need to be pampered . . . I've a message to launch and no one is my mother.
M. M.: Fortunately for you.
Jacques: In the land of my mother I do what I want, but elsewhere I've got my throat tied. (M. Mannoni, 1973b, pp. 116, 124, 125)

There is enough in this to fuel chapters of analysis. But my concern here is with one point alone, which bears upon Jacques's relation to the Russian and French languages.

Maud Mannoni explains that Jacques has chosen to speak and write in a foreign language so that he can himself be renamed. As Jacques puts it – 'Me, I'm a Russian citizen: Kalmaroff.' Jacques attempts to reject the 'Name of the Father' (which is an essential part of what Lacan calls the 'Paternal Metaphor'), and so avoid the interdiction on the union he both needs and dreads with his mother. From within this rejection he fantasises a new control over his mother tongue. He dreams of a new, impossible fluency.[17] Readers familiar with the work of Louis Wolfson will be reminded of how, in *Le Schizo et les langues*, this writer tells of his pathological aversion to his mother tongue. When Wolfson's mother speaks to him in English (his native language) he is lacerated by her words. It is, he writes, as if 'elle se fût décidée à frapper son fils simultanément avec la langue de sa bouche et celle des Anglais presque chaque fois qu'elle le [sic] pourrait' (p. 73). Wolfson tries to keep some grip on his sanity by shutting his ears. Beyond this, he regains some power of expression through an arduous apprentice-ship in foreign languages, which enable him to 'convertir ces mots de sa plus proche parente en mots étrangers et ainsi – peut-être comme subconsciemment il le voudrait faire – les détruire en quelque sorte' (pp. 123–4).[18] Wolfson, a New Yorker, writes the harrowing account of his life not in English but in French.

For Wolfson and for Jacques the mother tongue represents the site of maximum desire, and therefore maximum danger and impossibility. But lest their suffering does not spell out boldly enough the force of language, and the relation of language to the one who is often responsible for teaching it, then perhaps Roland Barthes's *The Pleasure of the Text* can be called upon once again. A pattern has already been pointed to which reveals writers as inhabiting a space which is tantalisingly perceived by certain of the patients of psychoanalysis, while being unavailable to them. Barthes now extends this pattern. After stating that no object can ever be in a stable relation to pleasure, he continues:

> For the writer, however, this object exists: it is not the language, it is the *mother tongue*. The writer is someone who plays with the mother's body . . . in order to glorify it, to embellish it, in order to dismember it, to take it to the limit of what can be known about the body: I would go so far as to take bliss in a *disfiguration* of the language.
>
> (p. 37) [j'irai jusqu'à jouir d'une *défiguration* de la langue (p. 61)]

In the light of Barthes's comments, it will be seen as no coincidence if many of the writers under consideration here – Kafka, Celan, Beckett and Proust (as I shall suggest in chapter 6) – have had a very special, and not unambiguous relation to their mother tongue.[19] Nor is Barthes's statement without relevance for his own career as a writer (a writer who was increasingly preoccupied with his status as a writer). For it is to his mother that Barthes returns in *La Chambre claire* (*Camera Lucida*). He returns to her illness and death, and writes of his rediscovery of her in a photo taken when she was a child. In what was to be his final book, Barthes achieves what is perhaps his most moving writing. It emerges painfully, beyond its ostensible preoccupation with photography, into the experience of loss and recovery of his mother. Psychoanalysis has already been coaxed (in § 2.7) into one imaginary space (between two stanzas of a Celan poem). Maud Mannoni's psychoanalytic practice can perhaps be characterised through a second imaginary space: between the words of Jacques (and of Wolfson) and that which the words of Barthes both say and show (argue and demonstrate). It is not a change of sets of preoccupations that

Maud Mannoni seeks to facilitate – any more than it is a change in the 'real' circumstances of a life. In his preoccupations Barthes is certainly very close to Jacques; and Maud Mannoni would not seek to repress this resemblance – how could she without a deal of self-denial? It is the representation and enactment of the preoccupations that Maud Mannoni seeks to change, in a direction at one end of which one might well find a Barthes (and beyond him the figures of such as Proust or Beckett). Jacques in his talk, Maud Mannoni in her writing, Barthes in his – all tell a not dissimilar story. Only, the point *from which* they tell it differs crucially.

I can now turn, as promised, to the case of 'Guy ou la mort du père', reported in *L'Enfant, sa 'maladie' et les autres* (pp. 149–60), in order to give a final indication of this overlapping of preoccupations, and also (in § 3.6) to develop a sense of this crucial difference. Unlike Jacques, Guy is not exceptional, and he has been chosen rather because he is so typical of the numerous brief case histories which Maud Mannoni recounts. Here is something of his story.

Guy is a child of six, a late developer in all respects, oligophrenic and schizophrenic. When Guy and his mother first consult Maud Mannoni, the situation is already grave. Guy's mother is isolated from her family owing to the jealousy of the father, a skilled factory worker on night shifts, who demands peace during the day. At the first consultation Guy delivers a monologue, and draws, speaks and acts like an automaton. Maud Mannoni agrees to take him into analysis, but, owing to the father's unavailability, without first seeing both parents. During the first three months of sessions, the child tells stories of castration in which the mother and then the analyst are hated as sorceresses. Guy leaves for a stay in a home, and his father commits suicide. The matriarchal maternal grandmother arrives on the scene, and demands that Guy be hospitalised. Maud Mannoni excludes this grandmother in order to allow Guy's primitive re-enactment of the drama of the father's death to continue. Guy presents himself as a partial, rejected object – 'pee, jobby, bathroom, willy' (p. 155). The parents had wished to keep Guy from desire, and to silence him. Guy believes they wanted to poison him. By the end of the second year of analysis Guy has concluded that he no longer loves his (dead) father and that it is when he is annoyed that he feigns madness (or 'plays the fool'). He rejects his family, and when his mother declines into depression he is sent to a foster family to allow her time to recover. On returning home, he decides he wants to have a child with his mother. He returns to the foster family, remains oligophrenic and unteachable. Yet he is able, notwithstanding, to find some satisfaction in work with artisans.

Maud Mannoni draws several analytic conclusions from the case, the last of which is that she was involuntarily complicit in the death of Guy's father. She tells a grim tale unforgivingly. However, rather than go further into her analysis of the events, it is other events I wish to pursue. Here, in brief, is another tale by another writer.

A young man sees a ghost of his father who has recently died, which tells him that he has been poisoned by his brother. The brother/uncle has meanwhile married the young man's mother. The young man suffers from a resultant radical loss of desire, but still decides to seek a form of revenge upon his uncle, after first making sure of his guilt. He attempts to do this by feigning madness and, later, by staging a play which is itself a close copy of reported reality. The young man kills several people, but not his uncle. He rejects his lover whom he sees as sexually tainted, accusing her of all kinds of debauchery. She ends up losing her wits and drowning herself. Her brother, seeking his own revenge, is employed by the uncle to kill the young man. This he manages, but not before he himself, uncle and mother have also managed to slaughter each other.

My synopsis of Shakespeare's *Hamlet*, though in most respects a horrible travesty, nevertheless offers a final confirmation of the fact that literary and psychoanalytic preoccupations can be contiguous, and that a case history can encompass many of the elements of tragedy. (It may have been the theatre, with its 'suspension of reality', that helped Freud to understand and describe the 'field of play' of transference.[20]) Yet despite the pushings of 'writing smugglers' such as Leclaire and Lacan, and despite the polemics of a 'theory as fiction', there persist certain radical differences between the two areas of preoccupation. The case of Guy was cited partly to highlight such differences, and it is to these I shall now turn.

§ 3.6

To go back to my crude summary of *Hamlet*, I may now say that what is significant about it is not just that it leaves out more than does my summary of the case of Guy. What is significant is that it leaves out *the essential*: that *this is a fiction*, however real the suffering, the family rivalry, and the incest may be (and however available these are to the incursions of Ernest Jones or one more subtle).[21] However real the events may appear, they will always be subservient to the need to create a drama, and to one individual's vision of all this implies. At its very simplest, this means that the events will be determined by the necessity that however the drama unfolds, it will have a form defined by a beginning and an end.

To turn to the audience's side, it should be noted that our experience will be defined by similar conditions and constraints. When we leave the theatre (or lay down the text, or complete the novel or poem) we may well find ourselves changed. The Greeks envisaged this, with their theory of catharsis (a theory that psychoanalysis was quick to adopt). But however powerful the change, the basic fact is that we do leave the theatre, emerge from the novel or poem. We experience fiction (and art in general) within certain parameters; even those of us whose lives are largely taken up with the reading (or experiencing) of it. Our 'real' lives may be so greatly modelled, scarred and enabled by fiction because, in the end, it does *not* refer us back to any *real* life. It refers us only to its metaphoric, or, in the broadest sense, symbolic life. We live *Hamlet* in the first and last instance – between which absolutes there is time and space for Hamlet and Laertes, Ophelia and Cordelia, time and space even for Shakespeare – as *our* drama. We do so because the context and conditions are such that we know *it is not*. We know (though we may forget) that it is not ours, nor, strictly, its author's, nor even Hamlet's. We know it belongs only to what may now be termed the 'potential space' between us.

I borrow the notion 'potential space' from the British psychoanalyst D. W. Winnicott. And I do so partly because it allows me to bring together again, this time in a clearer fashion, the moment which has been seen to be crucial in the development of the infant into childhood (and which was described as characteristic of ambivalence), and our adult experiences in culture. The 'potential space' is described by Winnicott as an invisible terrain of 'maximally intense experience', which should arise between mother and child. It is a terrain 'between me-extensions and the not-me . . . at the interplay between there being nothing but me and there being objects and phenomena outside omnipotent control' (Winnicott, 1974, p. 118). Within this terrain the child learns and grows through interaction with what Winnicott calls the 'transitional object', and through significant, creative *play*. Such play takes place across 'the theoretical line between the subjective and that which is objectively perceived' (Winnicott, 1974, p. 59). Play belongs to, and is the infant's prime means of exploring, that intermediate, wavering zone which was introduced in discussion of ambivalence: the zone of merging and separation (which serves for Freud as a model for so much of adult experience).[22]

Nor does the relevance of Winnicott's notion stop here. For the importance of the 'potential space' does not disappear as the child grows. If the conditions (of mothering and of trust) are right, play yields to cultural experience in general; and the transitional object, decathected, yields to the art-work in particular. For Winnicott the 'potential space' does not – indeed *must* not – disappear, nor do its ambivalent charge and scope alter greatly with age. It is simply inhabited by new activities and artifacts, most intensely by reading, writing, painting and creating: by art and its objects. It is through them that as adults we can re-explore the 'potential space': leave the confines of our language-worlds and our limited and limiting selves, and do so with assurance of change *and return*. Here, as art critic Peter Fuller has tried to show in relation to Modernism and abstract art, 'The existence of the boundaries (outlines) or limiting membranes of the self and of its objects are at once perceived and imaginatively ruptured' (Fuller, 1980, p. 11).[23]

As far back as in discussion of Kafka, I suggested (§ 1.4) that the processes of fiction depend on the fact that narratives do end, and depend on the separateness of reader and writer – what I termed the reader's 'ostensible inviolability'. I was at pains to emphasise the inviolability. Now it is time to remember the force of the ostensibility. Thinking it from the reader's side, it can be said that the line between the rapture of fiction and hysterical identification is a fine one.[24] It is nonetheless crucial – as crucial indeed as it is fine. Lest one forget this, Hamlet – protagonist and producer of his own play – is there to remind one of it, though his feelings of guilt blind him to the truth of his insight. Hamlet watches his player friend's rapid absorption into the drama of Priam's slaughter, and rues his own complacency, in one of his most poignant soliloquies:

> O what a rogue and peasant slave am I!
> Is it not monstrous that this player here,
> But in a fiction, in a dream of passion,
> Could force his soul so to his own conceit
> That from her working all his visage wann'd,
> Tears in his eyes, distraction in his aspect,
> A broken voice, and his whole function suiting
> With forms to his conceit? And all for nothing! . . .
> Yet I,
> A dull and muddy-mettled rascal, peak
> Like John-a-dreams, unpregnant of my cause,
> And can say nothing.   (II, 2)

Hamlet offers a wonderful description of the power of fiction. What he fails to see is that the player achieves his intensity not despite but precisely because he is acting out such a 'fiction'. For unlike the dilemma Hamlet is trying to resolve, a fiction has order, is bordered, has rules, exclusions, a beginning and an end. Hamlet does not see it, but he in turn will use a fiction, the 'play within the play', to ferret out the truth and 'unmask the real'.[25]

Going back again to my summary of Maud Mannoni's 'Guy ou la mort du père', it may now be agreed that it is in fact rather perfunctory. It omits details of Guy's fantasy world which are important, and omits the bulk of Maud Mannoni's interpretation. But whatever its inadequacies, it still contains grains of truth, and is at least aimed at the correct mark. The suffering, despair and manipulation within Guy's family may suggest this or that about the nature of control, of desire, and of parent–child relations. They may or may not correspond to concerns and worries of one's own (and as my own father died when I was Guy's age, there may well be more to my apparently random choice of him than I at first realised). But what is significant here is the nature, or the very fact, of this 'correspondence'. For no matter how close the sufferings, and how well they are told, even if they were to feel, while one reads, as if they were almost one's own, they remain in the first and last instance – between which one may make them however much one's own – ineradicably those of another (in this case the hapless Guy). During the analytic sessions there may have been – indeed almost certainly was – interchange of great intensity between Guy and Maud Mannoni. Their exchange catches at the force of Leclaire's need for an 'utterance that may be released . . . in a meeting with another utterance which is being born'. Yet despite this intensity, despite the risk involved, despite the critical interlocking of destinies and the surges of transference and counter-transference, their own 'real' lives remain separate from each other. The words that recount these sessions remain those, at a further remove, of the committed and scrupulously honest analyst, Maud Mannoni. The lives of patient and analyst not only remain separate from each other but also irremediably separate from that of the reader.

Within psychoanalysis, whatever the pressure upon words and their sharing, the investment of the analyst will at any moment be less than total. As I started to indicate with Leclaire in terms of the body, this is not because of some lack of generosity or latent megalomania on the part of the analyst. It is because of the necessities of the psychoanalytic process, and the necessity, above all, for *survival*. In art one can accept loss of oneself because one's experience of trust has paid off in the past.[26] The context and fact of fictionality assure one's return from the 'potential space'. For the psychoanalyst, on the other hand, there is no equivalent reassurance. And for the reader of the psychoanalytic text something of the same condition applies. Reading Guy's case history, whatever the reader's sophistications – which may dictate that a 'real' life does not exist just the other side of these graphic notations, or that if it did it would still be predicated upon the primacy of certain symbolic functions – he or she is returned to the otherness (and awfulness) of the referent (the life being described and analysed). This is not because of some further lack of generosity, on the part of the reader this time. Like analysts, readers too must look to their survival.

These distinctions might in one sense be more easily sketched by starting from the opposite end to that of the reader – from the end of the author and his or her intentions. However strong the urge, as J.-B. Pontalis has it, to 'communicate the psychoanalytic object', Maud Mannoni's project is still quite distinct from that of a Shakespeare. The commitment to writing is not the same. As Michel de M'Uzan puts it, in conversation with Pontalis, 'The analyst does not have to confront writing as an absolute commandment' (M'Uzan, 1977, pp. 25–6). This is so while the writer has, on the contrary, to stake his or her all on the act of writing.[27] Talk of commitment and intentionality can take one so far. But when taken any further, such talk tends to founder on the rocks of one's revealed assumptions, which had remained unthreatening so long as they were submerged under a sea of common sense and shared premises.[28] Shakespeare's intentions drew him to the artistic venture, Maud Mannoni's to the psychoanalytic – this much is obvious. But readers read writing, not the traces of another's wanting and choosing and committing. Whatever the intentions of a Shakespeare or a Mannoni, the necessary forms of their ventures are subsumed within the various possibilities afforded by language (and, I have suggested, afforded by their readers as well). This is to say that the forms of their ventures are themselves profoundly determining, and that these lie outside the scope of intentionality.

In preparing to move on to part II of the present work, and attend again more directly to literature, it may be useful to state that this is one of the questions which will be considered: how the work of fiction can be said to be a 'creative venture' when it is constrained by its borders, its exclusions, and its form which is dependent upon a pre-ordained beginning and end. Does this question define a simple contradiction, or does it contain a more complex sort of paradox? By holding for a moment to the example of Shakespeare, some leads may in fact be unearthed that will be worth following. However fierce Shakespeare's artistic purpose, and however revolutionary its drive, the conventionalisation of these into recognisable rhetorical and aesthetic patternings (of metre, rhythm, rhyme and plot) constrains this purpose. But are the constraints necessarily unwelcome? Few would doubt that Shakespeare leaves his innovative imprint not only upon one's consciousness but upon the course of English drama, poetry, creativity and language. Yet it is Shakespeare who, in *The Tempest* (his final complete play), adheres to the classical unities of time, place and action to a degree unknown since his first drama, *The Comedy of Errors*. And, as Gabriel Josipovici points out in his conclusion to *Writing and the Body*, one need hardly commit the Victorian critics' error of reading Shakespeare into Prospero to accept that in Prospero's epilogue is contained a sense of both the 'Freedom of the Poet',[29] the limitless scope of art and artifice, and the inadequacy, the formalism and impersonality of art. In

Prospero's epilogue is contained the frustration of a Prospero, or indeed a Shakespeare, who, in and of art, 'can never quite speak *in propria persona*' (Josipovici, 1982, p. 133).

Prospero's epilogue gives expression to ambivalence, directed now at literature itself. This ambivalence recalls the case of the boy with the painful head–leg, who could not speak 'in his own person'. If it points backwards, however, then it also directs forwards, towards the writers who will now be considered at greater length, among whom Marcel Proust and Samuel Beckett will be prominent. For there are some obvious connections between this ambivalence and the work of these writers. After all, the narrator of Proust's great novel cannot decide upon a subject for his book that will make it distinctively 'his own'. In Beckett's *The Unnamable* (as I began to show) there is no more abundant source of suffering than the inability to speak in other than another's words. Could it be that the very resistance of art can in certain cases become the substance of art? Could it be that the formal constraints of literature – signally the primordial need of a beginning and an end – are in some way generative or re-generative of literature? Could it be that the writers whose work appears most intensely their own, whose palpable physicality is most imminent, are those who have lived longest and closest to language's resistance to their unique selves and bodies? Rather than try to offer short or simple answers to these questions, I shall move on, while requesting my reader to bear these questions in mind.

Part II

Play it again

4 · *For to end yet again*

§ 4.0

ONE of the questions posed in the final paragraph of chapter 3 has an immediate relevance for Proust's novel, *A la recherche du temps perdu*. It is that which finds a relation between the formal constraints of literature – first and foremost the constraint of beginning and ending – and literature's generative power or creative scope. Proust's novel gives a twist, or series of twists, to the question. Perhaps more than any other novel, it confronts the reader with a sense of his or her own perpetual need to be beginning and venturing, into a work which embarrasses with the scope and weight of its achievement. If all the risking seems to be on the reader's side, then this is reinforced by the way the novel proffers itself, as a sort of repetition or going over of events which have been rediscovered through the benevolent intervention of 'involuntary memory'. Proust's novel is monumentally there. It may appear as the very antithesis of the work of one such as Paul Celan, in which achieving (as seen above, § 2.6) is impossibly distant, and in which words pare themselves down under a minimalist urge. Its sheer bulk and completedness cause an awkwardness which critics have been happy to overlook. I wish to confront this awkwardness, but before doing so, to point briefly to some other ways in which writing more generally can be on the one hand creative and venturing (involved in choice and danger) and on the other hand always already completed – as if constructed out of repetition – and available to the reader only through the performance of a further re-enactment that reading involves.

One may usefully refer again to T. S. Eliot, and particularly to the way he describes the poetic duty in his *Four Quartets*. For the duty of the poet is to be constantly rediscovering what is new, like old men who must be 'still and still moving' ('Burnt Norton' v). The duty is to perform 'a raid on the inarticulate / With shabby equipment always deteriorating' ('East Coker' v). It is not for the poet to concern himself with achievement, for all has already been achieved, 'by men whom one cannot hope / To emulate'. Eliot's words of conclusion net poet and reader alike: 'For us, there is only the trying' ('East Coker' v). Yet even as he asserts this, Eliot allows a different, perhaps contradictory impression to emerge. For in the very same poem he is at pains to point out that 'in my beginning is my end', and 'in my end is my beginning'. Nothing is new, apparently, not even the poem. Before the reader starts to read, the work is complete – and not only that, but even before the writer starts to write. Can this view of the poem be compatible with the poet's obligation to be 'venturing'? In the course of this chapter I shall return to Eliot and to poetry, to try to answer this question. For the moment I wish to indicate how broad the preoccupation may be with the dual possibility (which, for the sake of argument, can be simplified down to that between venturing and repeating, or 'becoming' and 'being'). I wish to suggest that it spreads not only to fiction and poetry, but to critical enquiry as well.

One example will serve to illustrate this. Few writers have been more able than Maurice Blanchot to give a sense of the unpredictable nature of literature, and of the writer's need to coax new meanings out of his or her art. Here, for example, is a short passage which is not untypical of the way he writes of narrative:

Narration is movement towards a point which is not only unknown, ignored and strange but such that it seems to have no prior reality apart from this movement, yet is so compulsive that the narration's appeal depends on it to the extent that it cannot even 'begin' before it has reached it, while it is only the narration and the unpredictable movement of the narration which provide the space where this point becomes real, powerful and appealing. (Blanchot, 1982, p. 62)

For Blanchot, narrative always exists in a 'present' which is suspended in uncertainty. Yet though it exists so, it exists not only so. For in Blanchot's words is intimated a familiar problem or paradox, when he suggests that narrative may have reached its destination before it begins – the implication being that narrative repeats something, or perhaps repeats *itself* (whatever this might mean). What is a hint in Blanchot's words is more unavoidably evident in the words of another pre-eminent critic, Walter Benjamin, when he turns his attention to storytelling and narrative. Benjamin writes:

The reader of a novel actually does look for human beings from whom he derives the 'meaning of life'. Therefore he must, no matter what, know in advance that he will share their experience of death: if need be their figural death – the end of the novel. (Benjamin, 1973, p. 101)

How can narrative be movement towards a destination unknown, and at the same time movement towards an inevitable and pre-ordained end? How can it be both a repetition and a constant searching for the new?

I shall deal with such questions (and such ambiguity and ambivalence) in this chapter. At the same time I shall try to develop a sense of the structure of Proust's novel. For despite the novel's achievement, there is a way in which it allows the reader to perceive that it *too* has an investment in non-achievement, in waste, and in the never-quite-started. Not all the embarrassment is on the reader's side. Proust's novel confronts one with the unavoidable risk required in daring to read. But it also requires a reading which is somehow a repetition. It emerges from a writing which is a perpetual new beginning. At the same time it is only ever an enterprise involving re-writing.

§ 4.1

I wish to take an indirect path into Proust's novel: one which leads by way of his earlier work, and before that by way of a writer whose characteristic form or genre contrasts with Proust's almost as dramatically as does that of Celan – Jorge Luis Borges. The contradictions or paradoxes which appear to inhabit writing – over venture and form, newness and repetition, risk and achievement, becoming and being – cluster round a single issue or question: that of time or temporality. It may therefore be appropriate, when attempting to unravel the cluster, to elicit the help of Borges's great timekeeper, 'Funes the Memorious', who comes to life in the story of that name.

The narrator of this story recounts that he has been asked to contribute to an anthology of recollections of Ireneo Funes. He recalls that he first met him as a youth, and that when Funes was asked the time, he replied with utter precision (but without the help of a chronometer). At first sight this is not so surprising, as one supposes it to be a case of two youths bantering and staking claims. But as one reads on one finds that the narrator grew to accept the absolute veracity of Funes's timekeeping. While pursuing the story – and this is further cause for surprise – one tends to accept it oneself. When the narrator next meets him, Funes has been paralysed by a fall from a horse. What Funes lacks in physical ability he makes up in psychic mobility. For he has graduated from the role of timekeeper so that 'now his perception and his memory were infallible'. The narrator explains:

We, at one glance, can perceive three glasses on a table; Funes, all the leaves and tendrils and fruit that make up a grape vine. He knew by heart the forms of the southern clouds at dawn on 30 April 1882, and could compare them in his memory with the mottled streaks on a book in Spanish binding he had only seen once and with the outlines of the foam raised by an oar in the Río Negro the night before the Quebrancho uprising. These memories were not simple ones; each visual image was linked to muscular sensations, thermal sensations, etc. He could reconstruct all his dreams, all his half-dreams. Two or three times he had reconstructed a whole day; he never hesitated, but each reconstruction had required a whole day. He told me: 'I alone have more memories than all mankind has probably had since the world has been the world.' And again: 'My dreams are like you people's waking hours.'   (Borges, 1970, p. 92)

As these amazing possibilities are whirring in the reader's mind, the narrator confirms his own belief once and for all, when he writes: 'These things he told me; neither then nor later have I ever placed them in doubt.'

Funes's abilities are truly remarkable. Yet it gradually becomes clear that the sum of his abilities is also the cause of his failings, and not just in the sense of his physical debility. From the start, the narrator has warned, 'but one should not forget that he was also a kid from Fray Bentos, with certain incurable limitations' (p. 87). The nature of these limitations becomes clearer as the narrator outlines Funes's two absurd systems, elaborated with such care, one for numbering, the other for naming. For they are scarcely systems at all, abandoned as they are to the infinite nature of the particular. They betray Funes's inability to see life in anything but its absolute specificity, its immanence, its perpetual originality. Funes 'was the solitary and lucid spectator of a multiform, instantaneous and almost intolerably precise world' (p. 94). When he is last encountered, though he is only nineteen years old he has achieved monumental status – 'older than the prophecies and the pyramids' (p. 94). Despite this, he dies twenty years later the most prosaic of deaths from congestion of the lungs.

How do we make sense of time? Of the past and its diversity? Of the present, therefore? Funes impresses that we do so not, as we might imagine, by our perceptiveness, still less by our fine memories. Rather we do so by our obtuseness and by our capacity for *forgetting*.[1] Funes's ability as timekeeper seems to come from his living in the continuous present. It thus adumbrates his gift for a recall so perfect that it returns the past to an identical present – a day remembered becomes a day. In Funes we find our truth as very different beings who live a present constituted of a mutilated past which has been plundered of implausible generalities, and a present which already contains a future which is premised on the absolute forgetting that is death. We punctuate time, and we protect our lives under the ashes of our forgetfulness, our death. Funes emerges from these ashes, and rises up as monumental through his futureless, memory-less present. He rises up *as presence*. His life exemplifies Blanchot's requirement of narrative that it be 'ever present in a beginning so sudden that it leaves one breathless' (Blanchot, 1982, p. 65). And herein lies Funes's delusion, his madness. For Blanchot is talking of narrative, not of life; and narrative exists in the space of creation, of illusion. As I showed when looking at *Hamlet* (above, § 3.6), fiction is so engaging and enabling precisely because it operates in ways which are unimaginable in life. Or perhaps 'unimaginable' is the wrong word. Borges has imagined for his reader, and Funes is his imagining.

Despite his abilities – or perhaps because of them – Funes is subjected to the much more limited and limiting faculties of common mortals. He is subject of an anthology, and so of men's partial and imperfect recollections. Nor do all the limitations come from outside. Superb linguist that he is, Funes is unable to tell a story, least of all his own. For stories work by way of generalities, exclusions, partial recallings and forgettings. Only by so working can they begin to fulfil Blanchot's criteria and reveal the astonishing potential of one such as Funes. How perfectly Borges indicates this to his reader, choosing carefully his imperfect narrator, submitting Funes to the caprice of a 'Highbrow, city slicker, dude' (p. 87). How neatly the story of Funes fulfils Benjamin's requirement that death confer meaning, that time be read backwards. For it is Funes's death which concludes the story, which has perhaps prompted the anthology, and which renders it meaningful. Within the pages of his story, Borges taps the reader's credulity, and convinces one of the life lived in an immanent present. His telling may even be the living replica of that immanence. But this is what Borges makes one believe, and this is what his narrative does and is, precisely because it is engendered by death. Its own end – its 'figural death' as Benjamin has it – is emblazoned into its very form. For this is, after all, not a novel, nor even an anthology, but a *short story*. One has scarcely started it before it ends, as one knows it will.

After he began his career as a poet, Borges preferred genre became increasingly that of the short story. It is a genre, I suggested, which seems leagues away from that preferred by Proust. Despite this, Borges does offer a track which can lead into *A la recherche*. With his capacities for remembering, Funes is a figure that may recall one in Proust's novel. I shall have to see how far the overlap of capacities is real or apparent. Staying with the shortness of the short story and the bulk of Proust's novel, there is another way of corroborating that they are not as chalk and cheese, incommensurable poles of narrative. It is the way that follows Proust's own path, through that abandoned work, *Jean Santeuil*. This is a work Proust chose never to publish, but without which the successes of *A la recherche* are hard to imagine.

Here is how this novel begins (if 'novel' it may justly be called):

Should I call this book a novel? It is something less, perhaps, and yet much more, the very essence of my life, with nothing extraneous added, as it developed through a long period of wretchedness. This book of mine has not been manufactured: it has been garnered. (p. 1; p. 181)

Jean Santeuil comprises a collection of approximately two hundred 'scenes', transcribed from life into art. As the narrator has it, 'I lived all the scenes that I am recounting to you' (Pléiade edition, p. 490). It attempts to map moments not unlike those lived by Funes – moments of insight and illumination which Jean undergoes (most famously before the lake at Geneva which returns him to a Beg-Meil seascape). It does so by holding to the untotalised, discontinuous narrative fragment. *Jean Santeuil* is full of interest for readers of Proust, because of the many crucial scenes, such as that at the lake, which grow and develop into features of *A la recherche*. Jean may be more directly Proust than is Marcel. Yet as Blanchot has shown (in his essay 'Proust'), this is precisely the problem. *Jean Santeuil* is a novel whose form tries to mimic the illumination and timelessness it wishes to describe. Its form has not been modified by the insight which *Contre Sainte-Beuve* everywhere displays, and which the narrator of *Jean Santeuil* declares, that 'writing a novel or living one is by no means the same thing, whatever one says' (Pléiade edition, p. 490).

What draws the reader into Borges's story, what allows it to create around Funes a space of utter plausibility, is the story's *distance from* Funes and from the miraculous phenomena it describes. A certain timelessness is conveyed by the rigorous temporality of the short story. *Jean Santeuil* is very different. It is as if this novel inhabits the impossible space of Funes's own creativity. Like Funes's creations (his number and word systems), it is 'senseless', yet 'betray[s] a certain stammering grandeur' (Borges, 1970, p. 93). It too is infinitely expandable, therefore interminable. Despite the efforts of Pierre Clarac, the editor of the definitive Pléiade edition, to impose continuity upon the volume, it goes on and on in a way that *A la recherche* never does. I believe that only the determined reader will read every page of *Jean Santeuil*. One is liable to long for an ending, to the exact extent that Proust denies this. One may even, taking Benjamin as one's witness, think Jean better off dead . . . But only until one remembers that Jean was in fact sentenced long ago, by the person who brought him into the world, and that he would have remained quiet had scholarly curiosity not resurrected him. (*Jean Santeuil* was published in its present form only in 1971, and I suspect the event caused Proust to turn an inch or two in his grave.)

Reading *Jean Santeuil* may be a dissatisfying experience, but it does confirm, among other things, that Proust lived directly the tension I have highlighted between an achieved and an open present, between being and becoming. It is important to have this in mind when turning to *A la recherche*. For it is more than mere historical fact (which privileges one with a vision of wholeness and completedness Proust's contemporaries did not have) that encourages a feeling, in front of *A la recherche*, that (through the twist I mentioned above) one is oppressively faced as reader with unassailable achievement alone. Staying for the moment with the reader's perceptions, it may feel as if all the 'being' were out there, on the side of Proust and his novel; while all the need to 'become' is in here, on one's own side. It is hard to do justice to the feelings of awe and diffidence that Proust's novel can induce. Roger Shattuck is doubtless right to acknowledge readerly hesitation in his introductory book on Proust. If he makes reading sound like mountain climbing, he is not far wrong. For Proust forces the reader to inspect his or her capacities (the adequacy of his or her language, desire and time), as mountaineers inspect maps and equipment. Proust's novel often seems to be there in much the way a mountain is there. And Shattuck is doubly right to insist on difficulty because, as I have said, it is hard to write from a position that fully acknowledges readerly difficulty – impossible to write of Proust except as a reader of Proust.

Such a condition of temporality, by which critical writing goes over that which has already been accomplished and repeats what is already in the past, may prevail over the attempt to articulate feeling about any writer. With Proust, again, the temporal twist is peculiarly significant, and troubling as well. For one is immediately set by the twist in one camp (the camp of 'being', as it were), as opposed to the other (the camp of 'becoming'). Thus one misses the tension or paradox between the two, to which I have been attempting to direct attention. It is something of such a troubling problem that is taken up in a joke that is worth mentioning here. The joke decrees that one should not say 'I'm reading Proust', but rather 'I'm re-reading Proust.' Cultural snobbery plays its part in this joke, no doubt. But there is more to it than this. The degree to which one may find it hard to wriggle free of the barb of the joke indicates this, as does the fact that Proust himself is also somehow hooked.

Proust was of course his own most assiduous re-reader. *Jean Santeuil* was interminable, and, as scholars have begun to show, *A la recherche* was also in a perpetual state of change and uncompletedness.[2] One should not miss the force of this remarkable fact – the impact of a life spent between being and becoming. Most people who have ever written will know the special satisfaction of completing a piece of work and surrendering it to another or others. This is a satisfaction which Proust cannot have known, in relation to his major work. For he died with the galley proofs of *A la recherche* in his hands. The reason why the anecdote is significant is not because it confirms a romantic image of the self-sacrificing artist, but rather because it confirms my hunch that, beyond any recalcitrance on Proust's part, there was something peculiarly sustaining and nourishing about the novel, something which made concluding less important. Blanchot talks of Proust's 'amazing patience', and in the essay 'Proust Palimpsest' Gérard Genette helps show how the novel 'incorporates' the years of its creation. But there is more to be said about the way in which Proust's novel is, for its reader as for its writer, both an achievement and a perpetual labour, a repetition and a venture.

Turning to the novel itself, I should like to suggest, by way of preliminary remark, that it charts the tentative and haphazard steps towards a point from which a beginning can perhaps be made. It inhabits a world – or a womb – which has not yet known conception. Telling of Marcel, it embraces both Ireneo Funes and Jean Santeuil in a time rendered 'senseless' by the failure of ambition and of the future. Almost as much as Funes or Jean, Marcel finds it impossible to get going on the system or story that would matter. The narration of *A la recherche* embraces Blanchot's edict that it tell only 'itself'; but it does so most powerfully because Marcel is *unable* ever to begin to tell anything else. *A la recherche* is a chronicle of non-achievement, of the failure not so much to get to the end as ever truly to get started. If this is true, however, then the converse is also and equally true. More than any other novel (and quite as much as Borges's short story of Funes) *A la recherche* has its end written into its beginning. Not only are the reader's doubts and worries written into the novel, but also the reader's accomplishment, tenacity, doggedness and control. One inhabits this tension and paradox of twisted temporality in reading, as one becomes that 'I' (Marcel) around which the vast novel forms.

I shall have to uncover more precisely the ways in which this tension is deployed, this paradox exploited, and the way in which the shift from *Jean Santeuil* to *A la recherche* reveals to Proust a temporality which enables him to venture while repeating, and to incorporate the past in a present which was present but not 'senseless'. But in doing this, it will be important not to lose sight of the Proustian joke on whose barb I was hooked. In writing about the novel one implies one's re-reading (and thereby asserts one's status as an accomplished reader). Proust too was perpetually re-reading. It is indeed hard to wriggle free of the barb. Might there perhaps be a way off it in the suggestion that Proust is doubly hooked as well? Is Proust not only re-reading, but also *re-writing* (and in a sense different from the literal re-writing implied in his devotion to the galleys)? Could it be that the very act of generating literature is already contained by repetition?

§ 4.2

I wish again to call on other writers – some familiar by now, some new – to help explore and perhaps answer these questions. In § 4.5 I shall come back to Proust and *A la recherche*, with a clearer sense of the way in which the formal constraints mentioned in relation to literary works result from and also require a repetition which is instilled with ambivalence. This clarity should help in turn to resist the understanding of repetition which the novel forcefully proffers. In § 4.3 and § 4.4 I shall focus primarily on two examples from fiction. Here, after glancing back to Franz Kafka in order to see if what has been said of him can help in the present context, it is largely to poetry I wish to attend. Certain poets have shown with admirable brevity and force the way in which the present tense of their utterance is suffused with the past, and even with a possible or hypothetical future.

One way of expressing the problem with *Jean Santeuil* is in terms of over-proximity: of timelessness described and interminability of the narrative, of existential position and artistic method, of Jean Santeuil and Marcel Proust. This worry about proximity is not a new one since I have already developed it in relation to Kafka. I suggested (in § 1.3) that Kafka's life, as exposed for example in the *Letter to his Father*, is perilously close to that of his creation, Georg (in 'The Judgement'). I also suggested that Kafka is to a crucial extent redeemed by the mobility which his fiction allows him, and which sets him off from Georg's fixity. Kafka's fiction is moving and resonant in its telling – its telling of an end, a death – where Georg's letter remains unfinished and unsent.

Georg is not very different from Funes (in Borges's story), whose past and future collapse into a present so present as to render him virtually impotent. What Georg is unable to do is turn the generations. His life is in this sense a cruel conflation of origin and destiny, since his father exists as his source and his scourge (his to give life and his to take it away). In his father's judgement what Georg has to submit to is an almost teleological compacting of beginning into end, which leaves no room for a start of his own originating. Georg is to have no fiancée or family.

Yet Kafka, with 'The Judgement', seems to give birth in a story which hollows out of implausibility the space of its telling. Though the content of Kafka's story is in some measure incredible, the tale still nets the reader's credulity, and quite as compellingly as does that of Borges. It moves in its unflustered way from beginning to middle to end. Kafka's writings, in which 'The Judgement' holds such an important place, have created their own ancestors, backwards and forwards in time, as Borges shows in his essay 'Kafka and His Precursors'. Borges is himself not the least of them. It is therefore important to stress the difference between Kafka and Georg; but it is important also not to overstate the case. For Kafka, I suggested, is supremely ambivalent about his own literary efforts – reluctant yet desperate to begin, desperate yet reluctant to end. Not all the difficulties with generation are on the side of his characters.

What is true for Kafka holds to an extent for T. S. Eliot, whose *Four Quartets* I have mentioned as exhibiting an apparent conflict between the need to be venturing and the need to be already completed. Beginning may be an operation engaged upon with extreme reluctance – as the famous opening lines of Eliot's earlier poem *The Waste Land* serve to recall. This poem opens, after a title about endings ('The Burial of the Dead'), on a beginning which is also a recurrence:

> April is the cruellest month, breeding
> Lilacs out of the dead land, mixing
> Memory and desire, stirring
> Dull roots with spring rain.

April is no blessing, but arrives as an irritant to disturb winter's somnolence. Desire – even for an end – is always a beginning, here one which is fraught with resistance. (As 'Burnt Norton' v later puts it, 'Desire itself is movement / Not in itself desirable.') Desire, the desire to begin, is prompted by nature. Yet desire is uniquely human, mark of a fall from grace. It is imbued, as psychoanalysts have it, with 'lack-of-being'. *The Waste Land* emerges despite itself, as if from some hollow chamber of the mind, as the recurrence of nature's onerous design upon humankind. The poem is the return, in words, of the drama – or trauma – of its telling.

In *Four Quartets* beginning and recurrence are also mutually implied, though in a way that signifies more positively. In 'East Coker' I, Eliot writes:

> In my beginning is my end. In succession
> Houses rise and fall, crumble, are extended,
> Are removed, destroyed, restored, or in their place
> Is an open field, or a factory, or a by-pass.
> Old stone to new building, old timbers to new fires . . .
> Houses live and die: there is a time for building
> And a time for living and for generation.

What 'East Coker' describes in such lines is the life of significant *return*: return which is itself double-facing, being return of (the seasons, the rites and rituals, the past as tradition) and return to (the earth, origins, base materiality). Through such descriptions the way is opened for Eliot's poetry to *enact* itself as significant return, as in 'East Coker' III:

> You say I am repeating
> Something I have said before. I shall say it again.
> Shall I say it again?

In the moment of becoming, the poetry draws attention to itself as already there and complete – for writer as for reader. Nor need one read Eliot's lines as abstract or mystical, for they bear directly upon the activity in which one is – if, as long as one is mouthing the words, unwittingly – engaged. They bear upon the activity of reproducing that is reading the poem. The past is present in the present of utterance; but both the present and the past were there before the repetition of the poem began. Or as 'Burnt Norton' v more elegantly phrases it:

> Or say that the end precedes the beginning
> And the end and the beginning were always there
> Before the beginning and after the end.

The poem – be it *The Waste Land* or *Four Quartets* – not only dramatises the play of beginnings and endings, and the temporal possibilities these imply. The drama of the poem's utterance – or its very 'being' – is precisely and primordially founded upon the play of these possibilities.

In Kafka's work (as discussed in chapter 1) it is often the ambivalence of endings which seems important. Here, moving away from Eliot but holding still to examples from poetry, what it is important to recognise is the ambivalence of beginnings. In a discussion of W. B. Yeats's poem 'Leda and the Swan', critic Geoffrey Hartman suggests that

Fiction is strongest as paraprophetic discourse, as prophecy after the event – an event constituted or reconstituted by it, and haunted by the idea of traumatic causation.   (Hartman, 1980, pp. 40–1)

Following Hartman's suggestion, it may be agreed that Yeats's poem is traumatically 'engendered' in telling of an 'engendering' (which death already haunts). The suggestion can be extended to propose that narrative (in poetry or in prose) typically builds a testament to the ambivalence of its building. Death (an ending figurative or real) is the defining bracket of this building, this ambivalence. As Benjamin puts it, 'Death is the sanction of everything that the storyteller can tell. He has borrowed his authority from death' (Benjamin, 1973, p. 94).

To move on, but still in the context of reluctant or traumatic beginnings, one may be made to think of Dante, who finds himself 'Midway in the journey of our life . . . in a dark wood, for the straight way was lost', and who finds 'how hard it is to tell what that wood was' ['Nel mezzo del cammin di nostra vita . . . per una selva oscura, / che la diritta via era smarrita . . . quanto a dir qual era è cosa dura']. Dante's poem is obliged into being by the closure of the direct and easy way to the stars above. It may be the case that epic, starting as it is famed for doing *in medias res*, under the impulsion of casualty and catastrophe (though catastrophe is classically a goal or dénouement), offers the archetype of narrative beginning. Certainly Homer's *The Iliad* begins on a grim note. In Richmond Lattimore's translation the poem opens:

> Sing, goddess, the anger of Peleus' son Achilles
> and its devastation, which put pains thousandfold
> upon the Achaians.

Nor does *The Odyssey* offer any greater comfort, as it starts —

> Tell me, Muse, of the man of many ways, who was driven
> far journeys, after he had sacked Troy's sacred citadel.
> Many were they whose cities he saw, whose minds he
> learned of
> many the pains he suffered in his spirit on the wide sea,
> struggling for his own life and the homecoming of
> his companions . . .
> From some point
> here, goddess, daughter of Zeus, speak, and begin our story.

The Odyssey is perhaps the most celebrated tale of return. It forms up as 'paraprophetic': as the return of the muse to the moment of 'traumatic causation'.

Poets utter, writers write, and as a consequence readers read, as it were, backwards. As a line from 'Crisscross to Infinity', a recent text by Samuel Beckett, conjures it: 'The way back was on and on was always back.' The present tense of literary production is constantly a return to a worrying beginning which is itself inferred from the traces of death, completion and fulfilment. Ending seems to be written into narrative by the very ambivalence of the fact of telling, when telling is founded on the need to tell and the suppression of the infinite possibilities which any particular telling necessitates. As one reads, one lives through the ambivalence of the act. Many fictions and poems will disguise this fact (and it is no coincidence that those discussed here rather expose it, to the extent of making it the ground of their functioning). However strange it may sound, readers read backwards. Narrative inhabits the space of a repetition which (to borrow from my description of authority in Kafka's work) is *always already there*.

§ 4.3

The strangeness of this proposition about reading and 'backward-ness' will be explored in this section and the following through two works. The first is a novel by Gabriel Josipovici entitled *The Echo Chamber*, the second a film-script by Marguerite Duras entitled *Le Camion*. Both works have been chosen because they show the way in which narrative depends upon and further constitutes a repetition: in the first case the repetition of a past, in the second of some sort of a future.

   Before turning to Josipovici's novel, it may be worthwhile pausing for a moment to consider the term 'novel'. In my willingness to combine poetry and prose have I been obscuring what is truly new or novel about the novel? In a persuasive article entitled 'On Repetition' Edward Said argues in a way which would imply that I have. He writes that by its very 'novelty' the novel genre marks a break with history, conceived of as a '*repeating* [of] the very reproductive, and repetitive, course by which man engenders and re-engenders himself, or his offspring', and as dominated by 'the genealogical and procreative metaphor' (Said, 1976, pp. 144, 152). Said writes that:

> To be novel is to be an original, that is a figure not repeating what most men perforce repeat, namely the course of human life, father to son, father to son, generation after generation. Thus the novelistic character is, I think, conceived as a challenge to repetition, a rupture in the duty imposed on all men to breed and multiply, to create and recreate oneself unremittingly and repeatedly. (p. 144)

Said's words strike a chord which has become familiar here, through Kafka. Yet he suggests a degree of willed break with 'genealogy' that, in relation to Kafka at least, is quite inappropriate. For Kafka, as for Georg, the 'novel', the break with the reproductive generational cycle, is bitterly tragic and never fully accepted. The novel genre may dramatise the search for origins. But in so doing it exemplifies its status within the larger bracket of return. In his book *Fiction and Repetition* J. Hillis Miller helps make this clear. He shows that in so far as it seeks to discover true novelty, the novel is doomed to failure, since this search is contained by the priority of repetition. One comment he makes can serve to give a sense of the direction of his argument. He writes that: 'What I read repeats or seems to repeat something earlier, something deeper in. That something hidden is brought back out into the open in a disguised repetition by what I see' (p. 69).[3]

Moving now from the novel-form to a specific instance of it, the very title of Gabriel Josipovici's *The Echo Chamber* confirms that the reader is on familiar ground. The joke about re-reading may yet reveal its kernel of truth, for this, almost as much as Proust's, is a novel to be re-read. Reading seems indeed to imply re-reading. The novel is the echo of itself. The present is the past which is already present to another past. It is difficult to describe how this is so; but this is part of what the novel is about – difficulty, the difficulty of recovery.

A man in his late twenties, Peter, arrives at a country house owned and run by his aunt. He has come to convalesce after what appears to have been a severe mental collapse with consequent amnesia; 'appears' because the amnesia is such, and the solicitousness of the house's inhabitants is such, that only slowly does the reader learn what his 'illness' has been. He has come to rest and recover, as his one real companion, Yvonne, reminds him:

'You mustn't think', she said. 'You must forget it. You must rest and recover. Then you'll be able to think about it. When you're strong enough. And free of it.'
'But it's maddening. To remember nothing. Except afterwards.'   (p. 51)

Recovery (like that in psychoanalysis) is dually faced in time: recovery of elements of the past, without which mental recuperation on which the future depends is not viable. Yet the world around Peter is intent upon filling his mind with chatter, activity and noise – so much forgetfulness. This at least is the case with the adults. For the children in the novel, unconstrained by politeness as they are, other conditions hold. But the children's curiosity and straight questions, though refreshingly honest, run straight into the wall of Peter's amnesia. As the amicability of the house's inhabitants starts to wear thin, Peter's impression that he can 'feel life going forward again' dwindles (p. 54). The past is catching up.

As I have described the novel so far, the elements are common to many psychological dramas and thrillers. It is from this point that the novel does start to differ and disturb. The contrast with a more conventional tale of amnesia, with for example Alfred Hitchcock's *Spellbound*, is an instructive one. What one finds in this film, one of Hollywood's earliest brushes with psychoanalysis (1945), is a young man (played by Gregory Peck) taking up his role as 'Dr Edwardes', the new director of a psychiatric institution (a role in which he is evidently masquerading). The Peck figure, who is suffering from amnesia, comes to believe he has killed the real Edwardes. He escapes, with the help of Constance (Ingrid Bergman), who is in love with him. She takes him to her former analyst, who uncovers the fact that he was skiing with Edwardes when the doctor fell into an abyss. But it is only by replaying the traumatic incident that the Peck figure has his full memory returned, with the further recollection that Edwardes's death (in fact caused by the retiring – and jealous – director) reproduced elements of the childhood death of Peck's brother which had been repressed out of guilt.

The film contains generational replacement, father figures good and evil (as Raymond Durgnat has pointed out in *The Strange Case of Alfred Hitchcock*, pp. 193–4). And within this frame is dramatised one man's return and recovery, made possible by love. As Rohmer and Chabrol put it: 'It is the illustration of a theme that is dear to Hitchcock and which might be formulated as follows: "It is necessary to descend twice, to follow the path a second time"' (Rohmer and Chabrol, 1979, pp. 81–2). Many elements of the film are thus relevant to the present argument. Yet – and here the contrast with Josipovici's novel starts to show – despite *Spellbound*'s being about time and return, at no point does it question the essential linearity of time. The relation of past to present, and their separateness, are never seriously in doubt.

With *The Echo Chamber* one is on altogether more uncertain ground, on which (to borrow another of Hitchcock's titles) 'vertigo' threatens, and threatens not just Peter (who complains of finding himself at a clifftop, of falling from a height) but the reader as well. For the narrative itself seems to move into a space which it has already occupied before it began, and it draws the reader with it. It describes a past which is already a present before it started its description. The moments which begin to filter into Peter's consciousness – a house, a bike in sunlight, people talking pleasantly, the future 'open in front of me . . . weary but satisfied, gradually recovering' (p. 143) – seem to describe less a past than the immediate present. He is living, as *déjà-vu* or imperfect recollection, a reality which is a past in a terrifying state of becoming. He starts to tell a story of himself which is already once completed. He knows that the moment of understanding is one with the moment of falling and amnesia. He is living a repetition not (only) of a past, but of a present which is a past as well.

We make sense of time, deploy memory to produce meaning, through our capacity for forgetfulness, as Funes teaches (and as psychoanalysis confirms, with its notion of repression and screen memories). This is a capacity which Peter cannot harness to himself and his story. As happens to Funes when he lives his total 'memories', past and present cease to be meaningful as *The Echo Chamber* becomes (in a way that gives the reader no superior perspective) the echo of itself, and as it moves into the space it has already inhabited and abandoned, once if not more often. Gradually, in a way that induces increasing panic, Peter's consciousness meshes with his memory and so with the world around him. He finds himself on the cliff of his crisis, and at last he 'sees'. But of course all his vision amounts to is what is there: '"Don't you see?" he said. "The house. The people. Laughing and talking"' (p. 151). He watches in despair as a little boy plunges, as he knows he will, to his death in the quarry below. The point of recovery becomes the point of collapse. Yet the reader knows now that this collapse is not the end, but is only the point of a new (re-) beginning:

The body plunged silently down the side of the cliff and Peter looked into the unblinking eyes and understood at last why he had come where he was and why it was not concern for the falling boy but for something else, something else, that caused him to sense the black cloud coming to envelop him and to welcome it and to know in the same instant that it too, alas, was not final either. (p. 152)

Peter's collapse is the terrible vindication of his first moment of consciousness in the hospital bed when he thinks that 'nothing had happened' – only the coincidence of reality with itself – 'And at the same time . . . as if something absolutely terrible had happened' (p. 114). What is terrible for Peter in this coincidence is the ambivalence of repetition, when the repetition is one which is the very condition of his being, as a creature in the process of becoming. What is terrible for the reader is that the repetition is one which is at the heart not only of this particular story but of storytelling itself. Borrowing Peter's words to describe movement through *The Echo Chamber* – and through narrative in general – I may now say: '"I want to know . . . It's as if my neck's twisted round the wrong way. I keep looking back"' (p. 114).

§ 4.4

The narrative of *The Echo Chamber* reveals several things about narrative in general. It reveals how the present may already be a repetition, and one which is ambivalent in its charge – as ambivalent as the pair of terms recovery and collapse. It reveals how this repetition is one which connects present to past; and it hints that the future is implicated in this entanglement of tenses and time-scales, that repetition is not only of a past but of some hypothetical future as well. The 'neck' of narrative may be 'twisted' backwards; but it may be 'twisted' forwards as well. One contemporary writer, Marguerite Duras, has revealed this, and in a way that is breathtaking in its simplicity. It is a way that Proust, with his appreciation of the use of tenses, would have enjoyed.[4] In most of her work since *Le Camion*, Duras has made maximum use of the conditional, perfect conditional and future perfect (or anterior) tenses.

It is in *Le Camion*, where the fact of telling is to the fore, that the implications of these tenses are most clearly perceptible. For *Le Camion* is a film which is less acted than *told*, by actor Gérard Depardieu and Marguerite Duras, as they sit round a table reading the script of a film which 'would have been'. As they say:

G. D.: It's a film?
M. D.: It would have been a film.
    It's a film, yes.

(p. 55)

The potential which is intimated in this choice of tense did in fact correspond to a real one, as Duras explains in a conversation with

Michelle Porte which is annexed to the film-script. For Duras had been going to shoot a film about a lorry and a woman hitch-hiker; but this project left her dissatisfied. She explains that she was saved by the fact that the two actresses she had envisaged in the leading role were unable to make themselves available. At this point she decided – and with her decision came a real commitment – to shoot a film of the reading of a script about a film which would (or could) have been. The film is, then, of Duras telling Depardieu about the woman who would have been hitch-hiking.

The woman is picked up by a lorry. Woman and driver stare out of the windscreen at the bleak winter landscape and at the sea. A relationship of sorts develops between them, though it will never come to anything. Interspersed with the assembling of comments on what the woman would have done are comments on what the film would have been like: cheaply produced and shot in monochrome. Interspersed with the comments are shots of landscape with a lorry travelling across it. The woman hitch-hiker would have spoken of many things: of geography, of death, the sea, the moon. Depardieu interrupts to ask Duras how it all finishes, and she replies: 'It is perhaps finished' (p. 23). He asks what else the woman says, and Duras replies:

> She says: everything is in everything.
> Everywhere.
> All the time.
> At the same time.   (pp. 25–6)

Past, present and future conflate (all time, at the same time) as the woman carries on travelling, speaking of class, the proletariat, love, and her reason for being there . . . Till, in the middle of nowhere, she asks to be dropped off, and the film ends. It ends on words which show her action to be an infinitely renewable repetition and at the same time to be executed for the very first time:

> Someone would have said: she's that sort of woman: every evening she stops cars,
> lorries, and then she recounts her life for the first time.   (p. 65)

Le Camion makes one feel the desperate poignancy of a woman's need to confer meaning upon the awful barrenness of her existence, and to do so by telling her story. Her story is the potential, or conditional, into which she must become, into which she must repeat herself.[5] Her very life seems to hang by the thread of a possible coincidence of her story as she is telling it with her story as she is living it. It hangs by the coincidence of her story as it is told in the conditional tense, with her story as it is being told by Duras in the present of her telling. It hangs by the thread of the 'if' which is the presumptive heart of the conditional. *Le Camion* reveals the agony and the liberating potential of that 'if', by revealing its scope and its impertinence. For this *is* the film (not the sketch of a film which might have been) – no ifs or buts. While viewing it (or reading it) one inhabits the present as the repetition of a conditional future which might have already been, and which may become again.

Within the first few minutes of the film Duras in fact says, 'No rehearsal of the text would have been envisaged' ['Aucune répétition du texte n'aurait été envisagée'] (p. 15).[6] In conversation with Michelle Porte she says that her fear was that if Depardieu had had a chance to read the script before filming (which in fact he did not), he would have been tempted to 'play' ['jouer']. *Le Camion*, spoken as Duras has it 'for the first time', delves into the space between the 'repetition' (or rehearsal) it has not been and the 'repetition' it is; between the 'play' it is determined not to be and the 'play' which, as I shall show, it intends to be. If Duras's fictions often feel as if they are haunted by an invisible ghost, what *Le Camion* makes clear, with its startling mode of direction, is that this ghost is difficult to locate because it is so familiar. The ghost (or *revenant*) hides itself whenever a narrative is told. For narrative is becoming at the same time as it is achieved or 'finished'. Duras's fictions live, and compel their readers to live, the pain of the twisted neck.

Yet ghosts and pain are of course not the sole reality in Duras's fictional world. It is rather ambivalence which is central and unavoidable, as can be seen in the idea of play in *Le Camion*.[7] For play may be forbidden, in the way I have pointed out. But it is not forbidden alone. Duras's epigraph to *Le Camion*, taken from Grevisse's entry in the grammar *Le Bon Usage*, suggests that the conditional is in fact intended to *open* the space of play. The tense is indeed a paradoxical one, containing within itself the possibility of a 'future anterior'. As Duras explains to Michelle Porte:

In the Grevisse grammar it is said that the future anterior is the conditional which precedes a game [conditionnel préludique] and which is used by children in their proposal to play. Children say: you would have been a pirate, you're a pirate; you would have been a lorry, they become a lorry. And the future anterior is the sole tense that translates the play of children: total. Their cinema. (p. 89)

What is true here for children may also be true for the woman hitch-hiker in *Le Camion*, for the speakers who are describing her, and for the listeners who are listening to the description. For as I indicated above (§ 3.6), the ground of children's play can also be the ground of more adult explorations.

Psychoanalysis confirms this (psychoanalysis which has been waiting in the wings of my discussion of recoveries and conditional futures). In the case of Serge Leclaire (in chapter 2), psychoanalysis attempts to return the world and the body as desiring. It seeks to do this through creation of a space in which patients can voice their own story for the first time: speak their becoming, and become in the space of their speaking. The order of the Symbolic, realm of desire, is founded upon the conditions of language. One enters it (and continually re-enters it) in accepting the primary substitution of the world by words which effect and efface their own conditionality. The psychoanalytic patient does not learn that the Symbolic is adequate or identical to the world. (It is the Imaginary which is more the realm of identities and adequacy.) The Symbolic, towards which the patient is pushing, confronts with the difference and even arbitrariness of language. In that very non-identity of language and its referents, in language's non-present presence, a freedom and *a future* are, conditionally, to be found.

Nor is Serge Leclaire's perspective upon psychoanalysis alone in being of relevance here. It was in discussing aspects of the work of D. W. Winnicott that I developed an understanding of the relation between play and art. His 'potential space' is coloured by ambivalence and paradox, which can be understood in terms of the individual's need to commute between being and becoming – the need to accept loss in order to gain, to move into the 'not-me' in order to be 'me'.[8] This ambivalence can now be further understood in terms of the way in which play (or literature, here) opens a present which is the repetition of a 'potential' future which already exists when the player starts to play (or the reader to read, the writer to write). Duras's work impresses that the conditional space of play may be haunted by the ghost of finality or 'futurity'. Thinking of Benjamin and what he says of death as authority, one could say it is haunted by fatality. Yet in this 'futurity' or fatality is contained the chance of playful becoming. Perhaps it is something of this that Blanchot is suggesting when he writes that 'It is as though being only existed through loss of being, or through lack of being' (Blanchot, 1982, p. 105). Certainly it is recognition of a need generated by such lack that prompts him to describe the writer as being committed to 'the nascent intimacy with the reader who is still infinitely future' (Blanchot, 1955, p. 267).

Writing inhabits the potential space which is offered, or promised, to and by reader and writer alike. In a discussion of Winnicott's *Playing and Reality*, psychoanalyst J. B. Pontalis suggests this, when he writes that 'The potential space evoked in *Playing and Reality* – and which is already present in the reading – makes us aware of a reality which we usually perceive *out of lack*. We develop a bond with the author, a renewed (and kept) promise of an encounter' (Pontalis, 1981, p. 154).[9] In the case of Duras's writing in *Le Camion*, the force of this 'encounter' is such that writer, talker, hitch-hiker and reader are all compelled into a potential space so narrow that we seem at times to share an existence and the 'conditions' of this existence. As we watch or read *Le Camion* and listen to the woman who is telling her story again and again for the first time, we are made to feel the fine line which is dividing us from her. We watch the screen. We exist in the potential space of a present which is the repetition of a conditional future, and of a past which has never happened. She watches the road. She tries to repeat herself into a being which has never existed, but perhaps nonetheless *will have existed*. The line dividing us from her is narrow. This is the line which the film (or text) itself constitutes. It is in and through the 'playing' of the work that the potential which is play (or art) and the potential which is the 'I' who am playing with and through it are divided: that (to borrow from J. B. Pontalis's argument cited above a dense, if un-translatable pun) 'jeu' is separated from 'je'.

§ 4.5

The very term 'I' may, then, be a sort of conditional – a repetition (or promise) of a future encounter between myself and myself. With this troubling thought I can appropriately return to Proust, for whose novel the 'I' is so crucial. To claim, as the joke runs, that

'I'm re-reading Proust' is therefore not necessarily to deny the fear and difficulties his work provokes; not when my own 'I' is only a potential (like that of Proust's narrator). A venture is no less a venture for being a repetition which has its end implied in its beginning. Proust himself is always re-writing: not just literally, but in a way that allows his narrative continually to re-cover terrain which it has already staked out. Proust's 'amazing patience' perhaps derives partly from the way narrative gives some purchase on past and future. In an illuminating essay entitled 'Freud's Masterplot', Peter Brooks makes a suggestion which would imply that the claim I have made – that Proust is only ever re-writing – would hold true for any writer. Brooks writes:

> Narrative always makes the implicit claim to be in a state of repetition, as a going over again of a ground already covered: a *sjuzet* repeating the *fabula*, as the detective retraces the tracks of the criminal. This claim to be an act of repetition – 'I sing', 'I tell' – appears to be initiatory of narrative. (Brooks, 1977, p. 285)

The poets that have been addressed, and the works by Josipovici and Duras, persuade the general truth of this (with the proviso that narrative also seems to be going over ground of a future which 'will have already been' covered). This can perhaps be called the primary repetition of and in narrative. Such a general account of repetition is a starting point. It leaves it to be seen how Proust's writing allows him to maximise his 'patience', or fully inhabit the space of this repetition.

When one tries to develop a sense of repetition more specific to Proust's novel – what may be called secondary repetition – one immediately faces a challenge. For against a sense that it is in the use made of the 'I' of the narrator that Proustian repetition takes hold, the novel asserts strongly that it is 'involuntary memory' that is the fundamental (and specifically Proustian) mode of recovery and repetition. This challenge cannot be dodged; and therefore only in § 4.6 shall I consider the way in which the Proustian 'I' juggles with temporality and repetition. First, in this section, I shall inspect the workings – and repudiate some of the force – of involuntary memory. This course is doubly necessary since not only does the novel assert involuntary memory most forcefully, but to this has been added critical consensus. What book on Proust does not contain statements about the vital significance of involuntary memory? (As Serge Doubrovsky says in his book on

Proust, aptly entitled *La Place de la madeleine*, 'With Proust one is overwhelmed before one starts by the weight of commentaries' (p. 21).)

One may recall how the novel is proffered. After the famous opening line about sleep the reader is enticed into several pages of reveries, with sleep hovering as their subject and their negation. Out of the various recollected half-wakenings form memories over which one takes precedence: that of the mother's nocturnal kiss at Combray (a scene which has about it, as I shall show in chapter 6, the elements of an originating 'traumatic causation'). The memory runs on till the night it illuminates becomes the model for all nights to come. This 'luminous panel, sharply defined against a vague and shadowy background' is a mere fragment, yet it is all that can be grasped by 'voluntary memory, the memory of the intellect' (1, 46, 47; 1, 43, 44). Marcel is led to reflect gloomily on the incompleteness of his memory of Combray: 'And so it is with our own past. It is a labour in vain to attempt to recapture it: all the efforts of our intellect must prove futile' (1, 47; 1, 44). The past is dead, so long as he relies on rationality to resuscitate it. 'Permanently dead? Very possibly' (1, 47; 1, 44). It is a possibility no sooner evoked than refuted. The past may in fact be reopened, as everyone knows (including those who have not read a page of Proust), through a cup of tea with a 'petite madeleine' soaked in it. Out of Marcel's teacup come flowers, houses, villagers, and Charles Swann: in short, 'the whole of Combray and its surroundings' (1, 51; 1, 48).

Upon this, section II of *Du côté de chez Swann* (*Swann's Way*) opens, with the word 'Combray'. The inference is there to be drawn (and critics have drawn it), that Combray, the novel therefore, is enabled and even engendered by the incident with the madeleine. The configuration of sterile-voluntary and fertile–involuntary memory seems quite as central to *A la recherche* as it is to *Jean Santeuil*. A deeper reality is intimated before the spires at Martinville and before the trees at Hudimesnil. Marcel apprehends fully his grandmother's death on his second trip to Balbec. The music of Vinteuil and the painting of Elstir induce a special bliss. The moments may be few and far between; but when one reaches *Le Temps retrouvé* (*Time Regained*) one finds that the scarcity is just the point. All the loving, losing, suffering, planning, despairing and learning that Marcel has been doing have been a waste, so much 'lost time' ['temps perdu'], until redeemed and 'regained' ['retrouvé'] by involuntary memory.

For to end yet again

On his way to the Guermantes' *matinée* Marcel steps on an uneven cobblestone which returns him to the Piazza San Marco. Inside the Guermantes' library he uses a towel whose texture returns him to the Grand Hotel at Balbec, and the noise of a spoon on a plate brings back his train trip from the sanatorium to Paris. Only, the despair he had felt on the train while looking at the trees – despair at being able, in Coleridge's words (from 'Dejection: An Ode'), to 'see, not feel, how beautiful they are!' – is converted to joy as the moment returns. Such moments, Marcel insists, are the source of the one true bliss and the only real recovery:

> But let a noise or a scent, once heard or once smelt, be heard or smelt again in the present and at the same time in the past, real without being actual, ideal without being abstract, and immediately the permanent and habitually concealed essence of things is liberated and our true self which seemed – had perhaps for long years seemed – to be dead but was not altogether dead, is awakened and reanimated as it receives the celestial nourishment that is brought to it. A minute freed from the order of time has re-created in us, to feel it, the man freed from the order of time.
>
> (III, 906; III, 872–3)

Involuntary memory offers a relation with time in which, it is claimed, there is freedom from time. *A la recherche* insistently promotes a mode of recovery which claims to connect beginning to end, to make new sense of middle, and to lead to the conviction that art is also party to this realm of essential moments – that it is therefore an artist Marcel must become.

If this is the most important conclusion reached in *Le Temps retrouvé* (and one to which I shall attend in the following section), it is, however, only one of many. For this book is full of verdicts, all of which are based on certain more or less convincing privilegings. In a discussion of *Le Temps retrouvé* Malcolm Bowie indicates some of them: 'intuition better than rational argument, synthesis better than analysis ... metaphors are superior to abstractions, art to science, being outside time to being inside it' (Bowie, 1987, p. 46). What Bowie also shows is that all these preferences hang upon one larger one: Marcel's privileging of part over whole. It is no coincidence, Bowie claims, that critics have tended to ignore the bulk of the novel (all those difficult, unpleasant bits, especially *La Prisonnière!* (*The Captive*)) and concentrate on *Le Temps retrouvé*. For this book is indeed seductive. Not only is it much more easily (and quickly) read than the other books, it is also pre-eminently quotable. In this book, which offers intense intellectual gratification, it seems one is on firm ground at last. *Le Temps retrouvé* proposes a Marcel who is able to *know*. Knowledge is of a new, sensuous kind, and it will have to be enacted (as will the writing of the projected novel) in profane time, but it is powerfully stabilising all the same.

How does this square with what has been seen of the ambivalent, vacillating nature of repetition? This is where the lines of force established by Josipovici and Duras can help. Peter in *The Echo Chamber* and the hitch-hiker in *Le Camion* both fail to discover the meaning of their repetition (or fail to contain their discoveries). The moment of narrative's return upon itself is lived by Peter as unknowing, a vertigo of illusion and loss. It is lived by the hitch-hiker as a desperate need which has to be endlessly re-enacted. By comparison, Marcel's knowledge is thoroughly neutral and neutralising. One may be inclined to ask: has Marcel tried to put a stop to repetition and paradox? Is the insistence with which his claim is asserted not in direct but perhaps inverse relation to its tenability? Though these are awkward questions, in that they run counter to many of the novel's conclusions, one does not have to distance oneself from Marcel and the novel to articulate them. Quite the opposite: for if he 'knows', then who says so? The answer comes back: Marcel, 'I'. A second question ensues: can one take such a person at his word (particularly when lying is so central a concern of the novel)? Malcolm Bowie has a way of suggesting an answer when he writes:

What is often overlooked is that all the narrator's theoretical pronouncements – including the celebrated 'une œuvre où il y a des théories est comme un objet sur lequel on laisse la marque du prix' – are caught up in the fictional texture, infused with desire from the remainder of the book as any other of its parts.

(Bowie, 1987, pp. 47–8)

Thinking back to what was said above about how the 'I' offers the promise of an encounter between self and self, past and future, it can now be added that the Proustian 'I' is itself 'infused with desire'. To the desire of this 'I' its own conclusions and knowledge do not necessarily correspond. One need hardly impute lying for Marcel's claims to elicit caution. As teller and told live under the one hat, does this mean the recovery which is offered is the reader's as well? If in one sense the answer must be 'yes' (for one reads only through the 'I') in another the answer is a resounding 'no'.

As one sits with Marcel in the Guermantes' library, one is not returned to Balbec through towels or sounds one has not felt or heard, nor to Venice through a flagstone of which one was ignorant. Still less do these former realities return in their sensual palpability. Involuntary memory may return the past to Marcel as he says it does. But this is of little note, since it does so much less for the reader. The claims made about it rather lodge as an attempt to put an end to the force of repetition and to ground it once and for all. They are an attempt to take what was and what would have been and solder them into a single appropriable present and a unified, present, stable – not potential – 'I'. *A la recherche* appears to offer a key to its own recovery (which includes recovery of the time lost in reading it). However, the very project of Marcel's 'recherche' (as much as the Homeric urge to the muse at the beginning of *The Odyssey*, or Peter's return to his aunt's house, or the hitch-hiker's renewed journeying) implies a degree of volition that runs counter to the thrust of involuntary memory. Repetition shares etymological roots with research (the Latin *re-petere*). As Leo Bersani shows in his book on Proust, the transforming of the experience of the past into the present of the work is a labour, a consciously undertaken task.[10] Marcel's claims about involuntary memory do indeed reveal desire rather than transmit achievement.

It is not my intention, however, to discredit involuntary memory or discredit the first and last books of Proust's novel. This would be a further substitution, of new parts, for the whole. Rather it is to see the proffered configuration of beginning and end as limited and limiting: as a return neither to nor of a common past; a way of trying to suppress the anxiety provoked by the potential of the future rather than a maximising of this potential. The mode of repetition through which, rather than live vertigo, the reader becomes a witness to knowledge is not primary or even secondary, but is contained (rendered tertiary perhaps) by the fact of narrative as repetition and by the 'I' which tells this narrative.[11] Yet if involuntary memory is not the *mode*, it may still be the *model* of repetition in the novel. It is a model which can help to show how the larger and more latent doubling that is contained in the 'I' draws the reader into its dizzying influence.

§ 4.6

Towards the end of § 4.1 I hinted that the feeling the reader may have in front of *A la recherche* – that all the work and risk of failure are his or hers – is not an entirely justifiable one, in that the novel is a chronicle of non-achievement. *A la recherche* does accommodate diffidence, doubt and inadequacy, and it does so partly by being about failure, waste and loss. My characterisation of the novel as an area of intense threat or difficulty (which the reader enters as arduously as a mountain climber) requires some modification. For entering the novel is also as easy as starting to read: 'For a long time I used to go to bed early' ['Longtemps, je me suis couché de bonne heure'] (1, 3; 1, 3). Ambivalence pervades the novel from the start – the writing and reading of it. If this ambivalence inheres in all narrative telling, it also emerges powerfully from the twisted temporality which is contained in the repetition implied by the joke about 're-reading' and 're-writing' – a joke, I suggested (§ 4.5), that is in turn connected with the division within the Proustian 'I'. In the play of attention across this division, ambivalence and specifically Proustian repetition take hold.

Marcel, the 'I' of *A la recherche*, leads a life in which his central, literary ambition is unfulfilled (as far as one knows). Yet at the same time he is a magnificent achiever. The novel is about all manner of things negative. Yet if this is what it is *about*, what it is *doing* is supremely positive. The reader is continually directed towards a site of failure; but where the reader is directed from is the site of success.[12] Both sites are contained by the single name 'I'. The teller (the 'I' which writes) and the told (the 'I' which fails to write) are one; and yet not one, following the play of readerly attention. We move through Proust's novel in a becoming, towards a being which already exists in the moment of reading. We are directed continually towards a possible beginning. We exist in the potential space of a conditional, in the gap which is opened between what would be and what is; when what is is what would be. We move forwards as readers through *A la recherche*, with our heads twisted backwards; but also backwards, our heads twisted forwards. Proust tells the story of one who cannot find a story to tell. His story is of one who finally finds that the story to tell is the life of the one who could not find (the story which has just been told).

Nowhere is this form of doubling more prominent or more crucial that in *Le Temps retrouvé*, where the bliss of involuntary memory provokes the need for artistic creation. Out of the experience in the Guermantes' library grows Marcel's dedication to a literature that will transmute the base metals of his life into the gold of art. The novel in this way becomes the chronicle of the 'birth' and the 'exercise' of a 'vocation', as Gérard Genette puts it (Genette, 1982, p. 222). At the moment Marcel finds his vocation, the novel becomes a tale of 'apprenticeship'. It is confirmed as the history of its own becoming, 'advent' of its 'event'.[13] Marcel quits his novel with the determination to write a novel which will incorporate time. Is this or is it not the novel the reader has just completed? The correct answer is, not surprisingly, a somewhat ambivalent one. For the novel the reader is holding both is and is not the one Marcel hopes to write. To read Proust is to re-read; but to re-read with a difference. The future encounter Marcel promises (between a reader and his book, between the 'I' he will write through and the 'I' he will write about) both is and is not actualised in the 'I' with which he has written. Repetition conjures with identities and presences. But in the end, as the novel's conclusion confirms, repetition is less a matter of reduplication than of the return of the same-in-the-different and the different-in-the-same.

If such a formulation remains rather abstract, the suggestion made above (§ 4.5) about how involuntary memory offers a model for the more latent repetition contained in the 'I' can now be exploited, to render the formulation more concrete. Inspecting his life, and how it seems to map that of others, Marcel notes the difference which inhabits repetition:

> For nothing ever repeats itself exactly, and the most analogous lives which, thanks to kinship of character and similarity of circumstances, we may select in order to represent them as symmetrical, remain in many respects contrasting.
>
> (III, 509; III, 499)

His insight carries over into involuntary memory. What Marcel makes clear as the successive returns overcome him in the Guermantes' library is that no two moments are alike. The noise or sensation or taste is 'identical', 'exactly [a]like' (III, 900, 907; III, 868, 874). But the sensation or moment from the past, by being freed of its affective fetters, is subtly but crucially transformed — into so much difference.[14] A brief contrast with Borges's Funes the Memorious makes this clear. For Funes, memory truly is a case of identities: the day returned takes a day. Funes impresses that memory's capacity to make sense of time comes from its forgetfulness. Marcel's involuntary memory is nothing if not forgetful.[15] Involuntary memory is an 'optical illusion' which unites 'a moment of the past that was incompatible with the present' (III, 906; III, 873). It follows the rules that Marcel attributes to the phenomenon of rhyming in poetry, in that its beauty derives from 'something that is at once similar to and different from the preceding rhyme, which is prompted by it, but introduces the variety of a new idea' (II, 47–8; II, 51).[16]

At times Marcel associates the idea of difference with voluntary memory and the succession of selves (and deaths) that he and his acquaintances have undergone. Nevertheless, the continuity which he imagines art will return to him is based not on eradication of difference so much as on its exploitation. Through art he will be one *and yet several*. Marcel's vocation returns in the way of involuntary memory. The novel Marcel will write is and is not the one the reader reads.[17] The 'I' which writes is both one and two. It is both the 'I' which has written and the 'I' which will write. It is the 'I' which will have written, when the 'if' on which that 'will have' depends is as ambivalent as is the repetition which the experience of writing or reading the novel involves.

In the Guermantes' library and in Marcel's discovery of his vocation the reader rediscovers the ambivalence which has pulsed from the beginning of the novel (and the famous first sentence), and even before that, from the time the novel's size is apprehended as both inviting (with the possibility of a world in which one may voluptuously lose oneself) and frightening (one might truly get lost). In the library Marcel not only discovers his vocation, but something of its direction as well. He discovers that the timelessness to which he is partisan and which he wishes art to open to his reader is only to be made available in profane time. The awfulness of old age, decrepitude and death which strikes Marcel with such a vengeance through the parade of ancients at the Guermantes' *matinée* cannot be ignored or forgotten. Marcel concludes that it is duration and continuity – the stuff of profane time – which will be at the heart of his new venturing. He thus draws a conclusion which matches the reader's own experience of the novel, and matches Walter Benjamin's judgements, cited above (§ 4.0), about how narrative gains its meaning from the profanity of time – from the fact that it reeks of finality and death. It is no surprise that Marcel takes his leave upon a resolution to work 'in the dimension of Time' ['dans le Temps'] (III, 1107; III, 1048).

Such a conclusion is very different to the verdicts reached in *Jean Santeuil*. For *Jean Santeuil* tries to map the magical moment of illuminated memory and timelessness. In it profane time inheres as so much seepage in what is intended to be timeless (but ends up seeming interminable). By contrast, *A la recherche* seems to incorporate the years Proust laboured on it, and the months or years one spends reading it. It is a monument to duration and continuity, 'This notion of Time embodied, of years past but not separated from us' (III, 1104; III, 1046). Yet if it is this, is it this alone? The novel matches its narrator's conclusions, but is this all it does?

I suggested that Marcel's claims are only claims. This holds true for Marcel's claim that his work is going to be created out of profane time. One cannot be sure if his claim, which runs off the final page, is ever converted into practice: if the 'I' which is written will obey the edicts of the 'I' which writes. And so, against the pressure of much of my own argument about the importance of conscious memory and research, I wish now to assert that Proust's novel (not Marcel's this time) *can* allow an experience of 'timelessness'. It can allow a precarious freedom from time as it is commonly known, and from the division and death which give this time meaning. This is the timelessness or temporality which is that of narrative itself. It is present, but in a present that is a repetition that includes the past and the future as well – as Marguerite Duras has it, 'all the time, at the same time'. According to Maurice Blanchot, this is a 'primary time' ['temps original'] that 'only exists in the story . . . the coincidence at a single mysterious point of present, past and – though Proust seems unaware of it, future as well.' (Blanchot, 1982, p. 70).

If such a possibility exists, of transcending time in time, and going through ambivalence beyond ambivalence, it does so *despite* claims either that it does or does not. It is not a possibility to which Proust can lay claim, and it emerges out of the *failure* of his narrator's enterprise with involuntary memory and timelessness.[18] Nor is it a possibility or moment that I can hope to possess or contain either, since it exists in the space of narration, the moment of reading – in the play and trans-individual interplay of that difference which distinguishes reader from writer when their words are the same. It is a possibility or moment which cannot be tied down to a word or name, but which one ventures towards through the repetition that reading demands. The temptation of course exists to give greater precision to such a nameless and unstable conclusion as this. But rather than yield to this temptation, I wish to end this chapter by deferring to the very precise and confusing words of a poet who has written about precision. The poem I shall quote in full is by Wallace Stevens, and is entitled 'Adult Epigram'. It runs, relevantly and bafflingly:

> The romance of the precise is not the elision
> Of the tired romance of imprecision.
> It is the ever-never-changing same,
> An appearance of Again, the diva-dame.

5 · Once is not enough

IF *A la recherche* is rich in claims made by its narrator, it is of course rich in other matter as well – is teeming with incident and passion. So far, I have tried to explore the way narrative broadly operates a primordial repetition, and to understand how Proust's novel redoubles this repetition. Now it is time to look at some of the more local, but scarcely less intense instances of ambivalence and repetition which populate the book.[1] There is any number of more or less obsessive or willed repetitions in *A la recherche*. Is such repetition the sign of a stagnation or a mark of change? Is it a negative or a positive force in Marcel's life? In what way does it spread, within the individual and across society?

These questions about repetition, taken more generally, have a relevance in the present context which is not limited to Proust. They also offer (from § 5.3) a way into discussion of works by Samuel Beckett – works which are quite as dependent on repetition as is *A la recherche*. If repetition leads forwards, discussion of it will also allow an earlier exploration (in chapter 1) of movement in and through fiction to be developed through the important insights into movement that Beckett offers. Of course, there is no single Beckett work that has the status within his œuvre that *A la recherche* has within that of Proust, discussion of which would illuminate to the same extent the life and the work. But I believe there is a way in which attention to certain of the local instances of repetition in Beckett's various works yields a sense of how these works seem to repeat each other and so form an enlarged repetition (which is at the same time a transformation and an innovation).

Starting with Proust, however, and thinking of specific moments in the novel, one it is hard to forget is that in which, while out walking with his grandfather and father, Marcel catches sight of a young red-haired girl, with black darting eyes. Though all he will retain of her is this image, the vulgar gesture she makes, and her name 'Gilberte', the memory of these will sear his life, and sear the novel too. The moment serves as an initiation into adulthood and into the troubled heartland of love. Gilberte's name rings out from 'Combray', across the pages of *Un amour de Swann* (*Swann in Love*), to sound with quite the same intensity when Marcel encounters it again in *Nom de pays: le nom* (*Place-names: The Name*). Marcel is on the Champs Elysées with Françoise when he hears her name. The effect it produces is prodigious:

The name Gilberte passed close by me, evoking all the more forcefully the girl whom it labelled in that it did not merely refer to her, as one speaks of someone in his absence, but was directly addressed to her. (1, 428; 1, 394)

Marcel is already in love with Gilberte and her name, and this love which has long been nourished in private will develop and expand through the pages of *Nom de pays: le nom* and *Autour de Mme Swann* (*Madame Swann at Home*), till it reaches its limit. Then it will slowly, painfully cease, to the point where, some months and some two hundred pages later, he can declare:

we are always detached from our fellow-creatures: when we love, we sense that our love does not bear a name, that it may spring up again in the future, could have sprung up already in the past, for another person rather than this one. (1, 658; 1, 611)

The two incompatible statements about Gilberte and her name both describe a reality of Marcel's heart; but a reality lived in time (and the second is none the truer for being a more measured reflection). It is hardly surprising that between the two is lived an intense and intensely conflictual love.

It is not possible to read *A la recherche* without becoming involved in conflict. It rears its head wherever intense feeling shows itself. While every reader will find his or her own nexus in the novel which corresponds to one within, no reader can avoid the most insistent configurations, which form up around the notion and reality of love. For as the narrator of *Jean Santeuil* has it, in a statement which echoes through *A la recherche*, 'Love teaches us much, but it also much corrupts us. It both assimilates and estranges us' (p. 735; p. 874). To this love, therefore – or rather to these various loves – let me now turn, though this means confronting repetition in its most rebarbative and destructive aspects.

§ 5.1

Marcel's love for Gilberte, which paves the way into adulthood, can be thought of as played out in three acts. From the moment he rediscovers Gilberte in Paris, Marcel's life revolves around his visits to the Champs Elysées, where he continually hopes to be in 'her side' for a *partie de barres*. The agony of not knowing whether she will come to play is moderated a little by the delight he feels when she gives him an agate marble and allows him to call her by her first name. Despite the gifts and concessions, however, Marcel realises that in the dialogue of love he alone is talking. The first act of Marcel's love – if act it can be called in which so little happens outside his fantasies and longings – closes with his malingering through the Christmas holidays in the desperate hope of her sending him some message.

The second act, beginning again with Gilberte's arrival on the Champs Elysées, is carried through by Marcel's multilateral invasion of her life. From being infatuated, Marcel goes on to be fatuous, when he mimics Charles Swann's ways and manners in his attempt to get close to Gilberte (Swann's daughter). It remains for him to become Mme Swann's faithful follower, a regular attendant at her *goûters*. Marcel's love develops, with the hiccup of an ejaculation experienced surreptitiously in a wrestle with Gilberte and the start of a letter from Gilberte when he is ill, into a thoroughly domestic affair, and it does so under the approving gaze of Charles and Odette Swann. The bitter pill of his longing is thus sugared. Gilberte is mastered, the unknown is colonised, strangeness is saddled by the quotidian. A period of neutrality is experienced – if it can be called happiness, it is certainly not the bliss Marcel had anticipated – before the third act begins. The period is brief, and is hardly established before the forces of destruction take over.

These come not from where Marcel had anticipated, not from outside, but from Marcel's own heart, which seems to reject the possibility of happiness. As Marcel confronts his solitude and the fact of separation (which are the reality of the third act) he concludes that love and happiness are indeed incompatible. Love is not a mere seeking for possession of its object. It is a volatile force which is always ready to yield to ambivalence. There are few more poignant accounts of love's instability than that which Marcel gives at this point, on the threshold of adulthood:

What makes us so happy is the presence in our hearts of an unstable element which we contrive perpetually to maintain and of which we cease almost to be aware so long as it is not displaced. In reality, there is in love a permanent strain of suffering which happiness neutralises, makes potential only, postpones, but which may at any moment become, what it would long since have been had we not obtained what we wanted, sheer agony. (I, 626; I, 582)

Stability neutralises not only unhappiness, but desire too, upon which the dream of happiness is founded. Satisfaction undoes satisfaction.

If this is, more or less, what the acts of the drama of Marcel's love for Gilberte Swann consist of, how is their sequence to be understood? Thinking of M. de Norpois, Marcel's mother is naively amazed that he should be so punctual though so busy, so friendly though so famous. Marcel notes, more perspicaciously, that '"although", with such people, is invariably an unrecognised "because"' (I, 472; I, 438). The insight holds perfectly for his love, which is intense though unrealisable, then vapid though realised, and intense again (in the epilogue to the third act) though renounced. As he concludes while waiting for the letter from Gilberte which might patch up their separation, but which Gilberte will never send: 'a single feeling is often made up of contrary elements' (I, 656; I, 609). Marcel renounces Gilberte in order to rediscover intensity of feeling. But his renunciation can only be enacted in time, and time brings with it forgetting, even of his intention in renouncing her. For the initial passion of unknowing is substituted, through time, the nostalgia of letters written in the past tense. Real interest will only be stirred when, years later, Marcel mistakes Gilberte for a libertine (Mlle d'Eporcheville). Until he correctly places her as Mlle de Forcheville, she briefly recovers a distance sufficient to render her mysterious and desirable once more.

Gilberte is Marcel's first adult passion, but she is not, of course, his last. Late in the novel he decides that 'a man has almost always the same way of catching cold, of falling ill' (III, 502; III, 502). He draws the appropriate conclusions for a man's way of falling in love. By then the reader already knows this, however, and less through Marcel's assertions than through the experience of the novel as it imposes and superimposes itself. The elements of Marcel's love which have been observed – enchantment, fascination with the name, insinuation, invasion, and then indifference – appear again and again. They reduplicate with almost mathematical precision his love for Gilberte in relation to the Duchesse de Guermantes. The urge to control the Duchesse is none the less powerful for being hopelessly unrealisable. Not only the declared struggle contained in Marcel's desire to debase grandeur and impoverish wealth is striking. The undeclared struggle is striking too: for one knows Marcel well enough to realise that if she were reduced to the scope of his power, the Duchesse would be simultaneously divested of her fascination. She is enchanting to the precise pitch of her unattainability, which fortifies her within her exclusive social world. *Le Côté de Guermantes* (*The Guermantes Way*), the book which occupies this world, tells of Marcel's painstaking colonisation of it – those endless *matinées* and *soirées*. It also charts the course of Marcel's disenchantment. To know is to defuse and de-eroticise. From the buffoonery of Marcel's early morning walks on which he meticulously plans his 'chance' encounters with the Duchesse, to the total accomplishment of the perfect gesture he deploys at the Prince de Guermantes' *soirée* (a gesture signalling resolute independence), Marcel masters the social code. It is a code which determines that to be wanted one has not to (or to pretend not to) want. As the demiurge M. de Norpois amply demonstrates, in the world, desire is its own frustration (except in the rare case, such as that of the Prince von Faffenheim, where the aspirant is able to find the key to another's desire). Marcel masters the code. But once the code is mastered, it too loses its interest. From the moment that, prompted by his mother, Marcel decides '"I am no longer in love"' (II, 387; II, 373), the doors of the Duchesse's almost superfluous friendship and support are open.

As much as they are conflictual in themselves, there is a depressing compatibility between Marcel's loves for Gilberte and the Duchesse de Guermantes. The loves run a parallel course, or seem to repeat each other in time. They thus prompt the question – is Marcel open to what psychoanalysts call a 'compulsion to repeat'? Marcel has his own roundabout way of suggesting an answer. It involves a comparison between his aunt Léonie and the sufferers in Dante's *Inferno*. I have already suggested, when speaking of Dante (above, § 1.6), that part of the awfulness of *Inferno* stems from the way its inmates are consigned to a repetition of the same. In view of the argument of chapter 4, in which 'the same' suggests the possibility of difference, this term should be replaced by the stronger and more accurate term, 'the identical'. For in *Inferno* the possibility of change and difference has eternally vanished. As far back as Combray, on his walks by the river Vivonne, Marcel has connected repetition with Dante's world, as he explains:

I would still find it [the water-lily] there, on one walk after another, always in the same helpless state, suggesting certain victims of neurasthenia, among whom my grandfather would have included my aunt Léonie, who present year after year the unchanging spectacle of their odd and unaccountable habits, which they constantly imagine themselves to be on the point of shaking off but which they always retain to the end; caught in the treadmill of their own maladies and eccentricities, their futile endeavours to escape serve only to actuate its mechanism, to keep in motion the clockwork of their strange, ineluctable and baneful dietetics. Such as these was the water-lily, and reminiscent also of those wretches whose peculiar torments, repeated indefinitely throughout eternity, aroused the curiosity of Dante. (1, 184; 1, 169)

Marcel's observation bears not only on the world around him but on himself as well. He is famous for the view that children step into their parents' shoes (the most renowned example being the way his mother slowly becomes like his grandmother). He notices at one point that he might be doing this himself (his expressions mimic those of his mother and grandmother; quite as much as it was for his father, his own life's gauge is the weather – the barometer with its man hatted or hatless). Less famous is the variation on this theme, by which Marcel threatens to reproduce his aunt. Her hypersensitivity, her illness, her 'unceasing monologue which was her sole form of activity' (1, 55; 1, 50), her adoption of a 'routine' ['train-train'] (the very phrase used to describe Marcel's social rounds in Paris), her commitment to a life spent bedridden – these are just some of the traits Marcel will sooner or later develop.[2] Of course, one learns nothing of any loves aunt Léonie might have had. But this is beside the point. The inference is there to be drawn, that Marcel's loves also develop the insistent repetitiveness of the 'water-lily' and the 'neurasthenic': the 'uniformity' of the events of Léonie's 'train-train', which repeat themselves 'at regular intervals and in identical form' (1, 119; 1, 110).

To the compulsiveness of Marcel's repetition in love cor-responds the mounting frustration of the reader, who cannot but be increasingly exasperated by Marcel's willingness to fall into the same trap over and over again. In the end, it seems that the only persistent fancies are the unrealised ones. Marcel's unachieved loves – for Mme de Stermaria, for the string of girls sighted on rides in the country, for the chambermaid of the Baronne de Putbus – are perhaps the only ones which escape the awful monotony of the same. Nor is the reader's frustration likely to be confined to Marcel. For he is not alone in the way he loves.

Repetition establishes itself across individuals and across society. It does so through one mechanism in particular, through that fantasy which takes hold and does not let go – the fantasy of jealousy. A repetition is imposed by jealousy on individuals, irrespective of their class, gender or age. If Marcel is a lover whose loves are either unattainable or self-defeating, he is not the sole, or most extreme lover of this sort in the novel; not when he is in the company of Charles Swann, Robert de Saint-Loup and the Baron de Charlus.

The love of Swann for Odette de Crécy first establishes that repetition – of a kind of loving despair – can be trans-individual. Swann's love is a supremely jealous one. It seeks, that is, to make known; but confronts an inexorable core of secrecy and unknowability. The more Swann knows, in fact, the more Odette eludes him. The tighter he makes his grip, the more easily she slips through his fingers. *Un amour de Swann* traces the consequences of jealousy, which include the humiliation of intelligence and refinement that are reduced to ignorance and crudity by the Verdurin salon, the reversal of values which can rate a Forcheville above a Swann, and the indignity of Swann's nocturnal prowlings and fingering of envelopes. The book charts, and this not once but repeatedly, the torment and utter self-defeat of jealousy. Swann can never know enough, because he wants so badly to know. He will know only when he no longer cares.

Jealousy proliferates, and few escape its contagion: not Saint-Loup, who is stricken by a rage of it for Rachel; nor the Baron de Charlus, who watches over the undeserving Morel with over-protective eyes; nor even the Duc de Guermantes, who, though a dotard by then, tries to cage the still elusive Odette. And of course, most importantly, not Marcel, whose relation with Albertine may be the fullest exploration of jealous love ever attempted. In the end, when the nature of this love is considered, it is less than surprising that critics have tended to ignore the middle sections of the novel. They are extraordinarily painful to read. Not even the possibility of discovery awaits the reader, for one senses with a chilling certainty that jealous love will never possess its object.

Marcel's jealousy repeats that of Swann for Odette. It will in turn be repeated by that of the Duc de Guermantes for the same woman. But if Marcel repeats, he will fail to heed Swann's advice about the futility of turning a mistress into a prisoner. Marcel does sequester Albertine, and for a second it seems he may neutralise his longing for her. Indifference (which is the eradication of her challenging difference) comes over him like a blanket. But lodged in his mind is the sea air, the seascape and the sound of gulls; as are the words of Doctor Cottard about Albertine's reputation. Albertine is a mystery, like the sea or the inhabitants of the air. Under her ostensible 'virtue' she may be hiding the heart of a rapacious *gomorrhéenne*. Montjouvain, and the lesbian scene he witnesses there, burns ever brightly in Marcel's mind. Boredom yields to the most urgent curiosity when Albertine proposes a visit to the Verdurin salon. Marcel employs Andrée to spy for him, but he cannot be sure that she (like his chauffeur) is not in league with Albertine, who in turn betrays herself by half-truths and by chance use of revelatory expressions (like 'casser le pot' (iii, 345; iii, 339)). Marcel increases his vigilance, proposes a separation (so in fact as to avoid one), and employs ruses and seductions to lead Albertine into total dependence . . . till one morning she leaves him (who could blame her?). She will not be tamed: this is her seduction. Marcel will never know if she has been faithful, or if she has shared her favours far and wide (with Léa, with Andrée, with the woman in the toilet at Cannes, with Mlle Vinteuil). The net of suspicion spreads so wide that she slips through its mesh.

Marcel's love repeats his own and others' loves. Within this it is a tireless re-enactment of the jealous scene which attempts to match surface with depth, inner with outer, words with meaning. Jealous love attempts to commandeer an identity which will eradicate otherness, but cannot stitch over the difference between knowledge and desire (between the lover and the loved one, or, as it may be, the 'name' and the 'place'). It tries to resolve the ambivalence that is formed by division. Yet it does so in a way that enshrines knowledge and power, and so confirms division (between the knower and the infinitely refinable and redefinable object of knowledge, between the tyrant and the victim).[3] A space behind appearances is hollowed out by jealousy, which allows 'the penetrating chill of an invisible pool' to be felt (ii, 1050; ii, 1018). To act upon it is to attempt repeatedly to halt repetition – and this when love knows only repetition. Jealousy opens the search for paradise, when, as Marcel asserts more than once, the only paradise is paradise lost.

§ 5.2

The edge of repetition can be a cruel one, and it is felt in *A la recherche* by almost all individuals in love. Yet repetition is usually double-edged. If jealousy offers so much that is negative, then this is not all it offers, for in its repetititve nature is contained the germ of its peculiar fruitfulness. Marcel's loves are cause for frustration, but they are also cause for rejoicing. Quite why and how this is so, and how Marcel manages to avoid certain of the excesses of fantasy (while at the same time exploiting fantasy to the utmost) I shall not try to explain.

As Marcel notes, jealousy is truly 'endless' (III, 81; III, 87). Even Albertine's death will not put a stop to the detective work of Aimé or the interrogations of Andrée. The reason for this, Marcel admits, is that 'Amorous curiosity is like the curiosity aroused in us by the names of places; perpetually disappointed, it revives and remains for ever insatiable' (III, 139; III, 143). Jealousy and curiosity are of the same order as the 'names of places' ['noms de pays']. They partake of the symbolic world. If they reinstitute the Fall which divides the sufferer from the world, they also give rise to an abundance of words and devices through which the world can be negotiated (and in the process become redolent with meaning and imagination). They give rise to complex structures of words and symbols, and to jealousy's avatars – induction, luring, detection, lying – with which the bland literal world is enlivened. As Malcolm Bowie notes, jealousy 'is a continuous journey towards a receding goal, an itinerary with no stopping-places and no landmarks; it is an appetite for knowledge, but knows nothing' (Bowie, 1987, p. 58).[4] Nor is this instability just a coincidental or irritating fact. It is rather the essence of jealousy which, as Gilles Deleuze argues, is a 'repetition oriented to the future, this repetition of the outcome' (Deleuze, 1973, p. 19). Drawing on my conclusions in chapter 4, I may say that jealousy is both a repetition of a past scene which is supposed to have taken place, *and* a rehearsal of a future scene, which is as infinitely rich and renewable as is the ostensible desire that it should stop. The tense of jealousy is characteristically a future anterior, which is dictated to the fevered imagination of the jealous sufferer by anxiety. If jealousy divides, it thus also repeats in such a way as to bring past and future in some measure together. If it separates individuals, it also brings them closer, as if in a club to which membership depends upon repetition of Charles Swann's errors. If the many descriptions of jealousy in the novel make for difficult reading, they also offer a recognisable path which the reader can follow, and which leads securely from one incident, one character, and one book to another.

I wish to argue that it is Marcel's ability to exploit the double edge of fantasy, and monopolise on the symbols which jealousy deploys, that allows him to write at such length on the subject of jealousy. Marcel is always one step away from full-blown enactment of the jealous scene. Or rather, his enactment is that of writing, which is itself an enormous sifting of the evidence of his life. This distance from the temptation to over-literal enactment is what frees him from the excesses and risk run by his partners-in-jealousy. As it is, however, a distance staked out by Marcel-the-writer, he cannot represent it to the reader as such. It is latent rather than declared, and for this reason I shall come to it after first discussing the reason Marcel offers for his ability to hold back from the excesses of fantasy. Marcel tries to demonstrate his distance and freedom by drawing attention to his intelligence. It is this, he claims, that allows him to read in the book of love, which tells him that contradiction and dissatisfaction are the rightful inhabitants of love's fortress.

Intelligence does not carry much weight in *A la recherche*, but it is not negligible either (as Marcel admits when he says, 'I felt, however, that these truths which the intellect educes directly from reality were not altogether to be despised' (iii, 935; iii, 898)). The aphorisms love attracts, which invade the pages of the novel, do *signal* (if not actually cause) Marcel's willingness to keep fantasy as fantasy. He invokes his mother's disapproval and Françoise's contempt by sequestering Albertine. He isolates himself from his social world. Yet such risks fall far short of those run by Charles Swann, Saint-Loup or Charlus. Swann commits an act of social masochism in his pursuit of Odette through the Verdurin salon. It is masochism that amounts to social suicide when he marries Odette. (His wife and child will not be received by the Duchesse de Guermantes – at least not so long as he lives and wants most for this to happen.) Robert de Saint-Loup risks fortune and position for Rachel, a woman Marcel could have bought for a few francs.

He loses his hard-won *croix de guerre* in Jupien's brothel. His patriotism is a more literal form of suicide, incited by his sexual unease and his sense of deviancy. Examples of love's folly are legion. The Baron de Charlus embodies, if not them all, then their largest portion. The wounds he carries on his back are the testament of this.

Fantasy, of which jealousy is a major representative, tends to aim in *A la recherche* towards the eradication of difference. The homosexual fantasy of one such as Charlus is no exception. Yet even a love acted out in terms of the *homos* (the same) cannot do away with the threat of the *heteros* (the other or different). The figure of the hermaphrodite through which Marcel tries to comprehend homosexuality posits an original identity. But, as Randolph Splitter has shown, this figure is quite inappropriate to the workings of *Sodome et Gomorrhe* (Splitter, 1981, pp. 51-6). The figure is revealing nonetheless, in so far as it relegates the fantasy at the heart of these cities (and books) to a mythic past. It reveals the impossible nature of the dream of oneness into which sexuality (which is sexual difference) has edged its way.[5] The scourging of Charlus in Jupien's brothel is the dramatic dénouement of fantasy, in that it exemplifies not just its dangerous excess, but its very nature – as fantasy (whose enactment can never be adequate). Charlus's torturer cannot be sufficiently vicious: not *although* he is being handsomely paid, but *because* he is being paid at all. The coins passed between masochist and sadist are the symbol, the wedge – the division once again – which are the inevitable undoing of the paroxysm of fantasy.

In his discussion of homosexual attraction in *A la recherche*, Randolph Splitter catches at many of its paradoxes and complexities. But he does not catch up the full force of its fascination for Marcel, on which all the tellings (and most importantly that of Albertine's supposed 'vice') are premised. If Marcel is one crucial step away from the perils of homosexual enactment, it is a step signalled by his intelligence, but constituted, I have suggested, by the symbol. His jealousy deploys symbols ad infinitum; and his writing on jealousy does the same. The step (much like that which divided 'jeu' from 'je' in § 4.4) is that taken by the text itself, when the text tacitly requires and engenders an overlapping fantasy involving the reader. This overlapping fantasy exists in the 'promise of an encounter': an encounter between Marcel and himself, in which they will be truly one and the same; and between writer and reader, when their words and their 'I' will be thoroughly shared. Marcel is enraptured by the sexual and homosexual affairs of others, by their search to close division. While his fascination betokens and multiplies division (through his striving to know), it also finds form in the enormous attempt which his writing undertakes – an attempt to repeat his life in such a way that it becomes indistinguishable from that of another (the reader). In his essay 'Unity Identity Text Self', critic Norman Holland describes an engagement through writing in a way that is relevant here, when he remarks that

Every time a human being reaches out, across, or by means of symbols to the world, he reenacts the principles that define that mingling of self and other, the creative and relational quality of all our experience, not least the writing of literature. (Holland, 1975, p. 821)

As was indicated in discussion of the 'I' in chapter 4, Marcel's 'mingling' with the reader is of the most urgent and insistent kind. Marcel's fantasy can be described as the most subtle and the most powerful 'homosexual' (or 'homosexualising') fantasy in the novel. It is a fantasy in which the reader indulges. One's ability to get through the novel – one's desire to move through the heterodoxy of the symbol (of words), to a 'mingling of self and other' – is the proof of this. When Marcel repeats the repetitious jealous scene in words, he rehearses this 'mingling', this dream that beyond division there 'will indeed have been' a moment when writer and reader 'will have been' the same. The repetitions in *A la recherche* which form up around love do open upon a dream and a possibility of unity (though each individual reader must decide if the dream becomes a reality).

This is the broadest or most fundamental way in which love's repetitions offer a hope of assuagement; but there are other more immediate ways which are worth noting here, before I leave Proust to turn to Beckett. Marcel's loves may be determined by a 'compulsion to repeat' – and my conviction that they are is liable to be strengthened when the love of Marcel for his mother is considered (as it is in chapter 6). However, it is not his intelligence alone which signals that his loves give rise to more than a drab succession of obsessive substitutions for his mother. Repetition can also give rise to the wonderful moment of unexpected release, and to the unique individual who cannot be understood or contained by the series of apparently replaceable objects of love.

Charles Swann suffers agonies of awkwardness in his advances to Odette, but the instant he stops looking at her flowers and summons up the courage to 'Do a cattleya' ['faire cattleya'] is all the greater a relief. Charlus has a strange way of taking pleasure, but he can sometimes find such solace in dominating a conversation that this alone can purge and quieten him to the extent of allowing his astonished visitor to leave under no further obligation. The beautiful fishing girl is 'possessed' by Marcel's parade of social superiority. Marcel may be secretive about the joy he gains from his wrestle with Gilberte, but the reader cannot claim his degree of ingenuousness. The incidents are not mere cyphers of each other, no more than are the actors in the incidents. Gilberte is no Duchesse de Guermantes; and Albertine is to both as the Vinteuil septet is to the sonata. She is sensual, loving, mysterious, unique. She changes and invigorates like the sea at Balbec. She grows in depth and appeal every time she enters the novel (and every time one re-reads the novel too). Her swan-like curves and sleeping poses, her coyness and her sensuality ravish Marcel (and can still ravish the reader as well).

Lest one remain in any doubt about the way love and its objects outrun all attempts to contain them, a single deeply upsetting incident can serve to allay this doubt. I am thinking of the moment when Albertine is rudely revived by a telegram which reaches Marcel in Venice. The undead are always worrying, of course. But the disturbance of the incident comes from elsewhere. It comes first and foremost from the fact of Marcel's nonchalance. Albertine has apparently been consumed by 'the general law of oblivion' (III, 659; III, 644). Marcel is pursuing an insight when he makes the claim, which dates back to *Les Plaisirs et les jours*, that 'This contrast between the immensity of our former love and the absoluteness of our present indifference . . . we, in real life, observe insensibly' (pp. 134–5; p. 119). Only in so doing he is neglecting the other half of his insight, which says that this contrast, *in art*, is 'so afflicting, so full of tears'. The incident of the telegram is introduced as third and final example of the law of forgetting, of the 'intermittences of the heart'. But Albertine does not obey the laws that have governed the fate of Gilberte or the Duchesse de Guermantes. The law is in this sense the counterpart of involuntary memory – it belongs to Marcel, not to the reader. How can one forget Albertine, whose death is divided from her revival by only a few pages? She leaps out of the telegram. The telling of Marcel's love for her is that much more powerful than his disavowal. When Albertine is killed off again, no amount of knowing that the error in handwriting has been adumbrated can paste over the gap which has momentarily opened between a Marcel who has loved and a Marcel who claims to have mourned: between telling and demonstrating; between a narrative *in* love and a narrative *about* love.

Albertine is incomparable. As Marcel must himself admit, 'situations, while repeating themselves, tend to alter' (I, 630; I, 568). Or, again:

People are never completely alike; their behaviour with regard to ourselves, at, one might say, the same level of friendship, reveals differences which, in the end, counterbalance one another [qui, en fin de compte, font compensation].

(II, 591; II, 569)

If Marcel were to have accepted the force of his own insight, one may suspect that he would not have revived Albertine just to kill her off again; and that, more generally, the account of his loves would make less painful reading.[6] But Marcel's action is never delimited by his apparent wisdom. When Albertine is thoroughly dead, he will try, but conspicuously fail, to replace her with a 'look-alike'. The search for the same will again serve to highlight dissimilarity. The narrative will fall into the space left by Albertine. It will fall into the hiatus of the sanatorium years, into the lost time between *La Fugitive* and *Le Temps retrouvé*. This is a time – years and decades – which is truly lost. It will never be recovered, either by Marcel or by his readers. For certain losses there is simply no compensation – not even in literature or in art.

§ 5.3

In an essay collected under a title which gestures towards Proust ('Charmes d'autrefois'), Serge Leclaire discusses fantasy in a way that is very apposite to what is true of jealousy in *A la recherche*. Writing of the elements that make up any given fantasy, he says that

Each of these elements is set out like a character or an object on the stage of a small theatre where only a single act is played (a single variation, a single phrase). The act is indefinitely repeated in an inevitable scenario of monotonous variations.

(Leclaire, 1981, p. 158)

If this describes Marcel's jealousy, however, it can equally serve as an introduction to a work by Samuel Beckett – *Play* – which it describes with surprising accuracy.

In her biography of Beckett, Deirdre Bair tells that while working on the production of *Happy Days*, Beckett explained to his assistants that 'he thought his work was best performed in small theatres' (p. 465). Audiences of *Play*, the work he wrote two years after *Happy Days*, would be likely to agree. Here one finds a single act played on the stage of a small theatre, and spoken in 'toneless' voices (as the stage directions have it). It is an act which is no sooner finished than it is repeated, not in any indirect sense, but quite literally, from beginning to end, either as an 'exact replica of first statement' or with 'an element of variation' (p. 160). If the conditions of *Play* match Leclaire's words, then the emotion impelling the mouths which speak *Play* is familiar as well:

*W*1: I said to him, Give her up. I swore by all I held most sacred –
*W*2: One morning as I was sitting stitching by the open window she burst in and flew at me. Give him up, she screamed, he's mine.   (p. 148)

Jealousy, and the rivalry of two women ('W1' and 'W2') over a man ('M') are what sustain *Play* (in its first half at least). Jealousy deploys its usual devices. A detective is employed, and then bribed off the scent. Insults are bandied. The man's desperate need for both women, his weakness and his incapacity to decide – all are exposed.

Such is the stuff of melodrama. But it should be mentioned how this melodrama is enacted: from within three urns from which protrude three heads. These heads stare fixedly forwards and, when a spotlight flashes on them, speak fragments of monologue that together make the drama. There is longing and anger, demanding and vituperation in *Play*; but expressed by monotonous voices, speaking from a total isolation of a time unimaginably distant. The voices start speaking all together, as a babble. Quite as much as the constructors of Babel, they are unable to 'hear' each other. Dialogue is out of the question. Fixity is the order of the day (every day). Movement, which (as indicated in chapter 1) is of all possibilities and metaphors the most connecting, has stopped for good. The light flashes on and off as a 'unique inquisitor'. The monologues are similar to those given in the dock. Like those of a plaintiff or witness, they go over an event which seems to have been gone over a hundred times already. When *Play* repeats itself, it confirms the repetition which its inquisition has already firmly established.

Jealousy is not so central a concern of Beckett's as it is of Proust's, but what jealousy gives rise to certainly is. For jealousy gives rise to interminability. It gives rise to the unfathomable depth of being which is horrifyingly literalised in *Play*, where the very possibility of knowing, recognising and understanding is reduced to a distant recollection by the urns and the spotlight. It is not just the figure of Belacqua (whom one first meets in 'Dante and the Lobster' and who is still there as late as *Company*) that signals that Beckett read and was forever marked by Dante. The pilgrim Dante, when he approaches the sufferers in *Inferno*, finds them unable to understand the cause of their condition. They cannot conceive of their sin or see the justice of their suffering. They are therefore unable to do anything but endlessly re-enact the conditions of their downfall. Dante approaches them and they are prompted to speak the words they have to say, in their voices that return from a distant past. The awfulness of these words is enshrined in their unknowing. For the first part of *Play* (which is a third part in the repetition) the voices are quite as consigned to an interminability of unknowing as are the inmates of *Inferno*.

Yet infernal suffering is only part of the story in *Play* and in Beckett's work more generally. In their eagerness to enlist Beckett as a spokesman of 'terminal despair', critics have often missed the more complex – and specifically more ambivalent – feelings his work both manifests and produces. There *is* change in *Play*, such as is unimaginable in Dante's *Inferno*. Unable to stand the situation any longer, the man ('M') takes action. What the action consists of is not known, but its result is that neither woman secures him, though both imagine the other to be with him. The cycle of jealousy is fractured. The isolation which belongs to the voices is actively taken on by them. They are left with their regrets, imaginings and fragments of memory; these and the irrepressible need to speak. The change which is brought about allows a situation 'less confused. Less confusing.' Nor is change in the situation alone. The voices which repeat *Play* are 'toneless', but the tempo is 'rapid throughout', and the rhythm is one which intensifies as the spot flashes on and off more rapidly. Fixity is literalised in *Play*, but to the degree that the bodies are static, their words come alive *for and in the audience* that recreates their drama of jealousy. The play of the voices of 'M', 'W1' and 'W2' after their life-change exposes the play (of jealousy) which was theirs before. 'M' reflects on his past and says:

M: I know now, all that was just . . . play. And all this? . . . All this, when will all this have been . . . just play? (p. 153)

The answer to 'M''s question is to be found in the time and space characteristic of play, which exist between individuals: between the voices as they speak, and the audience's ears and minds as they respond. 'All this' will have been play in the moment of its future anterior, the moment of its becoming-in-the-audience as that play which is *Play*.

§ 5.4

The relation of fixity to mobility in *Play* is by no means simple. Nor is it simple in the rest of Beckett's work. The nature of the complex relation will be one of the things discussed in the rest of this chapter. What is simple, however, and can be asserted with some certainty, is that in any single novel or play the possibility of easy movement belongs to a time before. And what holds true for a single work may also hold true for the œuvre at large.

In *More Pricks than Kicks*, Belacqua Shuah is capable of a wide peripety, but he is lame and walks with 'spavined gait'. His bicycling is none too efficient either. Watt's movements are of an extravagance that threatens to tear him limb from limb. Vladimir and Estragon, like the narrator of *First Love*, have terrible troubles with their feet. And things get worse. Movement in *How It Is* amounts to crawling through mud. Winnie, in *Happy Days*, is buried up to her waist, and then her neck, in a mound. By the time of *Company* all that the speaker is capable of is a foetal flexing of the hand and finally a batting of the eyelids. Going with this reduction in the scope of movement is the inevitable reduction of the available world: from the city and countryside of the early novels to the single room of much of the middle work, to the blank emptiness of the late work. The world reduces as grasp upon it dwindles. In the face of this dwindling, the work builds up nonetheless, and does so in a way that both requires and produces dramatic, unpredictable and exhilarating movement. In the face of interminability and dismal repetition, the work necessitates endings and finds in repetition the possibility of originality and newness. Nowhere is this apparent contradiction stronger – between what Beckett's work appears to offer and what it achieves – than in the *Trilogy*. For the *Trilogy* progressively pares away the possibility of movement, and offers books which in some strange way are repetitions of each other, while at the same time it permits an opening and an originality which become ever more urgent.

As one first meets Molloy he is in his mother's room, and it is clear he is there to stay. Despite his immobility, however, within the space of a few pages he is out on a hillside, crouching like Belacqua or Sordello (he forgets which), then careering round the countryside in a way so reckless as to make it unsurprising that he eventually runs down Lousse's dog. Molloy suffers temporary usurpation of his means of locomotion at Lousse's house, but he is soon on his way again, across countryside, to the sea, through mountains and towns and villages. Molloy is on his way home. He is heading towards his origins (in a way I shall develop more fully in chapter 6). But his body is rebelling and inertia is setting in, to the point where fifteen paces a day is an achievement, to the point where rolling seems the only option, and where, eventually, in the final pages, 'Molloy could stay, where he happened to be' (p. 91). Molloy gives up his journeying, and comes to a halt. Yet even this halt will not be an end, for Molloy is to be 'saved', and taken to his mother's room, whence his story emerges.

His story is what offers mobility, and it does so through the power of memory – even if memory is lame, so much 'muck' which can always be changed for other 'muck'. Memory is far from total recall, for it only remembers in order to enable it to get to an end. As Molloy says: 'For if you set out to mention everything you would never be done, and that's what counts, to be done, to have done' (p. 41). Memory is partial, the trace of a time and of a journey which do not quite connect beginning to end. It does not know how it got where it is because it is stricken with amnesia. For this very reason it can allow a *tale* of a beginning (and perhaps an ending) to issue forth. This is Molloy's tale, a tale of beginning. Once started, it implies an ending which is distant, but which is nonetheless almost already achieved in Molloy's mind. As Molloy explains on the second page:

> It was the beginning, do you understand? Whereas now it's nearly the end. Is what I do now any better? I don't know. That's beside the point. Here's my beginning. It must mean something, or they wouldn't keep it. Here it is.
>
> This time, then once more I think, then perhaps a last time, then I think it'll be over, with that world too. Premonition of the last but one but one.   (p. 8)

Molloy's tale of his travels is the repetition in words of a time which is 'once more', and 'last but one but one' – a penultimate time of premonition. His story cannot tell of the first or last. It does not know how it got to the place where it begins, and so it does not know how to make an end. But beyond what the story can tell, and what Molloy knows, there is what the story can and does do. It begins and it ends. The novel *Molloy* starts as it finishes, as so much amnesia – when it is amnesia that allows memory a great deal of 'muck' with which to play.

Given that Molloy is so involved in repeating himself, and given that detection is, I have intimated, a prime way of repeating, it is only appropriate that part II of *Molloy* should introduce Moran, who is a private detective (of sorts). Moran is setting out to write a report which will be a laborious going-over of the journey he reluctantly undertook at Youdi's orders: the report of his search (or 'research') for Molloy. In the course of his attempt to catch up with Molloy, however, Moran suffers an onset of decrepitude, and he too has to strap a leg to his bicycle to be able to pedal. Molloy seems to be catching up with Moran, not the other way round. In preparing his report, to which he cannot wait to 'make an end' (p. 175), Moran starts to repeat the person on whose journey he was supposed to report. Moran threatens to become Molloy – or almost.

The second part of *Molloy* presents itself as the unwilling reopening of a case which would have been better off closed. Its repetitions are almost as painful as those of *Play*. Yet the narrative of both parts of *Molloy* not only gives an account of reluctantly undertaken repetition but also demonstrates that repetition always goes beyond what can be accounted for or 'reported on'. The narrative tells of decrepitude and arthritis, but is itself irrepressibly protean. It is also inexpressibly funny, as any reader will testify. Laughter emerges from nowhere more abundantly than from the gap between that which is described – reluctance, pointlessness, decay and interminability – and that which is enacted – excitement, motion, finding, beginning and completion. If Molloy finds a place where he is content to stay, if he finds some solace from being in his mother's room and from being obliged to remember, then Moran also gets to a point where he discovers a sort of freedom. This is the freedom to repeat (and he repeats his opening sentences verbatim).[7] It is also the freedom to deny and to lie. It is the freedom to put an end to his report – and it is drawn from his new-found ability, which is that of inventing. He concludes:

in the end I understood this language. I understood it, I understand it, all wrong perhaps. This is not what matters. It told me to write the report. Does this mean I am freer now than I was? I do not know. I shall learn. Then I went back into the house and wrote, It is midnight. The rain is beating on the windows. It was not midnight. It was not raining. (p. 176)

If *Molloy* ends on the possibility of inventing, then *Malone Dies* takes up and explores the breadth and depth of the prime way of inventing, which is telling stories. As Malone puts it: 'Live and invent. I have tried. I must have tried. Invent. It is not the word. Neither is live. No matter. I have tried' (p. 195). Malone has taken a lesson from Marcel's aunt Léonie, who 'never remained for long, even when alone, without saying something' (1, 54; 1, 50). Alone, catatonia encroaching, his reach diminishing, Malone is determined to *tell himself* to death. He is writing down his story, and the story of those surrogates or 'pretexts', Sapo and Macmann. He is doing so in order to finish, and to find a way out of his amnesia. He is doing it also in order to reach the greater amnesia that death offers. As he awaits annihilation, the very strength of his determination cuts against death's encroachment. 'I could die today', he says. Then he adds, 'if I wished, merely by making a little effort' (p. 179). His desire is for the levelling of death, for that 'indifference', but his desire is itself a form of difference. This in turn promotes a remarkable sameness in his stories – of Sapo, of Macmann (who is Sapo), and of himself. Malone's stories are all testaments to his life-sustaining desire, and they all end up being about himself. However infuriating this fact may be, he is obliged to recognise its truth: 'What tedium. And I call that playing. I wonder if I am not talking yet again about myself. Shall I be incapable, to the end, of lying on any other subject?' (p. 189). Despite himself, Malone lives, lives on, and becomes a presence as intense as is his desire that he should be absent.

Everywhere one looks in *Malone Dies* one finds darkness, denial, stopping, sameness, lying down and giving up, refutation and bitter interjection. On the other side of this coin one finds wanting, yearning and novelty. To read is to flip the coin and watch the sides spin. One can only ever see a single side at a time, but without them both the coin would be virtually worthless. A later text conjures the double-sided reality with breathtaking concision in it title: 'Imagination Dead Imagine'. Malone writes his becoming-into-death. It is almost as if he were trying to win for his scribblings the authority from death of which Benjamin speaks (above, § 4.0). Of course, he cannot articulate his being-dead, cannot yoke the authority of death to what he is able to note down. Despite this, he can usher this being into existence, and leave a place for this authority in the margins of his notes. His death cannot be a claimed identity, as that identity will only ever be another's story (as he puts it, 'And on the threshold of being no more I succeed in being another. Very pretty' (p. 194)). It is an identity intimated by the breath which accompanies his last panting utterances:

> or with his pencil or with his stick or
> or light light I mean
> never there he will never
> never anything
> there
> any more   (p. 289)

As Macmann, Lemuel and their ship of fools take to sea, adrift for the first time on an element which accommodates the body in all its stiffnesses and catalepsies, Malone falters for the last time in his bed, and jots this series of negations. He exists, finally, where there is 'never anything'. He exists in the white spaces and in the silence which echoes in the novel's conclusion. He exists where he most thoroughly *is not*.

It may be that the only sure way to reduce the difference which animates desire is through death. However, all of Beckett's work is haunted by the horror that this might not be so, that even death does not put an end to it all – and no work more so than *The Unnamable*. Few readers of Beckett's *Trilogy* will not have felt that *Malone Dies* is a repetition of *Molloy*, and *The Unnamable* of *Malone Dies*. Equally few, I suspect, will feel confident to say in what way this is so.[8] It is as if each subsequent novel incorporates its predecessor and then refines out the world, leaving, ever more urgently, the word. What is left is not just any word, but that which seeks death-in-silence. For the Unnamable, who finds that his limbs and all possibility of movement have gone, there may never be an end to words. He says, 'I am obliged to speak. I shall never be silent. Never' (p. 294). Since his words may never end, it means that he may never truly have begun. He has only ever repeated himself: 'The best would be not to begin. But I have to begin. That is to say I have to go on' (p. 294). Words are all there is, from beginning to end. Words are never the beginning or the end.

Repetition fuels the nightmare aspect of Dante's *Inferno*, in which the sufferer cannot find the vision (and the humility) to allow him to *know* (and so become one with the divine order). Repetition impells the hubris of a solipsistic individualism. In the Unnamable's world, repetition fuels and is fuelled by the one available order – 'words, other's words' – to which and through which order he can never subject himself (p. 390). The Unnamable can never be satisfied he has made himself the subject of his story. Where Malone tries to speak of others but ends up speaking of himself, the Unnamable tries to speak of himself but ends up speaking of others. As he puts it:

But this is my punishment, my crime is my punishment, that's what they judge me for, I expiate vilely, like a pig, dumb, uncomprehending, possessed of no utterance but theirs. (p. 372)

As in *Inferno*, the crime is the punishment: the crime here being that of speech, which cannot find its way to silence, and cannot close the gap between its utterance and what it utters. Speech cannot but be a seductive way of passing time in going again over 'the old story' (p. 375). Speech cannot offer the Unnamable more than what has been called a 'promise of an encounter' between himself and himself. Or as he puts it: 'The mistake they make of course is to speak of him as if he really existed, in a specific place, whereas the whole thing is no more than a project for the moment' (p. 375). In his book on Beckett, Ludovic Janvier offers a long list of entries under various headings, most of which run for a page or two. The entry under the heading 'IDENTITY' is the shortest in the book. It runs simply, almost brutally: 'Does not occupy a space. Keeps moving' (Janvier, 1969, p. 102).

The Unnamable has always been speaking, and will never stop. This is the case unless 'the words have been said, those it behoved to say' (p. 373). These are words that would not be irremediably consigned to otherness. The possibility they would open is precisely that of an end and a beginning: 'it will be I, it will be the place, the silence, the end, the beginning, the beginning again' (p. 417). These are words whose condition is that they will be unknown as such: 'no need to know which, no means of knowing which' (p. 373). They are words which can no more declare themselves than Molloy can account for his being in his mother's room, or Malone tell of his own death. They are words which would tell the Unnamable's story, and so give him his name. The need to find them increases as *The Unnamable* draws towards its breathless conclusion. As the need increases so too does the possibility that the words are not to be found in some other world or script or text or story (as the Unnamable imagines), that they do not depend for their existence on some magnanimous 'if', but are the very ones the reader has been following – those so crammed with despair and denial. The possibility is bodied forth in the novel's final determined utterance, which resounds with ambivalent silence:

I'll go on, you must say words, so long as there are any, until they find me, until they say me, strange pain, strange sin, you must go on, perhaps it's done already, perhaps they have said me already, perhaps they have carried me to the threshold of my story, before the door that opens on my story, that would surprise me, if it opens, it will be I, it will be the silence, where I am, I don't know, I'll never know, in the silence you don't know, you must go on, I can't go on, I'll go on.

(p. 418)

The story which is to be told is the one the reader has just finished. The future (conditional) *has been*. Yet it has also not been. For the story is the one the Unnamable has still to tell, which exists in the promise of the novel's final silence. The story is both the said and the unsaid: the sum of sayable and unsayable.

The Unnamable may never have started and may never finish – his life a ceaseless repetition of repetition. One cannot be sure. But with *The Unnamable* one can be sure. For it both starts and ends. It changes, has its own undeclared rhythm and pulse. These are undeclared because it is the reader who must render them real, by speaking them with the voice. The Unnamable often recalls for us that it is all a matter of voices, but this is not a fact one can grasp with one's mind – only with one's voice. A. Alvarez's book on Beckett is an unconscionable series of misreadings, but nowhere is it more illuminatingly wrong than about *The Unnamable*. In Alvarez's view, this novel is infinitely expandable, and so expendable, 'self-indulgent and, like most self-indulgence, wasteful' (Alvarez, 1973, p. 69). It communicates a 'terminal' vision which can be more easily grasped from concise versions of the same (such as Hamm's in *Endgame*). Quite the reverse is in fact the case. Beckett transmits *in*terminability through a work in which beginning and end are dynamically linked, necessary and mutually implying. One cannot 'know' this, however, by 'understanding' a 'vision' (any more than Molloy can know how he got home, Malone know what death is like, or the Unnamable know where he is in the silence). One can only live it through the falterings, quickenings, rushings and relishings which are one's own when one reads.

§ 5.5

There is no avoiding the importance of the role of the voice in Beckett's work. As the world and mobility through it are reduced, the importance of the voice increases. This is the case, I suggested, not only within any single Beckett work, but throughout the course of the œuvre which seems to whittle itself down from dramas of action (however minimal) to dramas of voices and words.[9] 'Lessness', as one title has it. However, it is never wise to be formulaic when discussing Beckett. After the nadir of mobility of *The Unnamable*, and alongside the sheer inertia of *Texts For Nothing*, came, quite unpredictably, *Waiting for Godot*. It is not merely a matter of drama contrasting with fiction. After the formidable, cold, hard surfaces of 'Ping' and 'Enough' have emerged 'A Piece of Monologue' and *Company*. The voice is no less crucial in these two works; but the *tone* of the voice is startlingly new and different. It is as if a certain hollowing-out had (and has) to be achieved for the voice to rediscover the presence of a remembered or imagined past, and to allow it to flood – or rather trickle – back in.

Certain things can be named in these later works, and states described which, within the worlds of *The Unnamable* or *How It Is*, would be inconceivable. They can be named even if – or perhaps because – they are redolent of evanescence and absence. One may think, for example, of how insistently death has made itself felt in Beckett's work. Yet there is not much dying; or rather all dying and no death. Death is always there, before, or ahead, never quite reached. Not since the cynical demise of Belacqua Shuah and of Murphy has death been perceived in anything approaching finality (that is, from without). Not, at least, until 'A Piece of Monologue'.

Elements of the monologue are familiar: it is spoken in a fading light, and it tells of ghosts – death as so much lessness. Other elements are new: death is 'out there' too, and the perception of it seems to let in a possibility of grief or mourning. The 'speaker' watches from his window, and sees 'Rain pelting. Umbrellas round a grave' (p. 269). He watches a funeral – 'Funerals of . . . he all but said of loved ones' (p. 265). In the 'all but' the loved ones are brought back with a force and immediacy that is literally unutterable. It is not possible to tell which enables which to be articulated: funerals or loved ones, absence or presence. Perhaps it is the 'all but' itself that is enabling, in the way it summons the presence of an absence that is secreted in all utterance. Under the speaker's bed are 'thousands of shreds' of photographs (p. 266). They somehow evoke those photographed with a vividness no photograph (or described photograph) could achieve. Within the space of decrepitude and denial forms up, again, the most suggestive and connecting of declarings. And what is true on a small scale in 'A Piece of Monologue' holds on a wider scale in *Company*.

The scene upon which this novel opens is a familiar one, not very different from that of *Malone Dies*: 'A voice comes to one in the dark' (p. 7). The 'one' (as the central 'character' of *Company* is called) is alone, after he has walked and then crawled to his point of rest. He is immobile, but for his eyes which still open and close. A little mental activity is still registered, all the same, and it has the sole purpose of trying to create from the situation something or someone that might serve as company for it. The voice that is heard might be some sort of company, but is not enough, is only what is called a 'necessary complement' (p. 11). It is described thus by a 'cankerous other' which claims that the voice tells 'of a past' which is not necessarily his. This 'other' would have 'one' do his own remembering and so appropriate his own life. It would oblige 'one' to try to become the first person pronoun, as it implies when speaking of the voice:

Another trait its repetitiousness. Repeatedly with only minor variants the same bygone. As if willing him by this dint to make it his. To confess, Yes I remember. Perhaps even to have a voice. To murmur, Yes I remember. What an addition to company that would be! A voice in the first person singular. Murmuring now and then, Yes I remember. (pp. 20–1)

'One' cannot divide himself from his world – into the 'two' which would make a 'you' and an 'I' plausible. He goes through a bamboozling series of possibilities to try to divide his one-ness for company. He uncovers 'deviser of the voice' and 'devised', 'creator' and 'creature', 'W' and 'M'. But the divisions never become real, because they are always the fabrications of a 'Devised deviser devising it all for company' (p. 64). 'One' cannot become 'some one', nor can he become 'no one'. Silence and darkness are never reached, nor is true solitude. There is only a half-light, and a murmuring with no relief.

To read *Company* is to undergo the assault of the contradiction of inner and outer, the strangeness (a version of which was seen to pervade Proust's *A la recherche*) by which anyone is one-plus-one and still one. It is to explore, and get thoroughly lost in, the 'confusion', or paradox of the voice, which is ever audible but which never becomes one's own – or that of another (p. 34). The text builds like a series of refrains, or superimposed monochrome slides, each one altering the total image while confirming its sameness. 'One' is not able to find the object or image – not even a fly or a dead rat – which would allow him to perceive himself as other than 'one'. Unable to grasp alterity, 'one' is unable to remember or imagine anything (not even 'In another dark or in the same another devising it all for company' (p. 29)) which will truly be 'one's' own – separate enough, that is, to render the possessive meaningful.

Company takes the reader again and again through an ambivalence of the number one, which is both pronoun and numeral of impossible aspiration.[10] 'One' can never speak of the one of whom and to whom the voice speaks. He thus cannot be origin of himself, cannot be number one: 'Could he speak to and of whom the voice speaks there would be a first. But he cannot. He shall not. You cannot. You shall not' (p. 9). Because 'one' is one *and* one-plus-one, he is never really one *or* two. Repetition surges out of this fact (and its consequent ambivalence) through words which both do the job of telling and at the same time re-establish an unassailable difference between the 'one' and his 'cankerous other' (a difference which he cannot exploit). Words surge in a manner reminiscent of Maud Mannoni's patient Jacques (in § 3.5), who dreams of being one with his first love, his mother. Jacques does not have the available words to render his dream anything more than an incestuous fantasy. Beyond such a fantasy, however, I suggested that the preoccupations of Proust and Beckett may be located. I suggested that the words of these writers (as well as the words uttered in psychoanalysis) can offer a route not so much away from as through these fantasies – a route which renders them negotiable.[11] The route leads, unsurprisingly, through words that allow a gap (the gap of the ambivalent Symbolic which replaces Imaginary bliss or folly) to inhere in their uttering. In the analytic context, the words of the psychoanalyst must, as Serge Leclaire puts it, open 'the cutting edge . . . the cleft . . . the otherness of the literal space thanks to which pleasure can be repeated, if not regained [répété, sinon retrouvé]' (Leclaire, 1981, pp. 44–5). Proust's novel contains fantasies of oneness, some of which (as I shall imply in chapter 6) are incestuous in kind. Despite this, the novel operates always out of and back into the 'cleft' (as it might be, between the 'name' and the 'place', the 'I' and the 'I') by which Marcel's pleasure can be 'repeated, if not regained'. The 'one' of Beckett's *Company* cannot become 'one' or more than 'one'. Yet for the reader, many of the most startling words of *Company* emerge from precisely this impossibility, from the gap or cleft between one and one-plus-one. For this is the gap from which the voice appears to issue – the voice which transforms the monotony imposed by repetition into something unforeseeable and unique.

In *Company* the voice may be the irritant which disturbs the silence and entices with the prospect of company only to confirm solitude. I suggested, however, that Beckett's late work contains certain tellings that reverse the vision of his œuvre as a whittling-away. *Company* tells not just of lessness but also of release. I have spoken of the nothingness experienced by the undifferentiated one. This is only half the story. To show this, I should now give the novel's opening *in full*:

Psychoanalysis and Fiction

A voice comes to one in the dark. Imagine.
To one on his back in the dark.

That 'Imagine' calls less as an order than as an incantation (the French is 'Imaginer', not 'Imaginez'). Unplaceable, unregenerate, it opens a gap, a precarious space unbounded by the 'one' or the 'cankerous other' (which uses the third person). It is only a space, and it cannot be grasped by logical deduction (which always leads 'one' back to his isolation). It is glimpsed as if out of the corner of the eye, but it is fleshed out in other glimpsings – and not just those perceptions which are jotted and then left (with the interjection 'Quick leave him') as if they were too precarious to support inspection. The 'Imagine' seems to open a space for the voice. And though the 'one' may be unable to 'verify . . . if it is indeed to and of him the voice is speaking' (p. 9), this lack of knowledge is not debilitating. Quite the opposite: the 'one's' very ignorance is source of the voice's power to evoke. If the 'cankerous other' speaks of the awful sameness of all imaginings, the voice speaks differently. It is quite as true here as it was in the *Trilogy* that it is not enough to know *about* the voice. What the reader must do is give up the obsessive quest for knowledge which characterises the 'one' and the 'cankerous other', and yield to the force of the 'Imagine'. The reader must *incorporate* the voice, and in this way discover that what it offers is truly other – and though often marked with pathos and anger, not 'cankerously other' in the least.

The *tone* of many passages in *Company* is startlingly relaxed and relaxing; so much so that it allows rememberings and imaginings (when the line dividing these is hardly perceptible) of unparalleled luminosity to emerge. Who has read *Company* that can forget the walk from Connolly's stores when 'you', hand in hand with 'your' mother, asked if the sky 'is not in reality much more distant than it appears'? (pp. 12–13). Or the look exchanged between father bobbing in the water and his son who is summoning courage to dive from the board high above? Or the saving of a hedgehog from itself till pride turns to guilt and the hedgehog, trapped, turns to so much putrefying mush? Or the 'bloom of adulthood' experienced in the little summerhouse? Or the glimpsing of those distant hills across the sea, 'seventy miles away according to your Longman'? To feel the utter absurdity of A. Alvarez's claim that 'Beckett writes like someone who has never had a childhood' (Alvarez, 1973, p. 18) one need stretch no further than to any page of

Company. The moments the voice yields are of a childhood. If their flashing luminosity cannot be grasped within a continuity, or 'life', they do allow a plurality to emerge which, though it irritates 'one', alleviates the monotony of his half-life. Nor does memory account for all the moments: not for the father's mountain tramp in avoidance of his wife's labour, nor 'your' birth, 'in the room you most likely were conceived in' (a moment which is perfectly summoned, midwife and all).

'One' cannot know if these moments are true, or even truly his own. It may well be this very fact which allows them to be so startlingly poignant. 'One's' moments are never thoroughly his own. In this fact resides the possibility that 'one' can be (like Marcel in *A la recherche*) both 'one' and 'several'. The voice is a property which is most and least one's own. It emerges here, I suggested, out of the unplaceable 'Imagine'. In turn, it gives force to this incantation, for if there were no gap between 'one' and 'one's' voice (or moments, or past), there would perhaps have been no *need* to 'Imagine'.[12] Since the gap does exist, the reader can listen to the voice, and imagine. If one accepts to do this, then the voice and its moments are no longer merely his (or 'one's') but are one's own as well. And one plus one equals two – which is surely enough for company. How 'companionable' is the voice which remembers and imagines these moments, and tells them out loud?[13] So companionable that the desolation of the novel's final word – 'Alone' – is drastically modified as one finds oneself trying to *imagine* what this might mean. As the novel ends, it starts to reverberate companionably in the mind. What an addition to company *Company* can be!

§ 5.6

The voice is a property most and least one's own. In chapter 6 I shall indicate one of the reasons why it is the former of these (a reason not unconnected with a 'one-ness' which can be thought of as 'first' or originating). For now, I wish to note, through a final example of Beckett's work, that living in what Walter Benjamin calls 'the age of mechanical reproduction', we have a ready means to remind ourselves of the force of the latter (Benjamin, 1973, 219–53). Few of us will forget the shock of first hearing ourselves on a tape recorder. 'Is this what my voice *really* sounds like?' we may ask. The answer is – ambivalently – 'yes'; and (as shock recedes) 'no'. 'Yes' to everyone, but 'no' to ourselves.[14] There is perhaps no work which explores the continuities and dis-continuities of the self (the sense in which we both are and are not the sum of our past and our parts) so illuminatingly as *A la recherche* – unless that work is *Krapp's Last Tape*. Its way of doing this is to have as the second of its two 'characters' none other than . . . a tape recorder.

As Krapp is first encountered, in his 'den', he is in a state of agitation, which biting on bananas and popping corks are unable to assuage. These are just preliminaries, as Krapp settles at his table, to the job in hand. This consists of the reviewing in a ledger of the contents of old spools of tape, and the listening to tapes from the past – in particular that tape which announces a 'Farewell to love'. When Krapp puts the old tape on, it is the voice of the man on stage that is heard, only in a much younger incarnation, and 'rather pompous' (as the directions have it). Through the inflection of tone, the years are made to flit across the ears and attention of the audience.

The tape tells first of attempts made at renunciation, particularly of drink and bananas. In the face of Krapp's 'vehemently' shouted 'Cut 'em out!', continuity asserts itself again. The voice on the tape tells of listening to itself (on a further tape): 'Just been listening to an old year, passages at random. I did not check in the book, but it must be at least ten or twelve years ago' (p. 58). Listening to a tape recording of oneself may be bad enough, but a recording of a past self can be even worse. Krapp spits this out all too clearly when he says:

These old P.M.s are gruesome, but I often find them – a help before embarking on a new . . . retrospect. Hard to believe I was ever that young whelp. The voice! Jesus! And the aspirations! And the resolutions! To drink less, in particular.

(p. 58)

Through Krapp's embarrassed renunciation of past enthusiasms one inhabits for a second another's discontinuity, between a present and a past (which is a present to another past). Yet in the very moment one does so, repetition is forming up: those same bananas, same constipation, same drinking, same need to give them all up. If Krapp is proudly different from his former self, he is also humiliatingly similar. Similarity impresses not just between

Krapp and his tape, but between Krapp, his tape, and his recollected tape (and even, perhaps, another past which this recollected tape is already rejecting, in the words, 'sneers at what he calls his youth and thanks God it's over' (p. 58)).

The tape runs on, interrupted only by Krapp's need for more drink, and his brief burst of song. Where the recalled tape tells of his father's death, this one tells of the death of his mother. As she dies, Krapp (the voice) is left holding a rubber ball – 'A small, black, hard, solid, rubber ball. I shall feel it, in my hand, until my dying day' (p. 60). At the moment of loss, time 'stands still'. A rubber ball is all that matters. The supremely mundane returns to Krapp with irresistible force. It is so much more real than the great revelation which is intimated in the promise of 'The vision at last'. Krapp entices with the moment of vision – the moment of knowledge – in all its romantic trappings; but only to switch off the tape in impatience and wind forward. If one had any doubts left that in *A la recherche* the moments of true connectedness (or, conversely, of discontinuity) need not be those grand ones to which Marcel draws attention, Krapp in his own way helps dispel them. Quite as much as the Guermantes' library, the crashing breakwater is an ideal site for revelation. But who is interested in revelation? When there is still life to be lived, there are still stories to be told, and moments to be related? Not Krapp.[15] The force of his finger on the recorder cuts equally through the 'vision' as through the vehement renunciations. After all, how can a moment when life becomes clear be important when what he is doing is the same as he has been doing every birthday for what seems like an eternity? If repetition qualifies Krapp's renunciation, it qualifies similarly any conclusions or 'visions' (built upon exclusions and hidden repressings as these are) that he or I might seek to construct.

If the prospect of the 'memorable night in March' is tantalising, its lure yields to a new seduction through Krapp's finger on the recorder. The pulse rises as Krapp forgets talk of storms and miracles, to pay heed to the words which recall – 'My face in her breasts and my hand on her' (p. 60). As this moment develops, both forwards and backwards, it too becomes scene for an attempted renunciation (the 'Farewell to love' indeed): 'I said again I thought it was hopeless and no good going on and she agreed, without opening her eyes' (p. 61). The moment's sweetness is only intensified by the prospect of its loss, as the boat on which the lovers are rocking drifts into the reeds. 'We lay there without moving. But under us all moved, and moved us, gently, up and down, and from side to side' (p. 61). The 'Farewell', announced through the distancing mechanism of a tape recorder, brings back love's poignant intimacy with a directness unprecedented in Beckett's work. As Krapp returns to it, he of course tries to undercut it, by the disgust he expresses at 'that stupid bastard I took myself for thirty years ago' (p. 62). But fascination wins over disgust. The moment, like that experienced with the 'dark beauty' of the 'incomparable bosom', like that lived on the recollected tape 'with Bianca in Kedar Street', like the memory of her eyes – 'Incomparable!' – seduces Krapp out of his embarrassment. It asserts a new, loving continuity, and does so by permitting the voice to *appropriate* its *proprietor*.

One does not become united with one's voice in moments of knowing utterance. But perhaps one may do so – as Krapp shows despite himself – in moments of passion, abandon and loss. Submitting to the lure of the past, Krapp listens enchanted to himself. He becomes his voice. He forgets disgust and embarrassment, and crosses the years. Difference dissolves in the moment, which is itself made up of a mingling, a rocking on an accommodating breast (which may take him back to a still earlier sensuality). When Krapp starts again on his denunciation of his old self, it is, by a curious reversal, his voice *now* that risks sounding pompous and imposing. Until it too is scorched by the heat of the irrepressible memory: 'The eyes she had.' The Krapp of 'Twenty-six or twenty-seven' explodes back through the 'sour cud and iron stool' of the seventy-year-old, through the failure (the books unsold, the 'opus magnum'), the constipation, and the endless sameness of the days. Nor is Krapp done for yet. The word 'spool' can still move the mouth in pleasing ways. 'Viduity' is still worth the effort of lugging an enormous dictionary to the light. Though he has thanked God 'that's all done with anyway', he still reads his *Effie*, and imagines other possible romances. Fanny, 'Bony old ghost of a whore' that she is, still visits and rouses him to his old tricks – rouses him to a joke as well.

By the time Krapp draws to the end of his birthday account of the year, repetition has revealed its most oppressive and its most benevolent faces. We have been exposed to an awful sameness that has sought to impose its regime upon brilliant recollected moments. The uniqueness of these moments has been asserted, notwithstanding, in the very power with which they have been able to draw Krapp in – and draw us in too, so releasing us from *our own* uniqueness and isolation. In his book *Différence et répétition*, Gilles Deleuze argues that 'all reminiscence is erotic . . . it is always Eros the noumenon that makes us penetrate pure past in itself, and virgin repetition' (p. 115). Almost as much as the moments recounted, the fleeting possibility which Krapp's tape recorder opens up – of a voice which might speak and hear itself (as a repetition of simultaneity) – is hauntingly, rhythmically and mysteriously erotic.[16]

Krapp (whose name defies constipation) records his last tape (which is also not last, a precedent ever taken by the one before), and speaks his final words to the recorder. In his words is contained a glimpsed recognition of his dreadful need for the repetition which the recorder allows: his need to be one and more than one; to be once and more than once. He records:

Lie propped up in the dark – and wander. Be again in the dingle on a Christmas Eve, gathering holly, the red-berried. Be again on Croghan on a Sunday morning, in the haze, with the bitch, stop and listen to the bells. And so on. Be again, be again. All that old misery. Once wasn't enough for you. Lie down across her.
(p. 63)

Krapp's words echo in the silence. More than this, they act as a new permission. He snatches off the tape he is making, tosses it away, and puts back on the one recorded thirty years before. By this time we all know the passage he wants, and listen to the sensual familiarity of its refrain. This time Krapp can allow it to run on, to its final renunciation, its final denial:

Here I end this reel. Box – three, spool – five. Perhaps my best years are gone. When there was a chance of happiness. But I wouldn't want them back. Not with the fire in me now. No, I wouldn't want them back.   (p. 63)

As the tape runs on in silence, and darkness settles, there they are, want them or not – the years. Time moves backwards in the moment of moving forwards. We listen to Krapp listening to the silence. A poem of Beckett's, written in 1937, goes:

they come
different and the same
with each it is different and the same
with each the absence of love is different
with each the absence of love is the same.

(Beckett, 1977, p. 39)

Twenty years on, *Krapp's Last Tape* seems to be telling a similar story. But with a difference. As the tape runs on, if love is absent, it is also present before us and within us – in the darkness, in the silence.

6 · *In the beginning*

§ 6.0

THROUGH the work of Proust and Beckett, repetition imposes itself as a force which knows no origin and no end. Despite this, the work of these two writers, as I have indicated and as I shall explore further in this chapter, is suffused with a yearning for a time in the past or a time in the future when repetition's hold was or will be weakened. The yearning is a feeling that most of us who have written will recognise. For most of us who have written are aware as we take up our pen that we are only just beginning on the work that really counts – the work that will allow the crucial words to get said and our undiscovered potential to emerge. We know, equally, what tends to become of this knowledge when we get down to the work . . . We swiftly become frustrated and ready to give up. We may wonder if we should not have left the work where it was, or should never have started at all.

At the low point, when the future fails to yield the results we had hoped for, we may tell ourselves how once it was different – how before we had a fluency, how our best work is already done, and how all this struggling here and now is no more than an excuse for what once was easy. When we inspect our achievements more closely we may start to recall the flaws and the gaps, the cracks we papered over and the corners we cut. We may remember that producing was never as easy as we imagine. The power of the imagining seems nevertheless unreduced. It submerges, biding its time, to surface whenever we set out on another chapter, or essay, or letter, or poem.

The dual feeling is clearly expressed by painter and sculptor Alberto Giacometti in his conversations with James Lord, recorded in Lord's *A Giacometti Portrait*. Every day, as he settles down to paint, Giacometti sees an 'opening'. By noon he is frustrated and exhausted, wishes he had left the portrait as it was. Every day Giacometti rediscovers his hope and repeats his error. Every day he begins and fails to begin. James Lord recalls Giacometti's words:

'Youth', he said, 'doesn't necessarily mean much. I'm very young, whereas all my contemporaries in Stampa are old men, because they've accepted old age. Their lives are already in the past. But mine is still in the future. It's only now that I can envisage the possibility of trying to start on my life's work. But if one could ever really begin, if one could have *made* a start, then it would be unnecessary to go any further, because the end is implicit in the realization of the beginning.'

(p. 106)

Giacometti is constantly lured by the prospect of a beginning – a real beginning as he hopes every time – and so is lured into repeating himself. He paints, as we write, and as Beckett's characters walk – awkwardly, crippled. Gone is the fluency of movement for which Maud Mannoni's patient Jacques longs (in § 3.5), and which is encountered only in dreams. At the end of the day, Giacometti invariably wishes he could remove the paint which the afternoon has seen him add, and return to the relative simplicity of the work as it was.

To the very extent that common sense informs that painting and writing never were easy, that there never was a time before when all was well – to this extent we are ravished by the possibility that there was indeed, and will again be a time, and that painting and writing may be forms of ratiocination which lead towards it. This is a time when repetition had not yet begun, and when difference had not yet shaken the foundations of a first identity of our selves with our world and our words. To the extent that the tireless nature of repetition is exposed in the work of Proust and of Beckett, their work dramatises the alternative possibility – that repetition does have an origin, and that it may yet cease. The longing 'to be done', in Beckett's work, is matched in intensity only by the longing never to have started. The longing to start, in *A la recherche*, is matched only by the resistance to ever doing so. As I have begun to show, with Marcel and with Krapp, and will further develop by following some way the argument of Gilles Deleuze in his *Logique du sens*, these two strains (the two convictions about the nature and possibilities of writing and repetition) have bitten deep into human experience.

§ 6.1

In a chapter of *Logique du sens* entitled 'Simulacre et philosophie antique', Deleuze takes two such strains as characteristic of a fundamental divide in Western philosophy, between on the one hand Plato, and on the other hand Nietzsche. He suggests that the Platonic view starts from a notion of identity, from an original essence or model, and judges the world to be a copy of this. The Nietzschean view starts with difference, and judges the world to be a 'simulacrum' of this always extant 'first power'. Deleuze explains that:

It is a case of two readings of the world in so far as the one invites us to consider difference as starting from a prior similitude or identity, whereas the other invites us on the contrary to consider similitude and even identity as the product of a basic disparity. (p. 302)

After describing the two strains, Deleuze leaves little doubt that he is himself following in Nietzsche's rather than Plato's footsteps, and that for him the 'simulacrum' is 'a positive power that denies *both the original and the copy, both the model and the reproduction*' (p. 302). Deleuze is not alone in his choice of direction. For he is in company with his contemporary, Jacques Derrida, for whom difference ('différance' as he often has it) is so central, if complex a notion.

In his essay entitled 'Freud and the Scene of Writing', Derrida suggests that 'difference [la différance] . . . constitutes the essence of life' (Derrida, 1978, p. 203). He goes on to show how this can be so when essences are no longer valid as a notion, and how difference may be original when origins are redundant. His account strikes many familiar notes, when he writes:

To defer [*différer*] thus cannot mean to retard a present possibility, to postpone an act, to put off a perception already now possible. That possibility is possible only through a *différance* which must be conceived of in other terms than those of a calculus or mechanics of decision. To say that *différance* is originary is simultaneously to erase the myth of a present origin. Which is why 'originary' must be understood as having been *crossed out* [*sous rature*], without which *différance* would be derived from an original plenitude. It is a non-origin which is originary. (p. 203)

Derrida is grappling here with a world in which, as Maurice Blanchot puts it, '*in the beginning was the re-beginning* . . . to the extent that the word, even if it is that of the origin, is the force of repetition' (Blanchot, 1971, p. 205). The way he grapples requires him to make words work against words, and to put certain notions *sous rature*, in a manner that is by now recognisable, in so far as it represents the wish both to say and not say (to have his cake and eat it). Derrida's critique of Western metaphysics more generally – his attempt to reveal behind the myth or science of presence the absent present which is always already there — if it has far-reaching implications for philosophy, recalls also the early stages of the present argument. It recalls, for example, Kafka's story 'The Judgement'. I suggested that this story undermines the stability of identity and presence. It manages nonetheless to tell its conclusions in its untroubled, troubling way. It recalls Beckett's *Company*, in which the 'one' is unable to be origin of himself, and yet is able to hear the voice which tells its beautiful account of origins and birth, 'in the room you most likely were conceived in'.

It is not that the findings prompted by Kafka, Leclaire, Proust and Beckett are entirely incompatible conceptually with Derrida's formulations. Rather it is that life as spoken in psychoanalysis, or narrative as told in fiction, is not subject to a hierarchy which has at its head the conceptual. Narrative can reveal one thing to be the case while doing another, say one thing, show the contrary (and this without recourse to the inelegant sleight-of-hand of the *rature*). As Deleuze almost ruefully points out in his discussion of Plato and Nietzsche, narratives 'allow several stories to be recounted at the same time' (Deleuze, 1969, p. 300). Certain of the implications of this fact are drawn out to great effect by J. Hillis Miller in his *Fiction and Repetition*, in which he shows how the novel exploits the seductive lure of the Platonic model of repetition while at the same time revealing its inadequacy. Characters in novels are tirelessly in search of a 'first time', of their origins, which the novel is just as tirelessly frustrating, so that 'No originating first is recoverable, neither the first of fulfilled possession nor that of some traumatic loss' (p. 94). What Miller claims is that the novel represents 'in a skeptical age' the Platonic understanding of identities and repetitions, represents its opposite, then further endorses 'as a genre' the first belief. The consequence is that 'The relationship between the two forms of repetition defies the elementary principle of logic, the law of noncontradiction which says: "Either A or not-A"' (p. 17). Each novel J. Hillis Miller analyses seems to emerge out of the embrace of such contradiction, and does so by gathering the reader into the clutch of that embrace.

When one reads Kafka or Beckett, the fiction or poetry of a writer that moves us, one's consciousness may tell one that the words and narratives testify to anything but presence. The fictions which have been pursued here tend to draw attention to this fact and, characteristically, its awfulness. Yet, though this is something one can never prove (but then reading never needs to prove, proof belonging for that time to an alien hierarchy), the presence of the writer may still be felt – rather as the 'contraband' of Serge Leclaire's physical presence (his body) is gathered through his style (above, § 2.7). In his book on Proust, Randolph Splitter commends Derrida for his admonitions against the application of 'a metaphysics of presence to the universe of the written text'. Yet he continues by saying, 'can we deny that every writer (every text) *tries* to create – out of the difference between signifier and signified, between literal and figurative meanings, between presence and absence – a new presence?' (p. 76). Nor is one witness, as reader, only to the trying (as Splitter's suggestion might imply) – any more than in *A la recherche* one is witness merely to Marcel's failed ambitions.

When talking of Roland Barthes's critique of the 'realistic illusion' deployed by the first person pronoun (above, § 3.3), I imagined a situation in which he might tell of the illusion to one of Maud Mannoni's or Françoise Dolto's patients – the boy suffering from his mother's headaches, for example. It is not that Barthes is wrong, but rather that his remarks are, if true, a part-truth. The remarks are deeply irrelevant in the face of overriding *need*. Perhaps I can now imagine a comparable exchange between the psycho-analytic patient and Jacques Derrida, with his refutation of presence and identity. The conclusion to be drawn as to the truth and relevance of Derrida's refutation will be much the same as that drawn in the case of Barthes. The conclusion leads again towards a recognition of the way in which psychoanalysis, like fiction, does invoke a notion of identity, and a moment of original presence before repetition and ambivalence. The status of such a moment will be examined later (in § 6.3 and 6.4), but it can already be acknowledged that psychoanalytic practice is founded on the need which is directed at this (Imaginary) moment, and simultaneously the need for an escape in and through language from the absolute nature of its spell.

I have tried to show in the case of literature how on the far (or blind) side of a writer's trying, failing and ignorance, there may be a silent achieving. Even fiction which seems to move against any 'metaphysic' of Platonic origins or plenitudinous presence may yet be indelibly marked by the desire for these. This removes fiction some way from the panoply of Derrida's formulations. In her preface to the English edition of Derrida's *De la grammatologie*, his translator Gayatri Spivak writes that indeed 'Derrida seems to show no nostalgia for a lost presence' (Spivak, 1974, p. xvi). To the extent that this is true, Derrida reveals a startling degree of epistemological coherence. Yet to precisely this extent he also differentiates himself from the writers under discussion here. For these writers, though pushing in ways that Derrida's 'Grammatology' might endorse, nevertheless inhabit immeasurably different affective worlds. Their worlds are crowded with intolerable nostalgia, longing and craving – for a time before or after, a time of movement and fluency. Their *words* are crying out for an original time of presence.

I have already pointed to certain of the ways in which such nostalgia and longing represent themselves. Despite this, I feel I have not yet revealed their full force, as it was exposed, for example, by Maud Mannoni's patient Jacques. What was it Jacques desperately craved and at the same time bitterly rejected? What he craved was a version of a unity he had known with his mother. What he could not tolerate was to grow up and out of that unity. If there is a stage before repetition and ambivalence, Jacques recalls that it is in childhood (or perhaps in infancy) that it has been known. As we become adults we do not cease to be children. Childhood is waiting as a model of an original presence, and it pounces whenever we pick up a pen and start to write. It may pounce, equally, whenever we turn to psychoanalysis, or pick up the work of Beckett or Proust.

§ 6.2

There are not, in fact, many children to be found in Beckett's work, particularly when compared with the abundance of the elderly or moribund. Childhood is not a simple matter of years, however. It can also be constituted by a particular relation with the person who brought one into the world as a child.[1] Beckett is famed for his relation with his mother tongue. His renunciation of English never became total, but it did mark a radical redirecting of his writing – or a finding of true direction. Yet no viewer of *Not I* could think the tongue was unimportant to Beckett; and no viewer of either *Footfalls* or *Rockaby* (which were both written in English) could imagine the figure of the mother to have receded from his work.

Before there is any mention of a mother, *Rockaby* suggests her presence, through the rocking chair that provides the sole motion in the play. The mechanical insistence of the rocking of the chair imposes once again the harsh edge of repetition, and links up with the awful dissatisfaction of the old woman in the chair ('W'), and her reiterated cry for 'more'. At the same time it suggests a quite contrary reality. The stage directions indicate that the chair in which 'W' rocks should have 'Rounded inward curving arms to suggest embrace' (p. 273). The rocking of the chair offers the lulling rhythm of a cradle, of a mother's arms – 'Rockaby baby'. Rocking chairs go together with cradles, childhood with old age (the two which, turned masculine in *Worstward Ho*, become 'An old man and child . . . Hand in hand with equal plod they go' (p. 13)).

The voice ('V') in *Rockaby* comes to 'W' out of the darkness. It tells, in its rhythmical, repetitive, incantatory way, of the search 'for another / another living soul' – for company in fact. The search is 'for another / another like herself / another creature like herself'. It has proved futile, so futile as to merit stopping: 'time she stopped'. Despite this, the search has gone on, if for diminishing rewards, for 'another living soul / one other living soul / at her window / gone in like herself', and then finally for the trace of 'another living soul', 'one blind up no more'. There is not a trace to be found, and so the watcher must descend the steep stairs, into the place where her mother has been:

> right down
> into the old rocker
> mother rocker
> where mother rocked
> all the years.   (p. 280)

What the voice tells of, therefore, is the daughter's drift to the state she is in when the play begins. It tells of her adoption of the 'mother rocker', her reduplication of her mother. She cannot find 'another like herself', but she can become like another herself: become another daughter, being rocked off to sleep, another ancient mother, rocking herself to death. One need only remind oneself of the single real pleasure of someone from as far back as

Murphy to grasp the scope and charge of this possibility. Failing, while lying naked, to 'get a picture' in his mind of his mother (or of any other creature), Murphy takes himself to his garret and straps himself to his chair. As he starts to rock, he knows that 'Soon his body would be quiet, soon he would be free' (p. 142). In *Murphy*, the rocking chair counts for more than any picture. As in *Rockaby*, it allows a rhythm which connects the earliest sensations with those of decrepitude. *Rockaby* ends poignantly and characteristically upon an isolation which binds rocker to rocker, 'V' to 'W', speaker to spoken, daughter to mother. It ends upon a rejection of life which is resonant with life (and sexuality):

> rock her off
> stop her eyes
> fuck life
> stop her eyes
> rock her off
> rock her off.   (p. 282)

Beckett's work pushes repeatedly against the fact that there is no first repetition, that 'Again' (as the speaker of 'A Piece of Monologue' has it) is the order of the day, every day ('Birth was the death of him. Again'). The work intimates that there can, however, be a repetition which will allow an 'again' which is a return to – and of – an origin of sorts. Rationality decrees that narrative will tell of the adult world in which fusion is tantamount to incest or self-destruction. But narrative does not only *tell*. In *Rockaby* the voice does not declare that daughter becomes mother. Perhaps, as 'V' belongs to 'W', the rocker is herself a mother, telling of a daughter. The voice does not announce this multiple becoming. It allows it to falter into being through the participation of the audience's deductions. In the voice's very unknowing glimmers the possibility of a time which can be described by words of T. S. Eliot (taken from *Four Quartets*) as an 'echoed ecstasy / Not lost, but requiring, pointing to the agony / Of death and birth' ('East Coker' III).

The glimmering of this possibility is intensified by *Footfalls* (which was written some six years before *Rockaby*). As in Eliot's 'Burnt Norton' I, 'Footfalls echo in the memory' – echo like a ghost. In her biography of Beckett, Deirdre Bair informs that Beckett's mother (whose name was May) was insomniac, and took up the carpets in parts of the family house at Foxrock – which she was sure was haunted – to enable her to hear her feet pad while on her nocturnal prowlings (p. 19). When Beckett writes *Footfalls*, this May, his mother, is long since dead. Yet in the play a May is alive, listening to a voice ('V') – the voice which appears to belong to her ancient mother. May paces back and forth, and as she does so the voice tells of how it once did the same, and of how May asked it to take up the carpets, because she 'must hear the feet, however faint they fall' (p. 241). As May walks, she follows in her mother's footsteps. Yet she herself does not appear to know this. Rather than recognise any similarity, May feels compelled to offer what she calls her 'Sequel'. In this she tells of how 'she' (the voice, her mother), 'when she was quite forgotten', came to haunt the corridors at nightfall. May's only words which hint at recognition of her own ghostlike repetition come between two pauses, when she utters – 'The semblance'.

May is unable to tell of her return to her mother. But she can tell a story of one very near in name to her – Amy – who is herself a daughter, of Old Mrs Winter. This Old Mrs Winter sits down to supper one evening, and after a few mouthfuls bows her head, in wonder at the strange thing she observed at Evensong. What was the strange thing? Perhaps it was a ghost. If so, then Amy cannot corroborate, for she saw nothing. Though Mrs Winter heard Amy clearly, her daughter was not even there. We may wonder: did Mrs Winter perhaps see her mother? Or was it that she did indeed see her daughter? She cannot decide, and we cannot know or decide either. Like the voice of May's mother, Mrs Winter asks Amy (or Amy asks her mother – one cannot know this either): 'Will you never have done . . . revolving it all?'

May cannot see into her repetition, into her strange new identity which almost abolishes the gap between the generations. Nonetheless, she can tell the story of one who cannot see. Daughter and mother revolve in our minds, as we follow the footfalls, the 'Other echoes', as Eliot has it (in 'Burnt Norton' 1), which lead 'Through the first gate / Into our first world'. Words cannot tell of the passage back through that first gate, through which we passed to enter this, our second world. Repetition will always be of difference – of that which divides A–m–y from M–a–y, Amy from May. What the echoes of *Footfalls* remind us of is that this is so perhaps because, like May who cannot face 'The semblance', 'Human kind / Cannot bear very much reality' ('Burnt Norton' 1).

If it could bear the reality, and face the 'semblance', then it would not hear the echoes; and we would not have *Footfalls* to help us revolve it all . . . revolve it all in our poor minds.

The return to origins is pronounced in *Rockaby* and *Footfalls*, and it is even more dramatically enacted in *Molloy*. Yet if Molloy had awakened from his amnesia at the beginning of the novel to find his mother in the room with him, we might not have had *Molloy* either, to help to 'revolve it all'. He would, I suppose, have been too busy getting away from her – in order to be able to return to her – to have had time for telling his story. Let me recall how *Molloy* begins . . . 'I am in my mother's room. It's I who live there now. I don't know how I got there' (p. 7). Molloy, who will never move again, is back where he started – with his mother, or all that remains of her. He has reached home, the goal of all his journeyings. Despite this, he cannot reunite with his mother, for his occupation of her room is predicated upon her vacating it. He cannot find peace with her, can only take her place – the place from which he is able to tell his story. His story is of his journey to her, and to here. It is, I have said, a story which both is, and further compels, a repetition. It is also a story which moves forwards, as Molloy himself moves, despite impending paralysis, despite Lousse's seductions, towards its origin, where an end might be reached.

Beckett's work offers mothers (or mother figures) who are ever willing to evict (as in *First Love*), to reject or cut (as in *Company*) or to threaten (as in *Ill Seen Ill Said*). However, the lure they exert is no whit reduced by their ferocity or vindictiveness. Molloy's mother is too old to be up to such active hostility, or to be up to anything at all. She thinks Molloy her father. She is in her own way *sous rature* (just like the origins of which Derrida less hilariously speaks). But she is a mother to Molloy just the same. He explains:

> I called her Mag, when I had to call her something. And I called her Mag because for me, without knowing why, the letter g abolished the syllable Ma, and as it were spat on it, better than any other letter would have done. And at the same time I satisfied a deep and doubtless unacknowledged need, the need to have a Ma, that is a mother, and to proclaim it, audibly. For before you say Mag, you say ma, inevitably. (p. 17)

Molloy needs his mother quite as much as he needs to 'abolish' her. He ceaselessly visits and re-visits Mag, who tried to abort him and so 'spoiled the only endurable, just endurable, period of my enormous history', and who 'brought me into the world, through the hole in her arse if my memory is correct' (pp. 19, 16). He does this though he cannot tell why. Clearly, it is not to speak to her who is deaf, see her who is repulsive, or smell her who stinks. Nor is it for money, which has to be extracted by a code of raps on the skull. He visits her *because* he cannot tell why he does so, when that telling is *the most important of all*. He acknowledges:

And if ever I'm reduced to looking for a meaning to my life, you never can tell, it's in that old mess I'll stick my nose to begin with, the mess of that poor old uniparous whore and myself the last of my foul brood, neither man nor beast. I should add, before I get down to the facts, of that distant summer afternoon, that with this deaf, blind, impotent, mad old woman, who called me Dan and whom I called Mag, and with her alone, I – no I can't say it. That is to say, I could say it, but I won't say it, yes, I could say it easily, because it wouldn't be true.   (p. 19)

Molloy cannot tell why he visits, only that he must. No single visit can be final. He will get there, but only after he has ceased to move, and ceased to care. When he gets there she will be gone. Only now that she is gone can he truly start to become like her, as he admits:

Perhaps they haven't buried her yet. In any case I have her room. I sleep in her bed. I piss and shit in her pot. I have taken her place. I must resemble her more and more. All I need now is a son. Perhaps I have one somewhere.   (pp. 7–8)

Molloy's story of his journey emerges from his mother's room as the peculiar testament to her absence. The story is shocking, and side-splitting, in its *originality*. Perhaps, in telling his story, Molloy completes the cycle and becomes thoroughly a mother. Perhaps his story is that son he suspects he has somewhere, that son who is also a father: a 'Dan' who is also a 'Da'.[2]

§ 6.3

In the course of the present argument the connection has been repeatedly drawn between the birth of a word or story and biological birth (which, like most beginnings, is hardly a beginning at all). The connection can be so close, I suggested (above, § 2.7), as to merit being called 'symbiotic'. One further case of Serge Leclaire can serve to confirm this, and to offer an introduction to the way psychoanalysis has tended to view birth and the more general notion of origins. The case is that of Fabien, recounted in an essay entitled 'L'inconscient: une autre logique'. Where Molloy's relation to his mother and 'son' appears strange, that of Fabien to his parents and 'son' is truly perverse.

Fabien comes to Leclaire out of his psychic distress. However, with analysis under way, his suffering intensifies, and becomes increasingly somatic, to the point where he undergoes an acute attack of renal colic. It is only months later – nine months to be exact – that Fabien's symptoms reveal themselves as nothing other than a false pregnancy. It transpires that Fabien's father, a frustrated writer, had managed to make Fabien the carrier of his own 'ancestral wish' – 'that a child be born of man'. Fabien was to be, for his father, 'the son who would give birth to the book: a new, unique child born from the cerebral entrails of a man' (Leclaire, 1981, p. 71). Fabien's pregnancy, in which he suffers all the pain of labour, is of a book which is not his own. His own birth, consequently, has not yet been achieved, as separate from his father's fantasies of grandeur. Through analysis, under the 'difficult labour of bringing forth a phantom calculation', a quite separate gestation goes ahead, one articulated in Fabien's words, his formulae, his algorithms, his dreams, and his 'unconscious discourse', which are 'as determining for man as a genetic code' (pp. 71, 72). It is this discourse which will tell his own story, one it takes Leclaire nine months to be ready to hear and understand.

What Leclaire's account of Fabien makes clear is not just the power of the metaphor of birth, but also that psychoanalysis shares with fiction a precarious existence hunting for origins (for a moment before or beyond repetition and compulsion). It does this when for weapons the hunt has words, which are forever committed to a time after, a time of ceaseless substitution. Psychoanalysis therefore deals in two types of birth: a first which is the child's entry into the world; and a second which is into the realm of desire (of culture and language). It is in the space between the two that one can catch sight of a oneness and presence, shared typically with the mother. This space is so important to psycho-analysis that it has justifiably been said by Derrida that Freudian concepts 'without exception, belong to the history of metaphysics' – and hence to the myth of presence (Derrida, 1978, p. 197).

The Oedipus complex is just one of the most obvious of such concepts. It suggests what has been described in relation to fiction as a 'traumatic causation', and thereby implies a time *before* trauma.

Since the Oedipus complex was proposed there have been other, earlier moments of trauma which have been variously promoted, as psychoanalysts have increasingly recognised the importance of the mother–child relation. Lacan, among others, has helped turn the clock back. If (as suggested above, § 2.2 and 2.4) Lacanian desire inhabits the post-lapsarian realm of the Symbolic, this implies that there exists an Edenic moment before the fall – even if it is a moment which has to be surpassed. Might Lacan's mirror stage be seen as his 'traumatic causation', which establishes a Real that is put behind bars, and is thereby confirmed in its seductive and disruptive potential? Winnicott also suggests there is a time before, albeit a time in which the baby cannot be thought of as baby, being still an extension of the mother. His 'transitional moment' appears less traumatic than those different ones described by Freud or Lacan, but it shares their structural function. In his book *The Voice of Experience*, R. D. Laing turns the clock further back still (in a way previously suggested by Otto Rank), and proposes that the initial trauma is that of emergence from the womb. Nostalgias are thus amniotic. It remains only for a psychoanalyst to come up with the Shandyesque suggestion that the real moment of trauma is that of conception, and for the patient to complain, with Tristram: 'I wish either my father or my mother, or indeed both of them, as they were in duty equally bound to it, had minded what they were about when they begot me' (Sterne, 1967, p. 35).

Beneath my facetiousness lies an important realisation, which is that psychoanalysis, in its theoretical practice, staunchly upholds the need for origins, for a transcendental moment prior to repetition; and that it does so in dramatic exchange with the knowledge that it can only return its patients to a time after their second birth – to absence, and the 'lack-of-being' of the Symbolic. It should hardly be surprising that these two strains are dramatically engaged. How, when its self-appointed task has been to respond to the parallel strains in its patients, could psychoanalysis be expected to do other than enact a drama? If psychoanalysis does partake of a 'metaphysic' of presence, as Derrida suggests, it does so not for narrowly epistemological reasons. It does so for reasons that can better be described as ontological. For as I have shown, psychoanalysis seeks in some measure to correspond to the implausibility – the impossibility even – of any *meta-physic* which its chosen subjects or patients experience. In corresponding, it seeks to provide what is precisely a way out of (and only subsequently back into) the body. From a psychoanalytic viewpoint, desire or fantasy may trace a time of presence which once existed, and seek to eradicate difference; but the very form which desire takes exposes the 'fantastic' nature of that time. It is the ineradicable difference between the two times, and the two births, that gives rise to desire, as Serge Leclaire expresses when he writes (in a way that is bound to recall Proust) that desire 'is born of the difference between the memory of a first appeasement and the inadequacy to this mythical model of the satisfaction obtained: it is always nostalgia for a lost paradise' (Leclaire, 1981, p. 158).

Freud himself, while he is compelled to relinquish his idea that all children suffer from the trauma of parental seduction, perhaps never fully abandoned the idea that there is a real, primal event from which sexuality (and the principle of difference) originates. Maurice Blanchot, for one, believes this, and fixes on an ambivalence at the heart of Freud's project, when he writes (in an essay entitled 'La parole analytique') that 'What is striking is the sort of passion for origins by which Freud is driven – but which he experiences also, at first, in its reversed form, as a repulsion with regard to origins' (Blanchot, 1969, p. 345). Blanchot is not alone in his belief. In their essay, 'Fantasme originaire, fantasmes des origines, origine du fantasme', Laplanche and Pontalis also set out to show that Freud was fascinated by a 'moment of division between the *before* and the *after* which would yet contain the one and the other' (Laplanche and Pontalis, 1964, pp. 1864–5). They suggest that a 'screen memory' is just one of the more obvious ways in which the original scene can be divided from its mnemic trace. They go on to show that the original scene itself is only able to engender memory in so far as it is already divided, charged and sexualised. The original moment gestures towards another more complete, but evanescent moment which is ever more 'original'.

Blanchot writes that 'it is the force of analysis to dissolve all that seems first into an indefinite anteriority' (Blanchot, 1969, p. 347).[3] Despite this, he cannot deny the 'formative power' of the 'first'. He suggests that psychoanalysis must absorb this 'first', and transform it:

what counts is that, under the interrogative pressure of the psychoanalyst's silence, little by little we become able to speak about it, to make it into narrative, to make of this narrative a language that remembers, and of this language the truth that is given life by the ungraspable event (ungraspable because it is always missed or lacked – lacking in relation to itself). It incarnates itself in liberating speech precisely as a lack, and in this way eventually realises itself.

(Blanchot, 1969, p. 347)

In view of Blanchot's comments, the fact that Freud does not have much success in his search for origins is less important than his search itself, and what becomes of it. Nor should Freud be thought of as in any way eccentric in wanting to search.[4] For the origin of fantasy and desire (one's 'second birth') is itself bound up with an original and originating fantasy which, in the words of Laplanche and Pontalis, 'dramatise[s] as moments of emergence, as origin of a history, what appears to the subject as a reality of a nature such that it requires an explanation, a theory' (Laplanche and Pontalis, 1964, pp. 1854–5). We fantasise our origin by virtue of the fact that we originate in fantasy. We desire to rediscover it because we are desiring beings. We dream, like Joseph K., the Unnamable, or the 'one' of *Company*, of finding the birthright, the name, the law, or the 'first' which lies behind; and we do so because to dream is to know that there is nothing behind, that there is only sheer surface (of words, others' words). We know that not even our birth is in any absolute sense our beginning, nor our conception either, but our knowledge is weak (as Krapp shows) against the mythic power of the birthday.

Psychoanalysis recognises the original symbiosis of the infant with the mother, and recognises its impossibility – the very recognition a fantasy. This is a paradox which at times it tries to resolve. In the end, however, like certain of the fictions discussed here, it serves rather to extend it. The notion of ambivalence is one way of achieving this extension. For ambivalence can be seen (as above, § 2.1) as characteristic of a transitory phase of unity and parting, oneness and parturition shared between infant and mother. Nor does the paradox offered by ambivalence stop here. For if ambivalence is most intensely individual, it is trans-individual as well, and is carried down through the generations (as Maud Mannoni's entire work implies).[5] Quite as much – and as frighteningly – as in *Footfalls*, the generations repeat themselves and 'revolve' in psychoanalysis. The individual's story is written on the pages of his or her pre-history. To the extent that psychoanalysis recognises that this is so, it is also committed to allowing the individual to utter his or her unique story for the first time – even (or especially) if this story is itself haunted by the ghost of an original presence or paradise which has forever been lost.

§ 6.4

If the notion of ambivalence is one way in which psychoanalysis extends its paradoxical view of the nature of origins, then the notion of repetition, or return, is another. Nowhere is this extension more complex or crucial than in Freud's *Beyond the Pleasure Principle*, whose very title suggests the existence of a moment or 'principle' so fundamental or 'beyond' that it may be considered original.

Freud had already attended to the phenomenon of return, most thoroughly perhaps in his essay on 'The Uncanny', in which the recurrence of a repressed event is seen to induce fear because the anxiety of the repressing accrues to what was once *heimlich*, rendering it *unheimlich*. In fact, from the moment early in his career when he tries to understand hysterical trauma, Freud is already making sense of return. For an initial event becomes sexual, and so traumatic, not in the first instance, but when rediscovered or repeated in adolescence or adulthood. As J. Hillis Miller puts it, 'The trauma is neither in the first nor in the second, but in the relation between them' (Miller, 1982, p. 136). When the child makes its first essays at repetition, in the by now famous *fort/da* game discussed in *Beyond the Pleasure Principle*, it is finding a way of dealing with highly negative feelings. It is also and at the same time discovering a way of *protracting* these feelings (and it is this, Freud points out, which leads to the suggestion of a 'beyond the pleasure principle'). In Freud's thesis, passive experience is transformed through play into active. This transformation implies that the realm of the symbol rises up on the ground of loss. The compulsion to repeat (with which Freud had already engaged in his paper 'Remembering, Repeating and Working Through') becomes in *Beyond the Pleasure Principle* a puzzling amalgam – one which Freud never quite unravelled – made up of infantile pleasure and adult, neurotic acting out.

Psychoanalysis since Freud has continued to puzzle, and *Beyond the Pleasure Principle* has become in Laplanche's words, 'the most fascinating and most baffling text in the whole of Freud's œuvre'

(Laplanche, 1970, p. 163). Freud's short text has aroused an enormous volume of assent and dissent.[6] I do not wish to add to this volume, but rather to stay for a moment with the puzzle. Repetition leads Freud, as is recognised, to a 'beyond', and to the hypothesis of a death instinct according to which ' "*the aim of all life is death*" ' (*Standard Edition*, XVIII, 38). What is less clearly recognised, but should be becoming clear here through fiction (and Beckett in particular, with his characters who cannot wait to 'be done'), is that death is a *fantasy*, quite as much as is an origin or birth. Where Malone or the Unnamable must 'go on', so must everyone else, in and through life, towards that state of which nothing is known. Death is accurately described by Stephen Heath as the 'horizon' of repetition (Heath, 1981, p. 156). However long it is inspected, it remains elusive. Gilles Deleuze states a truth – if one that it is initially hard to accept – when he writes that 'Death has nothing to do with a material model' (Deleuze, 1968, p. 28). Death is to birth, that 'original fantasy', the true counterpart: the *terminal fantasy* perhaps. If, as Walter Benjamin suggests (above, § 4.0), death plays a vital role in conferring meaning in fiction, it can now be seen more clearly why it is that fiction so draws us. Benjamin adds that:

The novel is significant, therefore, not because it presents someone else's fate to us, perhaps didactically, but because this stranger's fate by virtue of the flame which consumes it yields us that warmth which we never draw from our own fate. What draws the reader to the novel is the hope of warming his shivering life with a death he reads about. (Benjamin, 1973, p. 101)

It is because we can never more than fantasise our death that the desire for death of one such as Malone is so captivating.

In *Beyond the Pleasure Principle* Freud is unable fully to accept that repetition is carrier both of the 'life' and the 'death instincts'. He cannot decide one way or the other, whether repetition cuts in a child's (or patient's) favour, or the opposite. Even Lacan, who is usually determined to present Freud as the paragon of clarity, has to admit an 'oscillation' in Freud's thought on this point: between a 'restorative tendency' and a 'repetitive tendency' (in *Le Séminaire II*, p. 85), or, as he has it (in *Ecrits*, p. 46) with Kierkegaard's essay on repetition in mind, an 'ancient and modern conception of man'. One may agree with Lacan, but also insist that it is Freud's very uncertainty which is fruitful. For repetition may 'echo' birth and death (as *Krapp's Last Tape* and *Footfalls* make clear); but birth and death can 'echo' only in repetition. Derrida expresses this elegantly when he writes that 'Death is at the dawn because everything has begun with repetition' (Derrida, 1978, p. 299).

If Freud cannot resolve the puzzle, he can write it out just the same, as he does in *Beyond the Pleasure Principle*, which Peter Brooks aptly calls 'Freud's Masterplot' (Brooks, 1977). If he cannot pinpoint a moment which is original, he can nonetheless originate a *version* of beginning (even if this beginning, like that with the child and the cotton reel, is always in the past). I have already suggested (in § 2.5) that Freud can be thought of first and foremost as a writer; and here the importance of this suggestion impresses itself again. For writing, as I have tried to show, is founded on a primordial form of repetition. It fascinates because it too is thus *unheimlich* – and Freud may well have perceived it as such.[7] Just as Benjamin urges that we need not be heartless to warm ourselves by the fire of fictional death, so I hope it will now be clear that if we warm to Krapp's compulsion to listen to his tapes, or to the 'revolving' of the generations in *Rockaby* or *Footfalls*, we do not do so as impassive witnesses to the blindness of others. If we take our warmth vicariously, it is because we are vicarious to ourselves, and to our own births and deaths – as vicarious as Krapp is to the voice on the tape. As May (in *Footfalls*) cannot see but must tell, so we cannot see but must listen. We too must hear the feet and the words, 'however faint they fall'.

In Freud's account of the *fort/da* game, the infant may at first appear to be impelled to play by the 'traumatic causation' of the mother's absence. It is, of course, the 'traumatic neurosis' of First World War sufferers that sets Freud's mind on the tracks of repetition (which looms initially as compensation or revenge). The *fort/da* game is complex, however. For it is also a form of rehearsal, as Lacan insists in his various commentaries on it, and a rehearsal not of a lost identity but of that which is new, different and ambivalent. When the child asks for a story to be told again, it is rather like a watcher of Beckett's *Play* on the re-run, in that it confirms the minute differences between the original and the repeat, the impossibility of ever achieving identical versions.[8] Lacan elaborates in *Le Séminaire XI*:

Whatever, in repetition, is varied, modulated, is merely alienation of its meaning. The adult, and even the more advanced child, demands something new in his activities, in his games. But this 'sliding-away' [*glissement*] conceals what is the true secret of the ludic, namely, the most radical diversity constituted by repetition in itself. (p. 60; trans., p. 61)

When the child throws the cotton reel it is not demanding the mother's return so much as re-enacting the alternation of her absence with a new trace of (absent) presence.[9] Quite as much as Krapp with his recorded voice, or May with her story, or as much as the reader of *Beyond the Pleasure Principle*, the child cannot *comprehend* repetition. But it can find the means of extending or re-presenting it with the cotton reel. As both Deleuze and Lacan in their own ways insist, repetition 'is therefore symbolic in its essence'; 'It is in fact from what *was not* that what repeats itself proceeds' (Deleuze, 1968, p. 140; Lacan, 1966, p. 43).

Psychoanalysis suggests that repetition gestures towards an original identity which both has and has not been known. In this it is similar to fiction. However, if Krapp and May are similar to the infant at play, to the adult under the sway of a compulsion to repeat, and to the reader reading, they are also distinct, in an important way. For within the world of fiction the act of reading – one's own voicing of the text – cuts into the knot of contradiction. Krapp and May exist only in and through their becoming-in-another (the viewer or reader). Their very existence is predicated on the founding of a new 'identity' across the gap which divides their fictional lives from the life of the reader. Their existence and their repetitions are always already taken up in that repetition – that ravishment – which excited reading implies. When can this be said to be true in any thoroughgoing sense of one's adult life and one's own repetitions? The answer is, no doubt – very rarely. But this is not the only answer. Psychoanalysis might respond, if asked, that there *is* a time when it can be said to be true. The response returns me to the heart of my earlier preoccupations with Leclaire and Marcel Proust. For it is a response which says that this may be the case when one *is in love* – that happy time when one plus one may be said to equal one.

As *A la recherche* amply bears out, love is itself full of contradictions, and takes the notion of repetition and returns it to the nerve-ends. Love may even be what, in a book appropriately entitled *Histoires d'amour*, Julia Kristeva calls a 'melting-pot of contradictions and ambiguities' (p. 10). What matters here is that love is this while at the same time it is grounded in the experience of a unity, a uniqueness and an acceptance which loosen contradiction and weaken the rule of the principle of difference. Love may take one's contradictions, repetitions, divisions and categories (including psychoanalytic categories) and roll them into a new sort of unity, a new sort of ball.[10] If this means, as Kristeva suggests, that love is a 'hallucination' of sorts, then there is nothing new in such an idea. Poets have been saying something similar for centuries. One might open an anthology of love poems at almost any page and find evidence for the idea. One poem in particular comes to mind, partly because it relates back to the discussion of origins, and partly because it is so short as to be quotable in full. It is by René Char and was included in his collection 'Le marteau sans maître'. It runs:

> Love
>
> To be
> The first there.
>
> [L'Amour
>
> Etre
> Le premier venu.   (Char, 1983, p. 12)]

The hope expressed in this poem is one that suitably belongs to lovers and to poets. However, it does not belong to them alone.

I have already argued (in § 2.5) that psychoanalytic practice has to exploit certain lovers' hopes (as Freud believed) in the transference. According to Kristeva, Freud was the first to make love the model of optimal psychic functioning (with transference 'the royal road towards the state of being in love') (Kristeva, 1983, p. 15). The possibility of a therapeutic relation between love and repetition is made explicit by Freud in his essay 'Remembering, Repeating and Working Through', where he writes that 'The main instrument, however, for curbing the patient's compulsion to repeat . . . lies in the handling of the transference' (*Standard Edition*, XI, 154). It is not that love abolishes repetition, but that (if the circumstances are propitious) it absorbs it and transforms it. It does so in just the way that the act of reading cuts into and across the paradoxes of presence and absence, self and other, allowing a new, less hostile, more playful space to emerge, such as that which can exist between lovers. Transference-love could not hope to abolish repetition – not when psychoanalytic practice is founded upon what is justly described as 'The Hour of Repetition' – 'L'heure de la répétition' (in an article of the same name, by analyst Annie Anzieu). Transference-love can only operate within what is termed 'the psychoanalytic frame', which itself 'is the most perfect repetition compulsion' (Bleger, 1966, p. 513). The psychoanalyst's willingness and capacity to listen, and the professional commitment to hear anything that is said, offers a process which in turn opens the space of a tentative loving. It does this only so long as this process is itself repeated.

Perhaps this space of psychoanalytic repetition can best be grasped where it is most desperately needed – as it is in the case of one Madeleine, who is the subject of Annie Anzieu's aforementioned article . . . Within the developing relation with her analyst, Madeleine is able to express her grief which she has long felt, by replaying the utter dejection she experienced when she was hospitalised at an early age. Through the analysis, it slowly becomes apparent that Madeleine's apparently regressive episodes are in fact a form of 'research' upon which she feels able to embark, under her growing trust in the sway of the transference. The research turns out to be for a lost time when she almost died. The intolerable experience is repeated by Madeleine, but each time she knows through the transference that she will survive it. Every time she returns to her earlier state, the event and its traumatic traces are subtly changed.

Madeleine's identity slowly reforms under the emergence of difference. As Annie Anzieu explains, 'The patient who is subject to the repetition compulsion quite clearly finds in it a means of each time modifying a tiny detail, and of bringing in a nuance which may be imperceptible' (A. Anzieu, 1977a, p. 174).[11] The words of the analyst which suggest the resemblance between Madeleine as she is now and a Madeleine as she was then affirm a continuity. This continuity (like that of Marcel in *A la recherche*) is a non-identity which spells the victory of life over the forces of death. As Annie Anzieu puts it, 'The passage from the *identical* to the *same* can only come about through the verbal mediation of the analyst. The repetition is only an allusion to a former state, it is not a reproduction of it' (p. 172). This passage through difference is made possible by the words spoken in analysis. It is also made possible by that further, impossible hallucination of identity which is offered by the transference.[12] Madeleine's need – or her ability –

to repeat, which 'already makes up part of the "request" for analysis' (p. 174), is what torments her; but it is also what subsequently frees her. In psychoanalysis repetition is a cross which must be borne. It also offers, in the end, the sole path towards salvation.

§ 6.5

In turning now a final time to the work of Proust, there may be a temptation to imagine scenes enacted and words deployed there in ways more sophisticated and crafted than have been found in the needy world of Madeleine and psychoanalysis. From the time of the early volume *Les Plaisirs et les jours*, Proust does conjure in his prose with a most knowing artifice and an ostensible grace and ease. Lest one take these imaginings too seriously – of the substitution of one world for another, control for struggle – it may be useful to stay for a moment with a story from this early volume entitled 'La confession d'une jeune fille' ('A Young Girl's Confession').

The story is a poignant little melodrama, in which a young girl is found lying on her deathbed after a suicide attempt which has not yet taken effect, but which is sure to do so within days. Her 'confession' tells mostly of her love for her mother, a love which was so absolute and absorbing that it left her without 'will' – to the point of being deprived of individuality. It tells of the protracted absences of her mother who, every summer, left her in the countryside. As the girl grows and moves into adolescence, it tells of her attempt to allay the suffering of being abandoned by abandoning herself to carnal pleasure. This pleasure turns out to be short-lived, and it brings with it a loss of self-esteem and a terrible guilt of desecration. Bouts of 'vice' alternate with those of 'virtue', until the daughter resolves to marry respectably at her mother's choosing. On the eve of her marriage she cannot resist a final fling with a lustful former lover. As she abandons herself to the call of her desire, she notices her mother on the balcony outside; and her mother, who is already weak of heart, is so traumatised by what she sees that she has an attack and dies. Upon this the daughter tries to shoot herself . . .

As with other stories in the volume, Proust milks this tale for certain prescribed effects, among which loss, nostalgia and regret are prominent. But under the stylised pathos a ferocious conflict of needs is being played out, and in a way so unresolved that it leads directly to perversity and death. Quite as much as in the later and better-known story (which actually cites the Oedipal legend) 'Sentiments filiaux d'un parricide' (in *Pastiches et mélanges*), violence and murder are the only plausible outcomes of this battle of inter-generational hostility and love. The daughter is subjugated in impotence to her mother, and to the over-adequacy of her love and kisses. She writes: 'I kissed my mother. Never have I recaptured the sweetness of that kiss' (p. 35; p. 87). The mother's nurturing alternates with as absolute a denying, as her daughter is left at 'Les Oublis' (a place which contains forgetfulness in its very name). To the mother's alternation corresponds that of the daughter, between her self-denial and her denial of her mother in her lustful episodes. In the end the alternation becomes too violent for either of them to contain. Both mother and daughter are killed. Only a hesitant life is squeezed out of the moments of dying, and out of the 'oubli': the life of the 'confession' which is the story.

This is not the first example of 'impossible' love to have been noted. There is that which Sygne feels for Serge Leclaire (in § 2.7), and that of which Kristeva speaks above, in terms of a 'hallucination'. Though these loves are also impossible, they are nonetheless expressible, and are fuelled and to an extent negotiated through words. The very definition of transference-love is, according to Kristeva, a love which 'intervenes on the couch so as to permit the scalpel of speech taken up by a subject to delimit the realm of his or her possibilities' (Kristeva, 1983, p. 16). In Proust's story the love is acted out not in words but in over-literal terms which cannot be rendered compatible with adult life in conventional society. When words do emerge, they do so too late. They become an epitaph for the daughter's life, and for that of her mother. As the young girl draws towards her conclusion which is also her death, she writes:

If I were not so weak, if I had sufficient strength of will to get up, to leave here, I would go to *Les Oublis* to die, in the park where all my summers were spent until I was fifteen. No other place is so full of my mother, so completely has her presence, and even more her absence, impregnated it with her being. For to one who loves, is not absence the most effective, the most tenacious, the most indestructible, the most faithful of presences? (pp. 30–1; p. 85)

The girl's words testify once again – and how poignantly – to the impossible longing for the homeland of the mother (which was introduced (in § 3.5) by Maud Mannoni's patient Jacques). It is a homeland which, as the young girl realises too late, is only ever available in the traces of its absence.

If they point backwards, the words of the 'confession' also point forwards, towards *A la recherche*. There are many love affairs in the novel, and Marcel's alone fill volumes. In the end, however – or more accurately from the beginning – one love seems to hang behind them all: that of Marcel for his mother ('je' for 'maman'). Marcel's mother goes about the business of being a dutiful wife and an accomplished hostess, a devoted daughter and a gently persuasive mother. She acts as a 'character' in the world and in the book. While she does all this, she also haunts the pages, and Marcel's life, with an infinite possibility which seems once to have existed, but now exists no longer. As Marcel turns to this woman and that, he is constantly in search of an appeasement of which his mother's kiss, conferred upon him in his childhood, is the model. In *Jean Santeuil* the kiss is described as 'that blest viaticum . . . a compress on his hot and feverish forehead just where the golden fringe fell on the delicate skin, striking inwards to his small heart' (p. 28; p. 205). Marcel awaits such a kiss with quite as much 'feverish excitement' as does Jean.

As Marcel moves from childhood and from Combray, he carries the past and the memory of the kiss with him, like so many flowers out of Eden. Yet every moment one is asked to recognise this – the completeness of his love for 'maman' – one is required to recognise the converse as well. It is this tension which (in Marcel's words) takes 'the coupling of contrary elements [which] is the law of life' and 'makes the amorous life the most precarious of all [la plus contrastée de toutes]' (III, 103, 75; III, 108, 80). The flowers Marcel carries with him from Eden are faded. The love he shared with his mother is revived not only in his moments of delight but in his anguish and jealousy too, as in his insatiable appetite for control and knowledge. *A la recherche* is (as Milton Miller claims in his book *Nostalgia: A Psychoanalytic Study of Marcel Proust*) shot through with nostalgia; but a nostalgia that is divided against itself. A single example will serve to illustrate this.

One night, when he is already deeply involved with Albertine, Marcel sits in his room waiting for her to visit, as she has promised she will do after her trip to the theatre. Albertine telephones, and searches for reasons to excuse herself from coming. Though he will never admit it to her, Marcel is devastated by her change of heart. He draws his conclusion as to why his emotion is so strong, when he says that 'This terrible need of a person was something I had learned to know at Combray in the case of my mother, to the point of wanting to die if she sent word to me by Françoise that she could not come upstairs' (II, 759; II, 733). Marcel's suffering returns him to his early past. In its own way it is a form of involuntary memory, for in the moment of crisis the 'old feeling' makes an effort 'to combine and form a single element with the other, more recent' (II, 759; II, 733). Marcel will try to find a way round this dilemma, a way which was not available to him in childhood: he will alter the conditions determining his anguish by rendering Albertine prisoner. But hand in hand with his increased power goes increased need, and as his need for control grows, so he is returned ever more forcefully to Combray and the impotence of childhood. One jealous scene with Albertine follows another, to the point where, after an embittered evening of recriminations with her, he is led to conclude that 'It was no longer the peace of my mother's kiss at Combray that I felt when I was with Albertine on these evenings, but, on the contrary, the anguish of those on which my mother scarcely bade me good-night, or even did not come up to my room at all' (III, 107; III, 111). As Marcel's loves offer the possibility of increased control and satisfaction, they threaten ever more doggedly to repeat themselves, and to repeat the love which seems at the origin of them all. Quite as much as in Beckett's *Footfalls*, the past (and its epigones, the dead) cling to Marcel. It is to Combray, to childhood, and to the scene of the nocturnal kiss that he is tirelessly returned as to a source.

As Combray rises up out of the early pages of the novel, it does so less as so much joyous remembrance than as so much suffering. The reason for this is that all Marcel's attention is focused on the potential awfulness of bedtime, 'when I should have to go to bed and lie there, unsleeping, far from my mother and grandmother' (I, 9; I, 9). To try to take his mind off the anxiety provoked by this prospect, various distractions are thought up: Marcel is given a magic lantern depicting the exploits of Golo the Knight. The distraction merely reduplicates his anxiety, however, by withdrawing the familiarity of his room, and profoundly upsetting habit (which is a form of repetition that purveys ambivalence into the very fabric of the material world, both the great panacea and the great deadener). The whole thrust of Marcel's anxiety, and of the pages which describe it, is that there is a single solace for the awfulness of separation, which is that his mother should come up to his room and be with him.

The evening which starts to be particularised from the mass of evenings spent at Combray is one on which Marcel does get what he wants, and has his mother spend the night with him. He does not achieve this without a struggle. For the dreadful possibility that she will be detained is made real in the 'double tinkle, timid, oval, golden, of the visitors' bell' which heralds the visit of the familiar stranger, Charles Swann (1, 14; 1, 14). With a guest taking up his mother's precious attention, Marcel is sent to bed alone. Unable to tolerate the separation and solitude, he chances his hand in a wild gamble, and writes an urgent note to his mother. When this fails, he ambushes her on the stairs, with the demand – '"Come and say goodnight to me"' (1, 38; 1, 35). Marcel takes a risk in making his request, but it pays off against the odds, and receives an unexpected blessing through the caprice of his father, who says, '"Go along with him, then"' (1, 39; 1, 36). Marcel is brought back from the brink of despair, and from the window out of which he had been prepared to throw himself. He is brought back to the bliss of his heart's desire realised: 'Mamma spent that night in my room' (1, 40; 1, 37).

In this way Marcel gets what he wants. But is it what he *really* wants? Into the moment of blissful triumph and possession a flaw has somehow insinuated itself: 'I ought to have been happy; I was not.' Marcel tries to explain this to himself:

It struck me that my mother had just made a first concession which must have been painful to her, that it was a first abdication on her part from the ideal she had formed for me, and that for the first time she who was so brave had to confess herself beaten. (1, 41; 1, 38)

Concession, especially when gained through an arbitrary paternal intervention, is not enough for Marcel. It implies a divergence of desire (which in turn implies that the satisfaction cannot be complete or original). Marcel soon starts to feel that he is almost willing to forgo immediate gratification, and ask his mother to leave, in order better to win her true favour and better to match her ideal. A gap has emerged between his vision (or anticipation) and the reality of fulfilment.

This gap points the way forward to all those loves in which possession fails to yield the imagined satisfaction. It points to the bliss Marcel can feel when he knows Albertine is on her way to visit him, the boredom he experiences when she actually gets there, and the agony he suffers when her interests prevent her from coming. Through the way the novel proffers Combray, and through repeated reminders, one is led to the unavoidable conclusion that Marcel's love for his mother is a model. But it is a model which serves to uncover early love's *double* edge – the way love offers the possibility of bliss, while declining ever to fulfil the offer. Marcel's plea for his mother (rather like the child's play with the cotton reel in Lacan's formulation) is therefore no mere demand. It is a form of rehearsal of an absence which has already taken its toll upon his young life. The reader of *A la recherche* is under a real pressure to view all Marcel's loves as displaced mother-love. While Marcel's feeling for his mother is unique, it is also indisputably emblematic. If only to the extent that one knows her as 'maman', his mother remains sovereign representative of a possibility which tantalises only to disappear when an attempt is made to catch it fully in vision. But if 'maman' is a model, she is an ambivalent one. She leaves behind her the traces of joy, but also of anguish and frustration. Proust reminds his readers more than once (and quite as forcefully as does Serge Leclaire) that *all* paradises are paradise lost: 'We dream much of paradise, or rather of a number of successive paradises, but each of them is, long before we die, a paradise lost, in which we should feel ourselves lost too' (II, 888; II, 859).

§ 6.6

The experience of Combray is, to an extent, that of a paradise lost. If this is so, it should not be forgotten that Combray has itself almost been lost. Marcel interrupts his account of the ordeal of his going to bed, addressing the reader from the depths of a later era and an older age, to explain that 'It is a long time, too, since my father has been able to say to Mamma: "Go along with the child." Never again will such moments be possible for me' (I, 39–40; I, 37). What is it that revives Combray and makes it retrievable? It is not the more famed sort of involuntary memory to which Marcel later draws attention, so much as the grief which, mixed with the joy, adheres to the memory of the night with his mother. Marcel's very misery is fertile in his memory. It alights on the recollection of the noise connected with the threat of separation – the bell which announces the arrival of Charles Swann. This bell announces a past which is irremediably separate and distant from the aged Marcel, but which is present still, so long as there is enough silence to be able to hear its perpetual relevance and resonance. Marcel continues:

Never again will such moments be possible for me. But of late I have been increasingly able to catch, if I listen attentively, the sound of the sobs which I had the strength to control in my father's presence, and which broke out only when I found myself alone with Mamma. In reality their echo has never ceased; and it is only because life is now growing more and more quiet round about me that I hear them anew, like those convent bells which are so effectively drowned during the day by the noises of the street that one would suppose them to have stopped, until they ring out again through the silent evening air.   (I, 39–40; I, 37)

A recovery is suggested here, but of a particular sort. What comes back to Marcel out of Combray is a voluptuousness of grief, which the bell announcing Swann allows to sound across the years.

This sound and these feelings point the way forward, as Marcel says, to the quiet and the experience of loss which pervade his later life, from which the novel is emerging (and which the novel is at the same time in the process of refuting). They point forward to the silent attention which writing and reading require if the resonance of the words which resurrect the memories is to be audible. Swann's bell sounds periodically through the novel, and it does so as a reminder of the fact that it is not fullness of (imagined) satisfaction that is pregnant and productive of memories and words, but anticipation, disappointment, and the need to find fresh compensations for what has been lost.

It rings nowhere more loudly and crucially than in the moment near the end of the novel when, in the Guermantes' library, Marcel is discovering his vocation (one he will fulfil in the silence of nightly vigil). It rings here with its old threatening sound, but it also rings with a significance implied not by Swann's arrival but by his departure. As the bell does not signify just one thing, but two or more, there is virtually no end to the various adjectives that can be attributed to its sound. The ringing (or the ambivalence which is contained by Swann's arrival and departure) is partly what makes the recovery of the years and the writing of the novel both possible and necessary. As Marcel explains:

This notion of Time embodied, of years past but not separated from us, it was now my intention to emphasise as strongly as possible in my work. And at this very moment, in the house of the Prince de Guermantes, as though to strengthen me in my resolve, the noise of my parents' footsteps as they accompanied M. Swann to the door and the peal – resilient, ferruginous, interminable, fresh and shrill – of the bell on the garden gate which informed me that at last he had gone and that Mamma would presently come upstairs, these sounds rang again in my ears, yes, unmistakably I heard these very sounds, situated though they were in a remote past. (III, 1105; III, 1046)

Across the pages written and read – across the life which has been lived – the bell rings. It tells of a time and a love which were not; but which, as long as the pages are in the process of being written and read, is nevertheless suggesting itself as original and determining.

This is not all the bell tells. For the fact that it announces Charles Swann is not insignificant. Making itself felt in Combray is the 'way' that Swann represents, which is to become one of the central alternatives of Marcel's life. Full of oppositions, irreconcilabilities and antinomies as this life is, no opposition cuts more deeply into it than that between the two ways, the 'côté de chez Swann' and the 'côté des Guermantes'. Swann poses an original threat to Marcel in Combray, but he is an originator in other ways too. He is both instigator and teacher, 'the unwitting author of my sufferings' (I, 46; I, 43). His love antedates and adumbrates that of Marcel for his mother, and subsequently for Albertine. As Marcel will realise late in life, Swann's way has, in an important sense, been the way of his life, and will be the way of his book ('the raw material of my experience, which would also be the raw material of my book, came to me from Swann' (III, 953; III, 915)). It comes as a great surprise to Marcel to find that this way is not exclusive of the Guermantes' way. It will surprise the reader much less than it does Marcel. For *A la recherche* teaches that wherever one might expect stability or simplicity, one finds conflict and ambivalence. The experience of the novel could even be described as the learning that the two 'ways' are not exclusive – that the principle of alternatives ever dissolves into that of alternation (or as Marcel puts it: 'Extremes, however, meet' (III, 327; III, 322)). It takes Marcel a lifetime to see this, and it takes the reader what may feel like a lifetime to read *A la recherche*. But only in the reading will the diverse and the antinomic – the life with its multiple 'lives' and 'deaths', the novel with its volumes and books – become changed to the point where they are all part of the same life and novel, the point where the 'I' which is writing (and will write) asserts a provisional continuity over the fragments and forgettings of the 'I' which is written.[13]

It is out of the experience of loss in Combray that the possibilities which Combray holds are able to emerge. In § 5.2 I indicated how out of the trials of jealousy comes the 'research' of detection, and along with it the abundance of words which this generates. In a similar way, here, it is out of the disappointment of his experience with his mother that Marcel's need emerges to move on from this disappointment – and to return to it at the last. Marcel's ability to build on his unhappiness is what marks him off from the 'young girl' of the 'Confession', and from the perilous excess of her oscillation between selflessness and selfishness. Marcel's love for his 'maman' is in the beginning – like most paradises which can be dreamt – but is not itself the beginning. As it is not the beginning, it is not the end either. Swann's bell, and Swann's way, come before and after. Swann and the way he represents are like a fruit on the tree of knowledge which grows from the flaw in the moment of bliss. In old age Marcel will gather this fruit in silence, and then turn it into words. However, his words are not the only fruit which grow on this tree.

When Marcel finds himself alone with his mother he cannot contain his grief. What does his mother choose to console him? She chooses the act of reading, and a book which was to have been his grandmother's gift: George Sand's *François le Champi*. One's early reading (or listening) experiences may be heavily risk-laden (as was implied above, § 3.6). They are also likely to be most nearly complete. *François le Champi* is the first novel Marcel encounters, and so every character and incident seems unique. He drifts off for pages at a time. His mother skips the passages on love. Yet Marcel is enchanted nonetheless, and for one night his remorse is almost appeased. Here is how he describes the experience:

When she read aloud the prose of George Sand . . . She found, to tackle them [the sentences] in the required tone, the warmth of feeling which pre-existed and dictated them, but which is not to be found in the words themselves and by this means she smoothed away, as she read, any harshness or discordance in the tenses of verbs, endowing the imperfect and the preterite with all the sweetness to be found in generosity, all the melancholy to be found in love, guiding the sentence that was drawing to a close towards the one that was about to begin, now hastening, now slackening the pace of the syllables so as to bring them, despite their differences of quantity, into a uniform rhythm, and breathing into this quite ordinary prose a kind of emotional life and continuity. (I, 45–6; I, 42–3)

There are other explanations for the excitement the reading engenders and the appeasement it brings than the reason Marcel offers (which resides in the wonder of the name 'Champi'). In his book *Proust et le monde sensible*, Jean-Pierre Richard shows that the mouth plays a role in *A la recherche* as mediator between inner and outer, and that food commutes across that divide (a 'gelée', for example, can function almost like a book). One thing Richard does not bring out fully, however, is the richness of this most important instance of oral sensuality, which can only reverberate all the more strongly when one recalls the delight Marcel derives from having his name pronounced by Gilberte – 'having been held for a moment in her mouth, myself, naked, without any of the social attributes which belonged equally to her other playmates' (I, 437; I, 403–4).

The mother's mouth, here in Combray in a curious reversal of the role of the mouth as instrument of feeding, becomes a source of nourishment to young Marcel. In what is a dramatic reversal of the horror experienced by Louis Wolfson (above, § 3.5) in relation to his mother and his native tongue, Marcel discovers a new peace and joy in his own language. Psychoanalyst Roland Gori (who has the case of Wolfson in mind) speaks of such a discovery in the following terms: 'To understand the mother tongue is to devour it, it is to take it into oneself, to incorporate it as an object that is *metaphoric* of other objects of Desire' (Gori, 1974, p. 303). Mother tongue and mother's tongue: in his mother's mouth and in the perfect confluence of voice and story, Marcel finds a new *identity* – one made of language and narrative. Through basking in his mother's voice, and through absorbing the story as a sort of 'metaphoric object', Marcel is perhaps introduced to the possibility of the 'metaphoric object' (or fiction) on which he will ultimately stake his life's ambition. This experience of appeasement in language is perhaps even more powerful and original than that of love, the inadequacy of which the story was designed to appease. This might explain the force Julia Kristeva gives to her assertions that: 'When the object that I incorporate is the spoken word of the other – precisely a non-object, a schema, a model – I bind myself to the other in a first fusion, communion, unification. Identification' (Kristeva, 1983, p. 31).

Marcel's joy at the 'incorporation' of his mother which her reading allows is so strong that he will never lose it. As he sits in the Guermantes' library at the end of the novel, his faith in literature seriously undermined by his recent reading of the Goncourts' *Journals*, Marcel notices a book and opens it: *François le Champi* once again. He now recognises that the book is in no way remarkable, yet he finds the child within himself revived by it nonetheless. The book has retained all the charm of 'the night that was perhaps the sweetest and the saddest of my life', in which 'my mother had read aloud to me at Combray until the early hours of the morning' (III, 920, 922; III, 884, 886). With the memory, the wonder of literature, 'that world of mystery', floods back in, along with a new confidence in his ability not just to read it (or have it read) but to write it as well (III, 919; III, 883).[14] As Marcel's desire hardens into vocation, and as the novel draws to a close, we are returned to Combray, to Marcel's mother, and to the mother tongue, of whose power to enrapture the words before us are the sovereign instance, as they reach backwards and forwards in time. We are perhaps made to think of the conditions of Marcel's early listening experience. For to have got to where we are (the end of the novel) we will have had to accept, like Marcel, that there are whole pages we read while half-asleep, that we skip passages, and that nothing we have experienced has prepared us for this novel which is in so many ways unique. Most of all, we will have had to accept that to read we must submit ourselves to the intoxicating tone and rhythm of another's voice, and the way it models, shapes, caresses and distorts its mother tongue.

The fact that Marcel's mother is prompted by his tears to read to him is therefore crucial, in the way it opens the possibility of an 'identification' with language and narrative. At this stage in my argument I do not, however, have the confidence of Kristeva to assert that this 'identification' is truly 'first' or original.[15] There is a prior exploration of the power of the written word which is in its own way a 'first' – the note Marcel sends to his mother to call her away from Charles Swann and to his bedside. This exploration has its own ramifications in Marcel's later eagerness to get into print,

and in the delight he experiences when at last *Le Figaro* publishes
his little monograph. Gilles Deleuze suggests that in *A la recherche*,
'repetition itself is always joyous', and Leo Bersani agrees, saying
that 'repetition in the *Recherche* is thus a mode of freedom'
(Deleuze, 1973, p. 72; Bersani, 1980, p. 30). If I have shied away
from such bold statements, there is one case where I can fully agree
with these critics, and it relates to Marcel's note. It is a case which
reveals the heart that drives the literary musculature, of which the
note is the first flexing. I need only recall that 'daily bread, a
nourishing food that had the almost sacred character of all flesh'
(III, 2; III, 10) on which Marcel has loved to feed, and which
consists of Albertine's tongue which daily she has slid into his
mouth, to feel the force of Marcel's joy at getting into print – a joy
he accounts for thus:

Then I considered the spiritual bread of life that a newspaper is, still warm and
damp from the press in the murky air of the morning in which it is distributed, at
daybreak, to the housemaids who bring it to their masters with their morning
coffee, a miraculous, self-multiplying bread which is at the same time one and ten
thousand, which remains the same for each person while penetrating innumerably
into every house at once.   (III, 579; III, 568)

Such an innocent, yet polymorphous and promiscuous repetition
is surely joy indeed!

If the note is a 'first', however, then even before Marcel has sent
it, he has encountered Golo, the magic-lantern Knight who makes
his way across curtain and door alike, confusing surface and
substance in a 'transvertebration' which delights and perturbs (I,
10; I, 10). Perhaps Golo is an origin of sorts, a first demonstration
of the power of representations, and their ability to lead into the
magical and disturbing world in which (as with the carafes Marcel
later sees in his cherished river, the Vivonne) container and
contained, inner and outer, are confused and reversed. Or perhaps,
in the end, Golo is not a 'first' either. Perhaps there is only one
'first' of which one can be truly sure – that in the beginning there
are the words – 'For a long time I used to go to bed early'
['Longtemps, je me suis couché de bonne heure'].

Sleep, or the moment of awakening from sleep, may be what
offers the original bliss. This is a moment when place and time
seem to wander, and when Marcel realises himself effortlessly as
what he will later call 'that ageless creature who has the faculty of
becoming many years younger in a few seconds' (III, 627; III,

613–14). The rest of the novel is perhaps an exploration and amplification of the possibility which is there from the start: there not for Marcel alone, but for the reader too, as in the opening pages we encounter Marcel young and old, Combray, Tansonville, Balbec and Doncières – were we but able to grasp their reality. These places are nothing more than names to us, nor are we able to comprehend the years of Marcel's life; and so we read on, and learn of suffering and loss, of an impossible love and the repeated attempts to render it possible. It is only much later, by the time that we are, with Marcel, in the Guermantes' library, that we are ready to accept that in the beginning the elements were there which offer a way out of loss and isolation. For only then do we see that in the beginning there are not just the places and people, but the crucial *relation* too – which is one of merging and gentle parturition – which contains a way out of intractable ambivalence and interminable repetition. This is a way out which is also a way in – into the novel.

I have already suggested (above, § 4.1) that there is a good deal of fear attached to opening *A la recherche*. This fear may dictate that the reader should expect a difficult or traumatic birth to this enormous novel. I have also hinted (above, § 4.6) that what one finds is quite the opposite. As Marcel sits in the Guermantes' library he realises that, in another reversal of the kind which brought him such pleasure from his mother's mouth, he will have to give birth and become a mother of sorts (like the idol of his youth, Bergotte, whose 'reproductive instinct' led him to 'the vegetative life of a convalescent, of a woman after childbirth' (II, 339–40; II, 328)).[16] If this will be a supreme act of will and sacrifice, it will also be as easy as falling asleep or awakening. The book Marcel will write will be a spoiled child, one which he will cherish and be allowed to 'cosset' ['suralimenter'] (III, 1089; III, 1032). He will love this child with the sort of love which he dreamed of when a child:

> What I had dreamed of, as a child, as being the sweetest thing in love, what had seemed to me to be the very essence of love, was to pour out freely, to the one I loved, my tenderness, my gratitude for her kindness, my longing for an everlasting life together. (III, 350; III, 344)

As a child and later as an adult, with his mother and with Albertine, Marcel has to learn the impossibility of this 'everlasting life together'. He has to accept the reality of ambivalence, the power of repetition, and the stark fact of the 'intermittences of the heart'. But who is to say if, in the book he sets off to write, Marcel does not find what he has been looking for? Rationality may decree that it could not be so. But rationality is blessedly limited, as the opening of *A la recherche* recalls. Perhaps, in the end, it is less than surprising that the writer of whom something *is* known – Marcel Proust – who, as far as is known, had no children, was reluctant to let go of *A la recherche*. Perhaps it is unsurprising that he chose to spend his life with his novel, and to die with his work and his life – his life-work – still coming into being in his hands.

Conclusion

IN a recent book entitled *Rencontre avec Samuel Beckett*, the poet and critic Charles Juliet gives an account of four meetings he had with Beckett between 1968 and 1977. During these meetings Beckett talks, among other things, of how he spends his time when at his country house near Paris. Juliet writes that: 'what he prefers is doing nothing. Staying for hours just looking out of the window. What he likes above all is silence' (p. 46). Immediately after noting what Beckett particularly likes, however, Juliet records that Beckett qualifies his statement by talking of the sound beetroot carts make when they pass by on the road. Silence is no sooner invoked than it is broken. Beckett has already explained (p. 31) that it is one of the facts of growing old, that hearing takes precedence over sight. If any single impression emerges from the meetings, and from Juliet's book, it is that of the intense silence of Beckett as he sits in the classic listener's posture: legs crossed, back stooped, the gaze averted. It is when he is faced with this intense silence that Juliet uncovers the depth of his admiration for Beckett the writer, and also a way of expressing this feeling to him. Beckett's silence is precisely that of a highly acute listener. It is a silence which exists as if in order to make heard that which would otherwise be inaudible. In conclusion to the second meeting, Juliet asks: 'But when nothing is happening, what do you do?' Beckett replies: 'There is always listening to be done' (p. 35).

The quality of that listening (what in French is more conveniently and accurately called the *écoute*) permeates all Beckett's major work. It hangs behind his words and gives them their resonance. And it finds expression in Beckett's 'characters', so many of whom are listeners: in Krapp, who is bent over his tape recorder, in the Unnamable, who listens to 'the words it behoved to say', and in the 'one' of *Company*, who listens to the voice in the dark. All three – and their author as well – listen to words which emerge, as if of their own accord, as a search for and a denial of silence. The tone of Beckett's voice is the tone of his ear as well, of his *écoute* – his silence. When Maurice Blanchot tries to establish what the idea of tone refers to in a great writer, it is the force of the writer's silence that he chooses to underline. He writes that tone refers 'precisely to the silence, the energetic power through which the writer who has renounced himself has achieved in this self-effacement the authority of a choice'. A writer's tone is thus, for Blanchot, 'the individuality of a silence he imposes on speech so that this silence is *his*' (Blanchot, 1982, p. 103).

When Beckett is quiet, he is also listening: to the quiet and to the impossibility of quiet. What Beckett's texts make audible is the way beetroot carts — and the like — *will* make themselves heard, the way 'there is always listening to be done'. Beckett makes his reader listen quietly: makes his reader quiet-to-listen; and he does so in order that the reader may hear the cart, hear the feet, and hear the words (as the voice has it in *Footfalls*) 'however faint they fall'. To the quality of Beckett's silence corresponds both the intensity of Krapp's need to listen to his tapes, and the intensity of his final wordlessness. To the double intensity responds the rapturous attention of the reader or viewer.

This correspondence explains a little the delight which Kafka took in reading aloud to an audience. From the depths of his own private attention to language was drawn the will to command an equivalent, public attention. Beckett is not alone in having drawn his tone from his silence. Most of the writers who have been considered here have been considered partly because they have been able to turn their capacity to listen into words which render audible their silence. Kafka's work is unimaginable without the long nights of vigil from which it issued. The quiet of the nightly haven is what is resolutely denied to his various characters who are perpetually harrassed by the noise of the day, of their suffering, and of their obsessive desires. It is only when such noise recedes that some peace is to be found, and that the summons to the act of writing is to be heard. This is what Marcel indicates at the end of Proust's novel, when he listens to the bell into the garden, whose ringing is calling him to his vocation. This is a vocation which he too (like Kafka) will fulfil in long nightly vigil, by descending into that most private part of himself where the bell into the garden is still ringing. Proust himself chose to write most of his work at night, and he is famed for his hermetic withdrawal from the world. He had his room lined with cork — in order to keep out the noise, no doubt. But perhaps the cork should also be understood as designed to keep his own silence in — the silence of the writer's attention to the bell into the garden and to the voice which calls ever more stridently from within him.

However, if the bell sounds within Marcel as a call to his vocation, it also sounds as an entry into the 'way' represented by Charles Swann. It reminds Marcel of his ambition, but also of how the world has constantly interfered with it. In the moment of attention which gives birth to writing, the distinction between private desire and public interference or corroboration is not as clear a one as my mention of Marcel or of Kafka's satisfaction at reading may have suggested. When Kafka reads his stories aloud he tries to cross the space between his voice and the attention of his audience. But when he sits alone at night, giving his attention to the words he has to write, he is already his own audience, already listening to himself as if he were another. In his diary the day after 'The Judgement' sprang forth, he writes: 'I, only I, am the spectator in the orchestra' (p. 213). If Kafka's essential and inimitable tone is to be traced to his silence and his listening (or *écoute*), then his words belong less to him than to some ill-defined 'other' that lives within him. Kafka has perhaps to share the experience of Krapp listening to his old repellent self, of the Unnamable listening to 'another's words', of the 'one' of *Company* listening to a voice which is not his own, or of Marcel in *A la recherche* hearing the bell which ushers in Swann, who is 'the unwitting author of my sufferings'. Writing, I have repeatedly suggested, comes to life vicariously. This vicariousness starts not at the point where the writing is yielded to a more or less responsive reader. It starts with and within the writer, who gives private voice to public language, and turns noise into words which (in terms I have already borrowed from Paul Celan) are thus 'dressed in the style of [your] silence'.

According to Celan, prose is 'too noisy' a medium altogether, in an era when poetry shows 'a strong tendency towards silence'. In what is therefore one of his rare prose works (the speech entitled 'The Meridian', from which these words come), Celan articulates beautifully the essential otherness which a poet's silence renders audible, the way a poem 'holds its ground on its own margin'. He writes that a poem 'speaks only on its own, its very own behalf'. Then he adds – 'But I think – and this will hardly surprise you – that the poem has always hoped, for this very reason, to speak also on behalf of the *strange* – no, I can no longer use this word here – *on behalf of the other* – who knows, perhaps of an *altogether other*' (Celan, 1986, p. 48). For Celan, the writing of a poem is a meeting with this other. It is a meeting with an other which is also a meeting with a self – which leads him to conclude, of the writing of a poem, that 'I had . . . encountered myself' (p. 53). Language becomes voice, and the poem is born of what another poet in another era (John Donne) calls a 'dialogue of one'.

The process of 'encountering' which writing entails does not stop at this. For as I have tried to show, the writer's voice is constantly in search of completion in and through another – not an 'absolute other' this time, but a proximate other, which is the prospect held out by the voice of the writer's audience. The writer's silence requires that writing be etched on the silence of the attentive reader. A poem, for Celan, 'intends another, needs this other, needs an opposite. It goes toward it, bespeaks it' (p. 49). Writing is always *towards*, or as Celan says, *en route*. It is towards a reader whose self-effacement is required quite as much as is that of the writer, if the 'dialogue of one' is to be repeated, and so become a sort of 'dialogue of two'. The writer's silence must solicit and command that of the reader. It must allow the reader to encounter his or her own 'absolute other', and it must do this through the proximate other of the writer's words. The present tense of the reader's utterance repeats the writer's encounter in a way that gives voice not only to the present, but to what the reader has been in the past and may yet be in the future (all that the reader 'will have been'). Only then is writing able, in Celan's words, to offer 'natural paths, outlines for existence perhaps, for projecting ourselves into the search for ourselves' (p. 53). Only then, Celan adds, does writing offer the chance of what he tentatively calls 'A kind of homecoming' (p. 53).

Such a homecoming, if it is the journey offered by writing, is not unlike the form of return offered by psychoanalysis. The poem, for Celan, if it is to permit such a 'homecoming', must discover 'reality' – reality which 'is not simply there', but 'must be searched and won' (p. 16). The 'reality', or 'truth', of psychoanalysis is no more generalisable or predictable than is that of poetry. But if the path that leads towards it can be indicated in any measure by a single term, then that term is: desire. Like the reality of poetry, such desire is traceable only in and through an encounter with an 'altogether other' (which, in the context of psychoanalysis, is partly what is meant by the unconscious). This is an encounter which psychoanalysis tries to render possible by contact with a more proximate other which is not the reader this time but the analyst. Like the poet in Celan's formulation, the analytic patient is 'racked by reality and in search of it'. Like the poet, whose search for reality is always made in company not only with his or her own silence but with the silence of the reader, the analytic patient's search for the reality of the desire by which he or she is racked is also made in company with silence – the silence of the other who is the analyst.

In one of the most quoted of his maxims, Lacan says that 'the unconscious is the discourse of the Other' (Lacan, 1966, p. 549). A full elucidation of this statement might involve chapters of commentary. But without further elaboration, it can be gleaned here that one thing this implies is that the unconscious (or unconscious desire) which psychoanalysis seeks to articulate is yielded to the patient in part at least by the discourse that is held by the other that is the analyst. This implies that the patient will discover, or 'encounter', his or her unconscious desire in the interpretations of the analyst. It also implies something that is more interesting and perhaps more surprising: that the patient's unconscious desire will be encountered in what is the predominant discourse of the analyst, which is invariably what might be called the 'discourse of silence'. The central fact of psychoanalysis – from the analyst's side at least – is the fact of this silence (quite as much as it is a critical factor in the tone of the writers to whom I have been attending). Not just any silence, but a silence which is alive with attention and *écoute*. For Lacan, the Other is thus, precisely, 'the place from which the question of his existence can be posed to him [the subject]' (Lacan, 1966, p. 549). The analyst no doubt often keeps quiet simply because he or she cannot think what to say. However, the analyst also keeps quiet in order to try to make audible that which is otherwise hushed under the noise and interference of the patient's resistance and repressions.

The tone of any given analysis is of course set by the tone of the analyst's interpretations (which are as variable as are the patient's words). It is also set, and crucially, by the tone of the analyst's silence, which perhaps serves even more than words to body forth his or her *own* desire. As Lacan insists, psychoanalysis is a practice where what is vitally in play is unconscious desire. As Lacan also insists, this desire is never that of the patient alone, but of patient and analyst both. The analyst's desire is given substance, or embodied, in his or her words, but also in the silence of listening, through which the patient is called upon to speak. For as long as the patient is speaking, the analyst's silence may be seen as required and even commanded by the patient. While the patient is speaking, the analyst's silent attention is the necessary other (or unconscious) which the patient is 'racked' by and 'in search of' – towards which the patient's words can be said to be 'en route'. The patient's words thus form a sort of ceaseless commentary on the silence of the analyst. The psychoanalytic patient is encouraged to encounter his or her desire in the words which give voice to the 'absolute other' of his or her unconscious, when this unconscious is 'dressed in the style' of the analyst's silence.

I have repeatedly suggested that the patient is in search of an 'I' with which to name him- or herself, and so begin to tell his or her own unique story for the first time. What I have implied, and should now emphasise, is that the patient carries out this search by way of the detour of the pronoun 'you'. The power of the transference, like the power of any love story, is rooted in the conjugating of these *two* pronouns: 'you' and 'I'. The 'you' which the patient utters in analysis will refer to the analyst, of course, and to all that the patient has been able to surmise about the figure in the chair. It will also, crucially, refer to, and establish its life in, the analyst's silence. 'You' is the name which can be attributed to this silence: to all the analyst cannot know or cannot declare, but which the patient can *suppose* the analyst to know and desire. It is a pronoun which renders silence audible, and opens a space for a reciprocal 'I' to take root and grow.

If there is a 'truth' of psychoanalysis, I have suggested, it is ultimately an unconscious truth. This means, of course, that such truth, while it can be sought, cannot rightly be 'discovered', in the way that treasure chests or gold nuggets are discovered. It cannot be known, retained, and then recycled. It can only be uttered, only encountered. It is less heard than overheard. For it is heard over the noise created not only by the patient's resistance, but also by the analyst's need to understand and interpret (which together contribute to the analyst's own form of resistance). It is encountered, like the 'reality' which Celan says all poems are in search of, on a path which leads 'from a voice to a listening You', when this path is at the same time a 'detour from you to you' (Celan, 1986, p. 53). Such an encounter is a return which may indeed offer the patient of psychoanalysis – and perhaps the analyst too – some sort of 'homecoming'. And if it offers a homecoming, it in this way offers a beginning. For as T. S. Eliot points out (in 'East Coker' v), 'Home is where one starts from.'

When as a reader one comes across the rare literary work that matters, it may also feel as if one has reached some kind of home, or new beginning. And a beginning is perhaps not a bad place at which to find oneself, for in a beginning there is the prospect of an ending. If one is not only a reader, but a scholar or critic as well, one may try to move forward, and furnish the home with knowledge and understanding: fill in the background, read the biographies, and elaborate theories. But when one returns to the work, its silence quickly drowns out most of the noise created by the urge to understand, and returns one to the quiet attention which is required for reading to start. In the significant silence one is perhaps always a beginner. One is less an impersonal or impartial intelligence than an intensely personal and vulnerable voice. One is less 'one', therefore, than 'I' – who am searching for a 'you', whose words are searching for me in turn. Every time I utter the words of the work that matters, the truth or reality I find is indeed one for which I have been searching. It is also one which I could never have anticipated and for which I am never prepared. I seem to stumble upon such truth with the surprise and wonder that are mine, for example, when walking on a beach I find a bottle with a message in it. For Paul Celan, a poem was always 'a letter in a bottle thrown out to sea with the – surely not always strong – hope that it may somehow wash up somewhere, perhaps on a shoreline of the heart' (p. 35). A writer begins to write (as a psychoanalytic patient speaks) in the hope that he or she may get to the finish – a finish which comes into sight when his or her words have begun to be *overheard*. Writing is always 'towards': towards an end, of course; but also towards a 'you' on a shore at the other side of a choppy sea, to whom all bottles – including this my own – are silently addressed.

Notes

INTRODUCTION

1 Two other recent works might have served almost equally well as examples of the blurring of the borders between psychoanalysis and fiction: Judith Rossner's *August* and Marie Cardinal's *The Words to Say It*. The first is a novel in which the major drama is offered by the psychoanalytic sessions in which a young woman is involved. The second is a 'fictional autobiography' which tells of a woman's recovery from the brink of madness.

For a general survey of the way psychoanalysis and psychoanalysts have been dealt with in literature, see Jeffrey Berman's *The Talking Cure: Literary Representations of Psychoanalysis*.

2 The influence of Lacan's work has not ceased to grow since his death, and the influence is now being felt abroad, particularly in Latin America. The effects of this influence on the various analytic institutions have been complex and varied, and the French psychoanalytic world finds itself extremely divided. (Readers interested in the recent history of French psychoanalysis can refer to Elisabeth Roudinesco's *Histoire de la psychanalyse en France*, vol. 2.) As for the legacy of Lacan the thinker and theoretician, which may be of more interest here, at least four by no means discrete ways exist in which Lacan's work is being developed and extended. As I do not believe all are equally fruitful (especially for the English speaker), it may be worthwhile trying to characterise them.

The extension into clinical practice has been mentioned. This extension is also a return to the source of Lacan's work. For Lacan was a major clinician and psychiatrist; only, he covered his clinical tracks so well that, except in his doctoral thesis, one hunts largely in vain for evidence of this in his work. A second way is offered by works of an introductory nature which may also modestly seek to relate Lacan to psychoanalytic or other traditions. This is an avenue which, with books such as Juliet Mitchell and Jacqueline Rose's *Feminine Sexuality*, Malcolm Bowie's *Freud, Proust and Lacan* or Bice Benvenuto and Roger Kennedy's *The Works of Jacques Lacan: An Introduction*, is currently being fruitfully pursued (in Britain as in France). A third avenue opens towards a synthesis of his work. The main problem with such global or totalising surveys is, I think, that they are mis-timed. They are simply premature, when of Lacan's twenty-five-or-so years of seminars, only six are currently available, even in French (the unpublished seminars are available in typescript, but there are serious problems in scholarly study of these). For the seminars are undoubtedly Lacan's major statements; and what the depressed reader of *Ecrits* should know is that the seminars are also the invaluable key to the formidably difficult, gnomic essays. A fourth avenue may be thought of as a strictly conceptual development: an extension of the concepts of Lacan, to increase their range or their depth. This also strikes me as problematic. For Lacan was the sort of thinker who took his own concepts to their breaking point, through constantly changing and honing them. Further developments – and they have tended to concentrate on Lacan's later, more mathematical work – can often look like mere imitations, or, worse, caricatures.

I. FATHERS AND SONS

1 Further on the subject of letters in Kafka's life and work, see Gilles Deleuze and Félix Guattari: *Kafka: pour une littérature mineure*, esp. ch. 4, sect. 1.

2 Speaking of Sigmund Freud's letters to Wilhelm Fliess, Masud Khan draws a picture which I believe holds perfectly for Kafka's letters to Felice. He writes: 'These years of acute stress [1887–1902], anguish, anxiety, distress, discouragement, and exultation of unmatchable discoveries were sustained for Freud by his relation to Fliess. This was a relationship sustained largely by correspondence, nourished sentiently by occasional meetings, which Freud christened their 'congresses'. Freud practised in Vienna and Fliess in Berlin. And it was just as well, because one wonders whether that friendship could have sustained the further strain of too intimate and frequent a relationship. Perhaps one attribute of genius is that it knows how to respect its limits of temperament and sensibility' (Khan, 1974, p. 107).

3 One should not doubt how highly Kafka rated the importance of paternity. In the *Letter to his Father*, he says that 'the utmost a human being can succeed in doing at all [is] marrying, founding a family, accepting all the children that come, supporting them in an insecure world' (In *Wedding Preparations in the Country*, p. 65).

4 See Kafka's diary entry for 14 Aug. 1913: 'Coitus as punishment for the happiness of being together. Live as ascetically as possible, more ascetically than a bachelor, that is the only possible way for me to endure marriage. But she?' (p. 228).

5 In a letter to Felice (p. 195), Kafka writes thus of public delivery: 'Nothing, you know, gives the body greater satisfaction than ordering people about, or at least believing in one's ability to do so. As a child – which I was until a few years ago – I used to enjoy dreaming of reading aloud to a large, crowded hall (though equipped with somewhat greater strength of heart, voice, and intellect than I had at the time) the whole of *Education sentimentale* at one sitting, for as many days and nights as it required, in French of course (oh dear, my accent!), and making the walls reverberate. Whenever I have given a talk, and talking is even better than reading aloud (it's happened rarely enough), I have felt this elation, and this evening was no exception.'

6 In his book, *A Remembered Future*, Harold Fisch talks in very similar terms of Kafka. His whole chapter entitled 'The Binding of Isaac' is of intense relevance, as in it he tries to show how father–son rivalry is an archetype or myth central to literature, and central particularly in the late nineteenth and early twentieth centuries. In discussing the importance of written testimonies for those who suffered and died in Auschwitz, he affirms that 'the written word transcends the seemingly terminal event; it breaks the seemingly completed cycle of death and sacrifice' (p. 93).

Of *Metamorphosis* and 'The Judgement' he goes on to say: 'Kafka perceived more clearly than anyone that the very penning of the record was his way out of the trap, out of the closed circle of the myth itself. He looked upon his writings as a "long-drawn out leave-taking" – a release from his father . . . Seizing the myth of the father who sacrifices his son in his hands, Kafka grotesquely dangles it before us. In so doing he makes his gesture of freedom: he tells his tale. He survives the syndrome, bearing the missive in his hand relating his trial and sacrifice' (p. 94).

7 Quite as much as Samuel Beckett, Kafka has incited critics to make him into the representative of a world view, be it the Decline of the West, the Dehumanisation of the Bureaucratic State, Judaism, Alienation, the Twentieth Century, or whatever.

It would be an interesting topic for study, why these two writers have provoked such an immense volume of lamentable, reductive criticism, where on the other hand Marcel Proust has brought out the very best in a great number of critics.

8 Such a view of the structure of comedy is upheld by Northrop Frye in 'The Mythos of Spring: Comedy' in *Anatomy of Criticism*, and in *A Natural Perspective*.

9 It is partly in response to this oversight that the part of Jocasta has recently been examined by Christiane Olivier, in her highly readable *Les Enfants de Jocaste*. And it is partly because of such a real oversight – or obfuscation – that Jeffrey Masson was able, though shadow-boxing, to create such a scandal and provoke such outrage with his book *Freud: The Assault on Truth*. (An account of the whole 'Masson affair' is to be found in Janet Malcolm's *In The Freud Archives*.)

10 On the subject of movement in *The Divine Comedy*, see John Freccero, 'Dante's Pilgrim in a Gyre', and Gabriel Josipovici, *Writing and the Body*, pp. 96–9.

11 Kafka's sister Ottla died in Auschwitz and his two other sisters died in other German concentration camps (as did his mistress Milena Jesenská).

2. DIFFICULT BIRTHS

1 In one of the few books devoted to the study of ambivalence, J. Boutonier's *La Notion d'ambivalence*, a similar emphasis is repeatedly placed on ambivalence's 'contradictions which are logically and sometimes ethically inadmissible'. The contradictions are such, Boutonier claims, that 'it is impossible for ambivalence to establish itself in the full light of consciousness; it only reaches it rationalised, justified, having lost its true identity' (p. 59).

2 Within the world of fiction, where one's expectations may be formally rather different, yet are dynamically very similar, there is no shortage of 'good stories' which go far towards satisfying such yearnings. It is in such terms that Leo Bersani describes Baudelaire's 'Tableaux parisiens', in a chapter of his book *Baudelaire and Freud*, with the slight difference that here the reader's yearnings find representation in Baudelaire's own 'ontological hunger'. Bersani writes: 'In the avid narcissistic appropriation of the other, we have a false prostitution of the self. The poet's availability to scenes from the external world is enacted as a process of partly willed, partly rejected self-recognition or self-identification' (p. 110). The task of many of the writers under consideration here might in fact be viewed as the carrying and frustrating of narcissistic readerly yearning.

3 In one of the best discussions of narcissism, 'Le moi et le narcissisme', Jean Laplanche says that narcissism is 'one of the most deceptive of notions' (Laplanche, 1970, p. 110).

4 As the notion of *jouissance* is central to the argument both of Leclaire and later of Roland Barthes, and as it does not strictly have an English equivalent, I shall often indicate the French term. The word commonly contains the notions of enjoyment, of possession, of bliss and of orgasm. *Jouissance* is distinguished from the idea of *plaisir*, which is seen as being a form of pleasure more constant, stable, seizable, and reassuring.

5 Lacan's essay is translated as 'The Meaning of the Phallus' by Jacqueline Rose in Mitchell and Rose (eds.), *Feminine Sexuality*. In addition to Lacan's essay, there are several useful short discussions of the phallus to be found in English: for example in Sherry Turkle's *Psychoanalytic Politics*, p. 56; in Anthony Wilden's 'Lacan and the Discourse of the Other', in *The Language of the Self*, pp. 187–8; in Martin Stanton's *Outside the Dream*, p. 35; and in Jane Gallop's *Reading Lacan*, ch. 6.

6 In an essay written in 1980, 'Le psychanalyste à l'envers', Leclaire describes the phallus as a 'Referent which has been publicly disavowed and theoretically ruined' (Leclaire, 1981, p. 10).

7 As one of Lacan's most famous maxims has it: 'no language can tell the truth about the truth, since the truth founds itself on the fact that it speaks and that it has no other means of doing so' (Lacan, 1966, pp. 867–8). Or as he puts it in his seminar on psychosis: 'If you understand, so much the better, keep it to yourself; what is important is not to understand, but to reach the truth' (Lacan, 1981, p. 59). What Lacan is suggesting, of course, is that the psychoanalyst can be master of knowledge, but not of truth. Speaking of this disjunction, in an essay of considerable relevance, analyst Patrick Guyomard comments: 'The analyst is not wedded to the truth. It is truth that does the catching.' Couching this fact in Lacanian terms, he adds that 'It is the formula for what is impossible in psychoanalytic discourse: it is impossible that knowledge should order truth. There is a disjunction between S1 (the repressed) and S2 (what the subject utters)' (Guyomard, 1985, p. 174).

8 The metaphor of 'contraband' is one previously used, to describe precisely the same phenomenon, by Catherine Clément in an article entitled 'Les nouvelles illusions perdues', which expresses a similar overall view to that of Pingaud.

9 The expression 'another scene' is borrowed from Freud, who used it (*anderer Schauplatz*) as one of his early descriptions of the unconscious, and in turn adapted the expression from Fechner.

10 In *Le Séminaire II* Lacan says with typical élan that 'We are of course all agreed that love is a form of suicide' (p. 172). It is no doubt significant in this context that 'Love' does not appear as a term in the 'Index raisonné des concepts majeurs' appended to the *Ecrits*.

11 I have used my own translation here as Richard Howard's seems flawed. The quotation comes from *Roland Barthes par Roland Barthes*, p. 144 (trans., p. 141).

12 In an essay entitled 'Un corps devenu récit' ('A Body Become Narrative'), Ivàn Almeida argues persuasively for such a view. He writes: 'And so the body is itself an unfinished fiction . . . it is true that the body is the source and the referent of all signs, but that it itself is not a sign as such since it is not in place of anything else. Yet in its own place it is nonetheless an endless fabric of

narration. In the beginning, if one may speak thus, there was perhaps narrative. Not the word, but a metaphoric narrative which set going the inexhaustible organisation of what one calls reality' (Almeida, 1983, pp. 16, 17).

13 On 13 December 1931 Freud wrote a letter to Ferenczi (published in Ernest Jones's *Sigmund Freud: Life and Work*, III, 174–6) in which he warned him: 'You have not made a secret of the fact that you kiss your patients and let them kiss you ... why stop at a kiss? ... bolder ones will come along who will go further to peeping and showing – and soon we shall have accepted in the technique of analysis the whole repertoire of demiviergerie and petting-parties.' For further discussion of Freud's quarrel and of Ferenczi's practice, see Ronald W. Clark's *Freud: The Man and the Cause*, pp. 457–60, and Vincent Brome's *Freud and his Early Circle*, ch. 14.

14 The force of this love and its relation to reality is usefully discussed in Octave Mannoni's article 'L'amour de transfert et le réel'.

15 Working with the *Standard Edition*, such an examination would in any case be limited, particularly if one accepts the force of the critiques that have been made of Strachey's translation, such as that by Bruno Bettelheim in his *Freud and Man's Soul*. Further warning on the dangers of Freud in translation and a detailed analysis of aspects of Freud's style are given in François Roustang's fine article, 'Du chapitre VII'. This includes a detailed bibliography of works on Freud's style.

16 In her essay 'Le discours médical pris au piège du récit', Françoise Gaillard shows this very convincingly. She demonstrates how medical accounts exploit principles of narrative; and, beyond this, how neurosis is an 'illness' which cuts against the conventions of illness (aetiology, diagnosis, prognosis and treatment) and so of traditional narrative. Neurosis is decentred and decentring, 'truly *the other of illness*'. It bears witness to – and may even be a product of – 'the bankruptcy of a certain conception of narrative reasoning'. To deal adequately with neurosis, therefore, Gaillard suggests that a new 'discursive ordering', a 'poetic discourse' must be forged (Gaillard, 1983, pp. 92, 93).

17 Similar implications may be drawn from Roy Schafer's article 'Narration in the Psychoanalytic Dialogue', in which he shows how the analytic procedure may amount for the analysand to the re-telling of a personal history under the aegis of a new narrative order. Such an order or style is not to be confused with mere technique, as Patrick Guyomard indicates clearly in his essay 'Le temps de l'acte: l'analyste entre la technique et le style'. Technique is something transmissible, a way of testing and experimenting with theory. Whereas 'what is aimed at by style' is nothing less than 'the subject' itself. Guyomard writes: 'The lesson of Lacan is that of style. The style of the analyst is what situates his technique as a necessary prop in his relation with the unconscious. A good technique without truth is possible, but there is no style without true speech ... An analyst must find his style and invent it' (Guyomard, 1985, p. 164).

18 Buffon's maxim is quoted as the opening of the *Ecrits*. Lacan's fondness for it is reported in Patrick Guyomard's entry on Lacan in the *Encyclopaedia Universalis* (Guyomard, 1984, p. 910).

19 François Roustang suggests something of this when he says, 'No doubt as

analysands or analysts we adopt Freud's style. But a style cannot be imitated, except in order to say nothing and do nothing' (Roustang, 1977, p. 95). Of relevance also is what Malcolm Bowie says of the shock caused by Lacan's style, which has to be understood in the context of 'The bland prosaicism of the international psychoanalytic journals' (Bowie, 1987, p. 145).

20 Since I shall be emphasising the divide between the two stanzas, it is worth noting that Celan's first verse finishes with a full stop, which Hamburger has preferred to change to a comma.

21 The original title is 'Unlesbarkeit dieser / Welt' (Celan, 1980, pp. 270, 271).

22 The poem is entitled 'Todesfuge', and the two quoted lines are 'Tod der Tod ist ein Meister aus Deutschland', 'Schwarze Milch der Frühe' (Celan, 1980, pp. 50–3). I borrow the term 'impossible possibility' from Philippe Lacoue-Labarthe, whose book *La Poésie comme expérience* consists of a series of valuable meditations on Celan.

23 The line about silence, 'Kristall in der Tracht deines Schweigens', is from the poem 'Below' – 'Unten' (Celan, 1980, pp. 94, 95). The line about the irises, 'ich verlor die Augensterne', is from 'Memory of France' – 'Erinnerung an Frankreich' (Celan, 1980, pp. 38, 39).

24 The title is '. . . Plashes the Fountain' – '. . . rauscht der Brunnen' (Celan, 1980, pp. 150, 151).

25 Lest the metaphor should therefore seem appropriative, let me call upon two women witnesses who share the conviction. Christiane Olivier writes that 'I carried this book within me like a child that society was preventing me from bringing into the light of day' (Olivier, 1980, p. 165). And Annie Anzieu, in her article 'Des mots et des femmes', puts it thus: 'Writing is a way of perpetuating oneself . . . something identical happens in a woman when she conceives and carries a child. Feminine writing replaces gestation for a woman, or continues it' (Anzieu, 1977, p. 167).

26 These words are taken from a contribution made by Lacan to a World Psychiatry Congress in 1950.

3. MOTHER TONGUES

1 Lack of space obliges me to assume that the reader has some familiarity with the Lacanian structuring of human reality into the Real, the Imaginary and the Symbolic. If this is not the case, however, helpful accounts are to be found in: Anthony Wilden's 'The Symbolic, the Imaginary and the Real'; Malcolm Bowie's chapter 'Lacan' (in Bowie, 1987); and Gary Handwerk's chapter 'The Irony of Double Vision: Lacan's Liquidation of the Subject' (in Handwerk, 1985).

Lacan's notion of the 'mirror stage' was first proposed in 1936, and finds its most famous statement in his paper 'Le stade du miroir comme formateur de la fonction du Je' ('The Mirror Stage as Formative of the Function of the I'). The notion was also developed in his seminars of 1954–5 (*Le Séminaire II*), and later in the (unpublished) seminars of 1960–1 (*Sur le transfert*).

2 Maud Mannoni makes this point very clearly in *Le Psychiatre, son 'fou' et la psychanalyse*, where she writes: 'Let us recall that the time when a structure is first put in place is tied by Lacan to the "mirror stage" . . . It is there that what

is shared out between the Imaginary and the Symbolic can be grasped. It is at this point that Lacan has an *I* surge forth from the Imaginary instance of the ego, and that he studies the relation maintained by this *I* with an image that is outside it. What belongs to the ego are Imaginary identifications. The *I* constitutes itself in relation to a truth of the Symbolic order; and Lacan shows how specular identification (absent in psychosis) only in fact takes place if a *word* [une *parole*] has offered to the subject the possibility of recognition of his image' (pp. 133–4).

3 The French original for this is even stronger. It runs 'Sans noms propres, pas de salut' (Beckett, 1953, pp. 84–5).

4 The one other occasion on which the name 'Marcel' is encountered also owes its origin to Albertine.

In referring to Proust, I shall give details first of the English edition (where available), and then of the 1954 Pléiade edition. Except where indicated, all references to Proust are to *Remembrance of Things Past* – *A la recherche*.

5 This is forcefully stated in George Craig's essay 'Marcel Proust: The "Petite Phrase" and the Sentence', in which it is written: 'the deepest and most enduring of the ways of construing the mass of words which is *A la recherche*: that somehow, and granted every possible qualification and reservation, it is *autobiography*' (Craig, 1981, p. 261).

6 This view of Celan's poetry is proposed by Martine Broda (Celan's principal translator into French) in an essay entitled 'La leçon de Mandelstam'. In this essay, using certain formulations of theoretical linguistics, Broda shows how the 'you' and the 'I' are utterly dependent upon one another; and how 'The search for the Interlocutor is therefore one of the strong channels of meaning in Celan's poems' (Broda, 1986, p. 34).

7 Olivier actually quotes statistical evidence (on pp. 77–8) from studies carried out on this, to show that girls are weaned significantly earlier than boys.

8 In an essay entitled 'The Concept of the Cumulative Trauma', Masud Khan suggests something very similar, if in different terms, when he writes that 'a mother should and indeed must fail the id, but never the ego of the infant' (Khan, 1974, p. 50).

9 In her early work, *Le Premier rendez-vous avec le psychanalyste*, Maud Mannoni states this conviction boldly: 'It is common to hear it said that to every problem-child there correspond problem-parents. It is indeed rare that one does not perceive behind a symptom a certain *family disorder*. Yet it is not certain that this family disorder has of itself a direct relation of cause and effect to the child's troubles.

What appears to be harmful for the subject is the *refusal* of the parents to see this disorder, and their effort in words to substitute for it an order which is no order at all.

It is not the confrontation of the child with a painful truth that is traumatic, so much as its confrontation with the 'lie' of the adult (that is to say with the adult's fantasy)' (pp. 121–2).

10 It is by just such mobility that Gary Handwerk characterises the Symbolic. He suggests that the Imaginary can be understood as 'a stagnation of the movement by which the Symbolic is characterized' (Handwerk, 1985, p. 146).

11 The investment which parents can have in their children's illness is vividly

displayed in Oliver Sacks's enthralling book *Awakenings*. Readers of this book will remember how his Parkinsonian patients, who have been suspended in catatonic states, often for decades, come alive again under the influence of the drug L-DOPA. The effect of this reawakening is usually traumatic for the patients' parents. The return from a state of total dependence to one of partial independence is often ferociously opposed by the parent whose life has been dedicated to the 'loving care' of the sufferer. Few pages make more poignant reading than those in which Leonard L. finds his sexuality rekindled, to the horror – if also titillation – of his aged mother: 'His mother – who, in a sense, was herself in love with her son, as he was with her – became indignant and "jealous" of Mr L.'s "new" thoughts: "It's ridiculous", she spluttered. "A grown man like him! He was so *nice minded* before – never spoke about sex, never looked at girls, never seemed to think about the matter at all . . . I have sacrificed my life for Ben: *I* am the one he should constantly think of; but now all he thinks of is those *girls!*"' (p. 185). The overlap between Sacks's and Maud Mannoni's work is only partial, however. For where Sacks's patients have been reduced to states of non-desire by an epidemic, an incontrovertibly physical ailment, Maud Mannoni's patients have often been consigned to that state by the very parents who are caring for them. The overlap is nonetheless illuminating in so far as it reveals the lineaments of ambivalence beneath the most self-sacrificial devotion.

12 Another of Françoise Dolto's cases quoted in the preface to *Le Premier rendez-vous avec le psychanalyste* illustrates this perfectly. Her child-patient says: 'Mummy's so unhappy with Daddy that I've really got to stay her baby so as to console her – her baby from the time when she and Daddy loved each other. And then she needs to devote herself so badly . . . I've really got to be ill, otherwise who would she stay home for? . . . and then that way it's me her almost-husband, it's me she loves, and I don't want anyone between Mummy and me' (p. 35).

13 A chronological list of Maud Mannoni's works is to be found in the 'List of Works Cited' at the back of this book.

14 Psychoanalyst and academic Pierre Fedida testifies to this in his intervention during Maud Mannoni's oral defence of her *thèse d'état*, when he says: 'What is the condition by which a theory becomes constituted for an analyst? With the ambivalences which match what this term provokes; ambivalences rather than ambiguities' (*Le Symptôme et le savoir*, p. 41). (This short book comprises Maud Mannoni's *soutenance*, or oral defence, of her thesis, in addition to various interventions from the examining jury.)

15 Lacan elaborates a similar notion of sacrifice of the analyst in his seminar of 1959–60, *Le Séminaire VII*, particularly in the final two sections.

16 Maud Mannoni concludes similarly in her commentary on her work in *Le Symptôme et le savoir*, saying: 'The normative order is confronted by the truth of desire. This question is that of analysis, but also that of creation' (p. 25).

17 In his paper 'The Mother Tongue and the Mother', Ralph Greenson tries to show how the need and ability to acquire a second language may be directly related to childhood fantasies of the mother (to the breast, to the action of

sucking, and to the role of speech as 'a means of retaining a connection with the mother as well as of becoming separated from her') (Greenson, 1950, p. 22).

18 It is with serious reservations that I translate Wolfson's words into English (in the notes, exceptionally, rather than in the body of the text). For it is hard not to see this translation as the negation of Wolfson's desire, a negation amounting almost to the sort of torture that his mother originally used to inflict upon him . . .

He writes that it is as if 'she had decided to hit her son simultaneously with the tongue of her mouth and with that of the English, almost every time she was able to'. In learning foreign languages, he writes, he is able 'to convert these words of his closest relative into foreign words and thus' – as he perhaps wanted subconsciously to do – 'in some way destroy them'.

19 It is worth adding that of these four writers, two – Beckett and Celan – rank among the great translators of the twentieth century. Proust was also a considerable translator from English (notably of Ruskin), and Kafka's choice to write in German rather than Czech is of some relevance here. Of the various studies on the choice of language made by these writers I wish to mention just a few: Deleuze and Guattari's 'Qu'est-ce qu'une littérature mineure?' in their *Kafka*, and Marthe Robert's *Franz Kafka's Loneliness*, esp. ch. 2; Didier Anzieu's 'Un soi disjoint, une voix liante: l'écriture narrative de Samuel Beckett', and Patrick Casement's 'Samuel Beckett's Relationship to his Mother-Tongue' (though neither of these essays on Beckett is very satisfactory, both relying too heavily on the authority of the Beckett biography); finally, on Celan, John Felstiner's 'Langue maternelle, langue éternelle'.

20 This suggestion is made by Octave Mannoni in his article 'L'amour de transfert et le réel' (O. Mannoni, 1982, p. 11).

21 Ernest Jones's famous book is entitled *Hamlet and Oedipus*. Also of note are Jean Starobinski's essay 'Hamlet et Oedipe', and Lacan's seminar of 1958–9, *Le Désir et son interprétation* (extracts of which are published in *Ornicar?* and translated by James Hulbert in *Literature and Psychoanalysis* (ed. Shoshana Felman)).

22 It should come as little surprise to find the 'potential space' being described by art critic Peter Fuller as coloured with ambivalence: 'Characterized by tentatively ambivalent feelings about mergence and separation, about being lost in the near, of establishing and denying boundaries, about what is inside and what is outside, and concerning the whereabouts of limits and a containing skin, so that the infant, while beginning to recognize the autonomy of objects, nonetheless feels "mixed up in them"' (Fuller, 1980, p. 164). If in fact, for Winnicott, hate as a properly differentiated affect develops fully at a rather later stage (when the infant is able to perceive a whole other person), the anxiety which belongs to the 'potential space' (anxiety over annihilation) is its prototype, as the ecstasy of union is the prototype of the child's more mature love. A discussion of hate is to be found in Winnicott's 'The Theory of the Parent–Infant Relationship' (Winnicott, 1965, e.g. p. 47).

23 Fuller's discussion of the artists Rothko and Robert Natkin are particularly useful: 'The Rise of Modernism' and 'Abstraction and "The Potential Space"' in *Art and Psychoanalysis*. His monograph on Robert Natkin, esp. chs. 1 and 7, is also of value, as is his more general essay entitled 'D. W. Winnicott'. It is only unfortunate that Fuller's impatience with Continental psychoanalysis blinds him to what could be a rich vein of insight, and one not always incompatible with his espousal of Winnicott's ideas.

24 Just how fine it is, Pascal Quignard's fascinating book *Le Lecteur* repeatedly shows. Of the thirteenth-century writer Claude de Moralles, Quignard writes: 'In the passion of reading he detected a mortal peril for the soul of the reader: reading was a kidnap of the soul. In the eyes of the Creator, this abduction was equal to total perdition, and even if it only lasted for as long as the reading, the flames of eternity could not cleanse this sin (this extraordinary, monstrous metamorphosis with respect to the statute of our condition), and could not regenerate what had died' (p. 29).

25 I borrow this expression from Serge Leclaire's book published in 1971, which is entitled *Démasquer le réel*.

26 George Craig shows this vividly in his essay entitled 'Reading: Who is Doing What to Whom?'. Craig explains: 'The decision to read is rather closer to any decision which puts the self at risk – a first dive, for example, or a musical solo – but, unlike these, it leads to no more direct involvement with the world, no externally sanctioned release. What is new, then, is that the apprentice reader has to decide to withdraw attention from the external world (including the book as object) *and* from his own internal world as a preliminary to an experience which is unpredictable and, in an important sense, unsharable. We can hardly be surprised that many gifted and sensitive children show reluctance to let reading get beyond the earliest stage. They are aware, even if in pre-verbal ways, that the recommended activity is one which involves a serious, because partial, lack of control, but brings no certainty of reward while offering no noticeable challenge (unlike say, rock-climbing). The reader must agree to a surrender before fighting the battle. What is surprising is that, on the whole, these children do learn to read, sooner or later, for they have hit on a central and uncomfortable truth, one that we find again as part of the force of these words, from a rather more experienced word-user [Mallarmé]: "Strictement, j'envisage . . . la lecture comme une pratique désespérée"' (Craig, 1976, pp. 17–18).

27 In his essay 'Les contrebandiers de l'écriture', Bernard Pingaud uses the metaphor of gambling to express a similar sense of the writer's need for commitment. He writes: 'At every moment [the writer] throws in his whole stake, in the same way as a stubborn gambler sacrifices his last pennies on the casino floor in the hope that, at the end of the day, something will come back to him' (Pingaud, 1979, p. 162).

28 Just how fatally tempting it is to stay, as it were, with the authorial side of events is borne out by volume sixteen of *Nouvelle revue de psychanalyse*, which has as its formidable collective title *Ecrire la psychanalyse*. The volume is full of insights, many of which I have benefited from and some of which I have referred to here. Yet the book as a whole remains peculiarly unilluminating; and the reason for this is that the articles in it are written almost entirely *by*

analysts, *from the analytic viewpoint*. In what at first promises to be the book's strength – that of offering insight 'from inside' – lies its weakness. The writers' failure to make an imaginative shift away from their professional positions towards that of the reader threatens to consign even their more humble and reasoned arguments to the borders of dogma and wish-fulfilment. In the end, one comes away from the volume with less of a sense of where literary and analytic prose overlap and separate, than of certain analysts' aspirations, satisfactions and frustrations.

29 The term is the poet John Berryman's, whose book *The Freedom of the Poet* contains a fine essay on *The Tempest*, entitled 'Shakespeare's Last Word'.

4. FOR TO END YET AGAIN

1 Some corroboration of this from the sphere of verbal learning is given by the article 'When Forgetting Helps Memory: An Analysis of Repetition Effects', by Lauren J. Cuddy and Larry L. Jacoby. Further, more compelling confirmation is to be gained from A. R. Luria's book *The Mind of a Mnemonist*. Luria tells of a man whose recall is so total as to oblige him to devise methods of disposing of redundant memories which are cluttering his mind, such as that of writing them down on pieces of paper which he subsequently burns.

2 This is amply shown by Alison Winton in her study *Proust's Additions: The Making of 'A la recherche du temps perdu'*.

3 J. Hillis Miller writes this in a discussion of Joseph Conrad's *The Secret Agent*. He develops his argument in an interesting and relevant way in reference to Emily Brontë, when he says: 'The most powerful form of repetition in fiction, it may be, is not the echoes of one part of the book by another, but the way even the simplest, most representational words in a novel ("1801 – I have just returned . . .") present themselves as already a murmuring repetition, something which has been repeating itself incessantly there in the words on the page waiting for me to bring it back to life as the meaning of the words forms itself in my mind. Fiction is possible only because of an intrinsic capacity possessed by ordinary words in grammatical order. Words no different from those we use in everyday life, "I have just returned", may detach themselves or be detached from any present moment, any living "I", any immediate perception of reality, and go on functioning as the creators of the fictional world repeated into existence, to use the verb transitively, whenever the act of reading those words is performed' (p. 72).

4 Gérard Genette helps to bring out Proust's sensitivity to tenses in his *Narrative Discourse*. It is a sensitivity brilliantly displayed in, for example, 'Journées de lecture' (in *Pastiches et mélanges*) and in 'A propos du "style" de Flaubert' (in *Contre Sainte-Beuve*).

5 In my discussion of Kafka (in § 1.4), I suggested that his narratives often seem to be underpinned by versions of the question 'What if?' I can now add that these questions are perhaps themselves underpinned by a pervasive 'if' or 'conditional' which is at the heart of all narrative telling.

6 One of the senses of the French *répétition* is that of a rehearsal. The difference in the direction in which the two variants appear to point – French pointing

backwards and English pointing forwards – highlights precisely the sort of complex temporality which I am trying to describe here.

7 Duras comes close to granting this status to ambivalence in her recent autobiographical novel, *L'Amant* (*The Lover*). Further comment on the 'fundamental duality' in Duras's work is to be found in an article by Elaine Michalski and Maurice Cagnon entitled 'Marguerite Duras: vers un roman de l'ambivalence'.

8 The stress Winnicott lays on paradox in *Playing and Reality* is paramount. He writes: 'My contribution is to ask for a paradox to be accepted and tolerated and respected, and for it not to be resolved. By flight to split-off intellectual functioning it is possible to resolve the paradox, but the price of this is the loss of the value of the paradox itself' (p. xii). In his seminar, Lacan often lays a similar emphasis on the possible fecundity of paradox, for example in *Le Séminaire II*, where he writes that 'It is the most paradoxical facts that are the most instructive' (p. 85).

9 In his discussion of Winnicott, Pontalis not only talks about risk but risks himself in a prose which, if it becomes the 'promise of an encounter', does so only through paradox. When he goes on to write of the possibility of successful analysis he does so in terms which are very evocative of *Le Camion*: 'In a sense, all analyses, especially perhaps those which "work well" and in which, contradictorily, "nothing happens", make us perceive a deserted space, a vain and laborious filling-in, which is interpretative on one side and associative on the other. This gap . . . is, through its presence–absence, "witness of a non-experienced": a demand, too, for it to be recognized for the first time, for one to encounter the gap at last so that what could be given no meaning can be given life. "It is through non-existence that existence can begin."' (Pontalis, 1981, p. 152).

10 Leo Bersani's illuminating study is entitled *Marcel Proust: The Fictions of Life and of Art*. There he elaborates: 'The narrator's book cannot be written in the ecstatic trance induced by the taste of the *madeleine* or the sound of a spoon hitting a plate. And by making his hero and his narrator the same person in *À la recherche*, Proust draws our attention to the difficulties of being faithful to the moments of involuntary memory in writing about the past. For we are constantly reminded that the man who has the involuntary memories has lost them at the moment we read of his having them; it is *his* voice that is now making the effort to remember moments in which remembering required no effort. The chance experience must be transformed into a deliberate investigation, a conscious *recherche*' (p. 215).

11 In his dense but invaluable *Différence et répétition*, Gilles Deleuze makes a suggestion which has a bearing on the relatively low status I am conferring on involuntary memory. He writes: 'Repetition is a condition of action before it is a concept of reflection' (p. 121).

12 In his essay 'Marcel Proust: The "Petite Phrase" and the Sentence', George Craig puts this clearly when he writes: 'If we must indeed follow what is pointed at in this novel (how else can we read?), we must expect that something crucial will be happening in what is being pointed away from. And this something is the writing. As the temptations offered by the world appear to draw Marcel continually from his chosen task, so the temptations offered by

the novel draw us from the reality of its *composition*. For us too there is revelation in the sudden awareness that this is not the recital of a failure – a recital punctuated by glimpsings of others' success – but a unique *achievement*' (Craig, 1981, p. 271).

13 The notion of the 'apprenticeship' is fully developed by Gilles Deleuze in his *Proust and Signs*, esp. ch. 3. The expression about 'advent' and 'event' comes from Maurice Blanchot's essay 'Proust' (Blanchot, 1982, pp. 66–78).

14 In an essay entitled 'Imagination and Repetition in Literature: A Reassessment', Edward Casey describes a process very similar in terms of 'imaginative repetition'. He explains: 'This has to do with the way in which imagining can effect an active re-creation of possibilities – possibilities which have been *predelineated*, but not necessarily actualized, in previous experience. The imaginer seizes upon such possibilities, actively reconstituting them as authentic psychic presences' (Casey, 1975, p. 254).

15 Walter Benjamin points this out in his essay 'The Image of Proust' (Benjamin, 1973, p. 204). Samuel Beckett agrees, and expresses his feeling with characteristic brevity, writing in his essay *Proust* that 'Proust had a bad memory' (p. 29).

16 The dangers of misreading Proustian repetition are exemplified in one of the few sustained enquiries into repetition in literature, Bruce Kawin's *Telling it Again and Again: Repetition in Literature and Film*. This book is fatally wounded by its failure to follow Marcel. For Kawin, repetition is a return of and to the identical, which does away with both temporal distinctions and the differences between people. Kawin goes hopelessly awry when he contends that 'the repetition of earlier events abolishes the dead intervening time', and that 'Proust founds a religion of time whose basic rite is transcendent repetition' (p. 92). To support his contention Kawin is of course obliged to ride roughshod over the reader's experience of the novel, and over the insights of Marcel's own intelligence as well.

17 Towards the end of his book *Marcel Proust*, Leo Bersani undercuts many of his finer insights when he declares that 'I have, of course, been assuming throughout this study that the book we are reading is the book the narrator speaks of writing in *Le Temps retrouvé*' (p. 244). But Bersani's view is a popular one, espoused by most commentators (including Harold Pinter, for example, in the introduction to his *The Proust Screenplay*).

18 The French have an expression 'Qui perd gagne' ('loser wins'), and nowhere is it truer than in relation to Proust (unless perhaps in relation to Beckett). One of the ways in which it is true is brought out by Gérard Genette in his essay 'Proust Palimpsest', where he shows how Proust's success is 'of having succeeded in the failure of his undertaking, and of having left us the perfect spectacle of that failure, namely, his work' (Genette, 1982, p. 226).

5. ONCE IS NOT ENOUGH

1 In his essay 'Freud's Masterplot', Peter Brooks suggests that local instances of repetition are circumscribed by the repetitious nature of narrative *per se*. He writes: 'Narrative must ever present itself as a repetition of events that have already happened, and within this postulate of a generalized repetition it must

make use of specific, perceptible repetitions in order to create plot, that is, to show us a significant interconnection of events' (Brooks, 1977, p. 288).

2 Marcel notes a series of stark contrasts between his aunt and himself, but only then to admit that he has grown increasingly like her (III, 71–2; III, 78–9).

3 Marcel explains: 'It is one of the faculties of jealousy to reveal to us the extent to which the reality of external facts and the sentiments of the heart are an unknown element which lends itself to endless suppositions. We imagine that we know exactly what things are and what people think, for the simple reason that we do not care about them. But as soon as we have a desire to know, as the jealous man has, then it becomes a dizzy kaleidoscope in which we can no longer distinguish anything' (III, 529; III, 519).

4 In his *Proust, Freud et l'autre*, Jean-Louis Baudry provides a similar view of jealousy when he writes: 'Jealousy, which is a form of madness, is first of all a discourse, and an interminable discourse. It overwhelms whoever is prey to it by resources of an inexhaustible inspiration, and, while it offers itself as an object of infinite investigation, it at the same time presents to the one who has placed himself in the position of writing (of which I have spoken) certain clear analogies and something like a model' (pp. 24–5).

5 It is worth noting that in *Beyond the Pleasure Principle*, in which (as I show in chapter 6) Freud tries to locate a first moment of division – what Marcel calls, appealing now to Christian mythology, 'what the Creation made separate' (III, 74; III, 79) – he too entertains the figure of the hermaphrodite (*Standard Edition*, XVIII, 57–8).

6 In an article entitled 'Proust, Deleuze et la répétition', M. Ferraris and D. de Agostini argue, similarly, that repetition undermines the intentions and willed identity of the author, breaking the latter down into 'numerous "*I am*"s that are autonomous and resemble one another' (Ferraris and Agostini, 1978, p. 72).

7 The opening sentences of Moran's narrative are: 'It is midnight. The rain is beating on the windows' (p. 92). Precisely the same sentences are found, and then refuted, at the end of his report.

8 In an unpublished dissertation entitled 'Style in Beckett's Prose: Repetition and the Transformation of the Functions of Language', Elisabeth Segres argues that 'The very structure of *L'Innommable* is based on repetitions' and that 'the changing proportions of repetitions from work to work indicate Beckett's dramatic moves to maximize the use of repetitions' (Segres, 1976, pp. 105, 285). Segres's thesis is a valuable guide to repetition in Beckett's work, though it does not try to relate the instances of repetition to a larger significance of repetition as a whole.

9 A similar course can be noted in the work of Marguerite Duras, which has shifted broadly from (a) representing action, however useless, trivial or repetitious, to (b) fictions where action is either botched or perverse, or (c) capable of signifying only to an onlooker or voyeur; to a final stage where (d) action is talked about. Examples of the four overlapping stages might be: (a) *Moderato Cantabile*, (b) *Dix heures et demie du soir en été*, (c) *L'Amour*, and (d) *L'Homme atlantique*.

10 In an essay entitled 'Suture', psychoanalyst Jacques-Alain Miller locates a paradox in the number one, a number which for him signifies 'the concept of

identity to a concept . . . Which means that this function of the number 1 is repetitive for all things of the world.' The fascination for arithmetic which Beckett's work displays reveals itself a little under Miller's argument, which sets out to show how all numbering is premised in the number one (and the zero): 'The central paradox to be grasped (which as you will see in a moment is the paradox of the signifier in the sense of Lacan) is that the trait of the identical represents the non-identical, whence is deduced the impossibility of its redoubling, and from that impossibility the structure of *repetition* as the process of differentiation of the identical' (J.-A. Miller, 1977–8, pp. 27, 29, 32).

11 According to Serge Leclaire, the institution of psychoanalysis is itself beset by a fantasy of an original unity which operates a 'first bolt – the narcissistic one' (Leclaire, 1981, p. 10).

12 In his essay 'Proust and Indirect Language', Gérard Genette discusses a way in which Proust's work might be seen to emerge from a comparable gap, which he locates between a 'first' or direct language and the 'second' or indirect language of the writer. His words catch at the force of the expression 'Qui perd gagne', where the winning here is Proust's, but might also be both Beckett's and the reader's: 'The work, for Proust, like the "line" for Mallarmé, "makes up for what is lacking in language". If words were the image of things, says Mallarmé, everybody would be a poet, and there would be no such thing as poetry; poetry is *born* from what is lacking in (for lack of) languages. Proust's lesson is more or less parallel: if "primary" language were truthful, secondary language would not be necessary. It is the conflict between language and truth that *produces*, as we have seen, indirect language; and indirect language is, above all, writing – the work' (Genette, 1982, p. 286).

13 The text uses the word 'companionable' on pp. 43, 60 and 79.

14 In a book made up of meditations on the voice, entitled *Les Hasards de la voix*, Alain Arnaud speaks of this shock, saying: 'One cannot hear one's own voice. It is foreign to the body that proffers it, and it thwarts all recognition that the body tries to gain of it. There is a hiatus between the mouth and the ear of the same body. Technical artifice makes no difference to this. One does not recognise one's recorded voice either' (p. 94).

15 The fact that one knows from various sources (including the Beckett biography) that this moment corresponds to one which is said to have been of crucial importance to the author – a moment in which he realised his work had to be created out of his 'stupidity' – lends force to the way the reader feels tantalised, and force also to the rejection of the wisdom which might be thought to emerge from any such moments of revelation.

16 It may be of some relevance that Beckett chooses for his French title of *Krapp's Last Tape* the explicitly sexual, if ironic, *La Dernière bande*.

6. IN THE BEGINNING

1 I have referred (in note 6 to chapter 1) to the relevance of Harold Fisch's book *A Remembered Future* to my discussion of fathers. In another chapter of this book, entitled 'The Absent Father', Fisch discusses the figure of the mother in a way that is very pertinent here. He suggests that the threat posed by the

father in nineteenth- and early twentieth-century literature is largely taken over by that of an over-present, over-loving mother. Not surprisingly, he uses the example of Proust to illustrate this (though I believe he overlooks the way in which Marcel's love for his mother is always flawed – in a manner I discuss in § 6.5 and 6.6).

2 In an article entitled 'Watt à l'ombre de Plume – l'écriture du désoeuvrement', Etienne Rabaté describes a very similar process, in relation to *Watt*: 'The whole forms a spiral to which nothing puts a stop . . . the text without origin thus makes up a cause for itself, a birth certificate . . . a blank voice, articulated on an absence, that ceaselessly repeats the journey of its origin' (Rabaté, 1984, p. 185).

3 In an essay entitled 'Some Considerations on Repetition and Repetition Compulsion', Hans Loewald proposes that the Oedipus complex is 'already a repetition of pre-Oedipal experiences' which are 'repeated not just in puberty but throughout life' (Loewald, 1971, p. 60).

4 Freud's search for origins was least of all eccentric in a Darwinian age which, for example, saw George Eliot open. *Daniel Deronda* (1876) with the line – 'Men can do nothing without the make-believe of a beginning.' On the more general and historical relation between Darwin's search for origins and that carried out in fiction, see Gillian Beer's book *Darwin's Plots*.

5 Maud Mannoni writes that: 'Very often the stakes have been placed before the birth; two generations earlier the nets have been woven with a thread by which the child is going to find itself caught, and driven towards psychosis' (M. Mannoni, 1970, p. 43). Notwithstanding the way the fate of the individual is predetermined, Maud Mannoni is committed to allowing her patients to make their story their own. This paradox is one she recognises, and of which she writes: 'In looking, through the cure, to distinguish the fantasies of the child from those of the mother, I am leading the subject to take on his own history, rather than stay alienated in that of the mother. The history of the child nonetheless remains one that is spread out over several generations' (M. Mannoni, 1964, pp. 84–5).

6 Some interesting examples of responses to Freud's text are Hans Loewald's 'Some Considerations on Repetition and Repetition Compulsion', Edward Bibring's 'The Conception of the Repetition Compulsion', and Jacques Derrida's 'Spéculer – sur "Freud"'.

7 In his *Proust, Freud et l'autre*, Jean-Louis Baudry suggests that Freud was very receptive to the way writing creates an effect of the *unheimlich*. Baudry suggests that: 'It is perceptible from the time of his first letters that Freud was sensitive to the particular rhythm that the position of writing imposes. He liked that relation to the self, which is to say he liked the relation to language as much as to the meanings it carries. He was sensitive to the echo that prolongs the words there on the page, the way reading redoubles sentences that are written, whose inscription has already created a strange effect of doubling' (p. 84).

8 In keeping with repetition as I have discussed it, in a letter to George Devine (included in *Disjecta*, p. 111), Beckett asks for a modulation, a 'slight weakening, both of question and of response' in the repeat of *Play*.

9 Lacan goes on to summarise the infant's action thus: 'The activity as a whole symbolizes repetition, but not at all that of some need that might demand the

234

return of the mother, and which would be expressed quite simply in a cry. It is the repetition of the mother's departure as a cause of a *Spaltung* in the subject – overcome by the alternating game, *fort-da*, which is a *here or there*, and whose aim, in its alternation, is simply that of being the *fort* of a *da*, and the *da* of a fort' (p. 61; trans. pp. 62–3).

10 Kristeva spells out the way love can confuse and conflate psychoanalytic categories when she writes: 'The experience of being in love indissolubly binds the *symbolic* (what is forbidden, discernible and thinkable), the *imaginary* (what the ego holds up to itself to enable it to maintain itself and grow) and the *real* (which is what is impossible, when the affects aspire to everything and when there is no-one to take account of the fact that *I* am only a part)' (p. 14). In a persuasive article entitled 'Réflexions métapsychologiques concernant l'état amoureux', Christian David argues similarly, claiming that love releases a 'new soul born of the fusion of love' and that 'The state of being in love represents a new birth – not just the repetition and as it were the transposed melody of some forgotten experience' (David, 1966, p. 217).

11 In *Le Séminaire II* Lacan expresses a similar conviction, if in more abstract terms, when he writes that 'the object' (as it might be in this case, the traumatic object of Madeleine's past) 'is met and is structured in the way of a repetition – regain the object, repeat the object. Only, it is never the same object that the subject meets' (p. 125).

12 For a different but illuminating perspective on the role of transference in the journey into the past, see Stanley A. Leavy, 'The Recovery of the Past in Psychoanalysis'.

13 In his essay 'Proust et la répétition', Georges Poulet describes such a continuity as being: 'no longer a continuity of the Bergsonian type, nor an overall homogeneity, but simply a juxtaposition of elements which, though they belong to different moments and places in the action, will be placed alongside each other in the sequence of the text, like a series of paintings having all to do with the same story' (Poulet, 1972, pp. 9–10).

14 In *Words* Jean-Paul Sartre also describes the immeasurably important experience of being read to as a child by his mother. He says that in being read to, 'it was as if I were every mother's child and she were every child's mother' (p. 34). What does Sartre go on to do as a consequence of the experience? He goes on to read for himself – 'Reading' ['Lire'], as the first section of *Words* is entitled. He explains that 'I became jealous of my mother, and I decided to usurp her role' (p. 34). After that, and only after that, comes the task of 'Writing' – 'Ecrire' (as the book's second section is called).

15 Proust originally intended his *Contre Sainte-Beuve* to function by means of a similar reversal, in which the recumbent narrator would deliver a series of talks to his mother (as explained in *Contre Sainte-Beuve*, p. 823, note 1). Alain Buisine suggests (in *Proust et ses lettres*) that in fact the mother is the imaginary *destinataire* of all Proust's letters – and of all his fictions as well.

16 In his notebook for 1908 Proust confirms this necessity, saying that 'Work makes us a bit like a mother.' He goes on to express his doubts about his own maternal capacities in the following terms: 'feeling the child that was forming in my flanks, and not knowing if I would gather the strength necessary to give birth to it . . .' (*Carnet de 1908*, quoted in Buisine, 1983, p. 42).

In his book *La Place de la madeleine*, Serge Doubrovsky expresses Marcel's need to give birth in the following (psychoanalytic) terms: 'Given the lack of a liberation – which is impossible at the level of the real and forbidden at the level of the imaginary (with Gilberte or Albertine he weaves repeatedly the same web in which he was caught) – *creating himself means (re)producing himself in the symbolic register*, by an imaginary maternity that is a real neurosis' (p. 60).

Works cited

Almeida, Iván. 'Un corps devenu récit'. In *Le Corps et ses fictions*, ed. Claude Reichler, Paris: Minuit, 1983, pp. 7–18.

Alvarez, A. *Beckett*. Glasgow: Collins/Fontana, 1973.

Anzieu, Annie. 'L'heure de la répétition'. In *Nouvelle revue de psychanalyse*, 15 (1977a), 163–75.

'Des mots et des femmes'. In *Nouvelle revue de psychanalyse*, 16 (1977), 151–67.

Anzieu, Didier. 'Un soi disjoint, une voix liante: l'écriture narrative de Samuel Beckett'. In *Nouvelle revue de psychanalyse*, 28 (1983), 71–85.

Le Corps de l'œuvre. Paris: Gallimard, 1981.

Arnaud, Alain. *Les Hasards de la voix*. Paris: Flammarion, 1984.

Bair, Deirdre. *Samuel Beckett: A Biography*. London: Jonathan Cape, 1978.

Barthes, Roland. *S/Z*. Trans. Richard Miller, New York: Hill and Wang, 1974.

Roland Barthes par Roland Barthes. Paris: Seuil, 1975.

Roland Barthes by Roland Barthes. Trans. Richard Howard, London: Macmillan, 1977.

The Pleasure of the Text. Trans. Richard Miller, London: Jonathan Cape, 1976.

A Lover's Discourse: Fragments. Trans. Richard Howard, London: Jonathan Cape, 1979.

Camera Lucida. Trans. Richard Howard, London: Jonathan Cape, 1982.

Baudry, Jean-Louis. *Proust, Freud et l'autre*. Paris: Minuit, 1984.

Beckett, Samuel. *Proust*. London: John Calder, 1976.

'Dante and the Lobster'. In *More Pricks than Kicks*, London: Pan/Picador, 1974, pp. 7–19.

Murphy. London: Pan/Picador, 1973.

Watt. London: John Calder, 1976.

First Love. In *The Expelled and Other Novellas*, Harmondsworth: Penguin, 1980.

L'Innommable. Paris: Minuit, 1953.

Molloy, Malone Dies, The Unnamable (The '*Trilogy*'). London: John Calder, 1976.

Waiting for Godot. London: Faber and Faber, 1956.

Texts for Nothing. London: John Calder, 1974.

Endgame. London: Faber and Faber, 1958.

How It Is. London: John Calder, 1964.

Krapp's Last Tape. In *Collected Shorter Plays of Samuel Beckett*, London: Faber and Faber, 1984, pp. 53–63.

La Dernière bande. Paris: Minuit, 1959.

Happy Days. London: Faber and Faber, 1963.

Play. In *Shorter Plays*, pp. 145–60.

'Enough'. In *Six Residua*, London: John Calder, 1978, pp. 23–31.

'Imagination Dead Imagine'. In *Six Residua*, pp. 33–8.

'Ping'. In *Six Residua*, pp. 39–44.

'Lessness'. In *Six Residua*, pp. 45–51.

Not I. In *Shorter Plays*, pp. 145–60.

List of works cited

Footfalls. In *Shorter Plays*, pp. 237–44.

Collected Poems in English and French. London: John Calder, 1977.

Company. London: John Calder, 1979.

Compagnie. Paris: Minuit, 1980.

'A Piece of Monologue'. In *Shorter Plays*, pp. 263–70.

Rockaby. In *Shorter Plays*, pp. 271–82.

'Crisscross to Infinity'. In *College Literature*, 8 (1981), 310.

Ill Seen Ill Said. London: John Calder, 1982.

Worstward Ho. London: John Calder, 1983.

Disjecta: Miscellaneous Writings and a Dramatic Fragment. Ed. Ruby Cohn, London: John Calder, 1983.

Beer, Gillian. *Darwin's Plots: Evolutionary Narrative in Darwin, George Eliot and Nineteenth-Century Fiction*. London: Routledge and Kegan Paul, 1983.

Bellow, Saul. *Mr Sammler's Planet*. Harmondsworth: Penguin, 1972.

Benjamin, Walter. 'The Storyteller: Reflections on the Works of Nikolai Leskov'. In *Illuminations*, trans. Harry Sohn, ed. Hannah Arendt, Glasgow: Collins/Fontana, 1973, pp. 83–109.

'Franz Kafka: On the Tenth Anniversary of His Death'. In *Illuminations*, pp. 111–40.

'The Image of Proust'. In *Illuminations*, pp. 203–17.

'The Work of Art in the Age of Mechanical Reproduction'. In *Illuminations*, pp. 219–53.

Benvenuto, Bice and Roger Kennedy. *The Works of Jacques Lacan: An Introduction*. London: Free Association Books, 1986.

Berman, Jeffrey. *The Talking Cure: Literary Representations of Psychoanalysis*. New York: New York University Press, 1985.

Berryman, John. 'Shakespeare's Last Word'. In *The Freedom of the Poet*, New York: Oxford University Press, 1965.

Bersani, Leo. *Marcel Proust: The Fictions of Life and of Art*. New York: Oxford University Press, 1965.

Baudelaire and Freud. Berkeley: University of California Press, 1977.

'Déguisements du moi et art fragmentaire'. In *Recherche de Proust*, ed. Gérard Genette and Tzvetan Todorov, Paris: Seuil ('Points' collection), 1980, pp. 13–33.

Bettelheim, Bruno. *Freud and Man's Soul*. London: Chatto and Windus with The Hogarth Press, 1983.

Bibring, Edward. 'The Conception of the Repetition Compulsion'. In *Psychoanalytic Quarterly*, 12 (1943), 468–519.

Blanchot, Maurice, 'La lecture de Kafka'. In *La Part du feu*, Paris: Gallimard, 1949, pp. 9–19.

L'Espace littéraire. Paris: Gallimard ('Idées' collection), 1955.

'La parole analytique'. In *L'Entretien infini*, Paris: Gallimard, 1969, pp. 343–54.

L'Amitié. Paris: Gallimard, 1971.

'Proust'. In *The Sirens' Song: Selected Essays by Maurice Blanchot*, ed. Gabriel Josipovici, trans. Sacha Rabinovitch, Brighton: Harvester Press, 1982, pp. 66–78.

Bleger, José. 'Psycho-Analysis of the Psycho-Analytic Frame'. In *International Journal of Psycho-Analysis*, 48 (1966), 511–19.

List of works cited

Borges, Jorge Luis. 'Funes the Memorious'. Trans. James E. Irby, in *Labyrinths*, ed. Donald A. Yates and James E. Irby, Harmondsworth: Penguin, 1970, pp. 87–95.

'Kafka and his precursors'. Trans. James E. Irby, in *Labyrinths*, pp. 234–6.

Boutonier, J. *La Notion d'ambivalence: étude critique, valeur séméiologique*. Toulouse: Privat, 1972.

Bowie, Malcolm. *Freud, Proust and Lacan: Theory as Fiction*. Cambridge: Cambridge University Press, 1987.

Broda, Martine. 'La leçon de Mandelstam'. In *Contre-jour: études sur Paul Celan*, ed. Martine Broda, Paris: Cerf, 1986, pp. 29–48.

Brome, Vincent. *Freud and his Early Circle*. New York: William Morrow and Company, 1968.

Brooks, Peter. 'Freud's Masterplot'. In *Literature and Psychoanalysis*, ed. Felman (1977), pp. 280–300.

Buisine, Alain. *Proust et ses lettres*. Lille: Presses universitaires de Lille, 1983.

Canetti, Elias. 'Kafka's Other Trial'. In Franz Kafka, *Letters to Felice*, trans. James Stern and Elizabeth Duckworth, ed. Erich Heller and Jürgen Born, Harmondsworth: Penguin, 1978, pp. 7–94.

Cardinal, Marie. *The Words to Say It*. Trans. Pat Goodheart, London: Pan/Picador, 1984.

Casement, Patrick. 'Samuel Beckett's Relationship to his Mother-Tongue'. In *International Review of Psycho-Analysis*, 9 (1982), 35–44.

Casey, Edward. 'Imagination and Repetition in Literature: A Reassessment'. In *Yale French Studies*, 52 (1975), 249–67.

Celan, Paul. *Poems*. Selected, trans. and intro. Michael Hamburger, Manchester: Carcanet Press, 1980.

Collected Prose. Trans. Rosmarie Waldrop, Manchester: Carcanet Press, 1986.

Char, René. *Œuvres complètes*. Paris: Gallimard (Bibliothèque de la Pléiade), 1983.

Clark, Ronald W. *Freud: The Man and the Cause*. London: Jonathan Cape and Weidenfeld and Nicolson, 1980.

Clément, Catherine. 'Les nouvelles illusions perdues, ou lettre à un ami analyste qui écrit aussi des livres'. In *Nouvelle revue de psychanalyse*, 16 (1977), 203–12.

Coleridge, Samuel Taylor. *Poetical Works*. London: Oxford University Press, 1967.

Craig, George. 'Reading: Who is Doing What to Whom?'. In *The Modern English Novel*, ed. Gabriel Josipovici, London: Open Books, 1976, pp. 15–36.

'Marcel Proust: The "Petite Phrase" and the Sentence'. In *History of European Ideas*, 1, no. 3 (1981), 259–76.

Cuddy, Lauren J. and Larry L. Jacoby. 'When Forgetting Helps Memory: An Analysis of Repetition Effects'. In *Journal of Verbal Learning and Verbal Behaviour*, 21 (1982), 451–67.

Dante Alighieri. *The Divine Comedy*. 3 vols., trans. Charles S. Singleton, Princeton: Princeton University Press, 1970.

David, Christian. 'Réflexions métapsychologiques concernant l'état amoureux'. In *Revue française de psychanalyse*, 30 (1966), 195–225.

Deguy, Michel. 'Un lecteur vous écrit'. In *Nouvelle revue de psychanalyse*, 16 (1977), 213–20.

Deleuze, Gilles. *Différence et répétition*. Paris: Presses Universitaires de France, 1968.

Proust and Signs. Trans. Richard Howard, London: Allen Lane, 1973.

Logique du sens. Paris: Minuit, 1969.

Deleuze, Gilles and Félix Guattari. *Anti-Oedipus: Capitalism and Schizophrenia*. Trans. Robert Hurley, Marc Seem, Helen R. Lane, New York: Viking Press, 1977.

Kafka: pour une littérature mineure. Paris: Minuit, 1975.

Derrida, Jacques. 'Freud and the Scene of Writing'. In *Writing and Difference*, trans. Alan Bass, Chicago: University of Chicago Press, 1978, pp. 196–231.

'Spéculer – sur "Freud"'. In *La Carte postale: de Socrate à Freud et au-delà*, Paris: Flammarion, 1980, pp. 277–437.

Dolto, Françoise. Préface, in Maud Mannoni, *Le Premier rendez-vous avec le psychanalyste*.

Doubrovsky, Serge. *La Place de la madeleine: écriture et fantasme chez Proust*. Paris: Mercure de France, 1974.

Duras, Marguerite. *Moderato Cantabile*. Paris: Minuit, 1958.

Dix heures et demie du soir en été. Paris: Gallimard, 1960.

L'Amour. Paris: Gallimard, 1971.

L'Homme atlantique. Paris: Minuit, 1982.

Le Camion, with 'Entretien avec Michelle Porte'. Paris: Minuit, 1977.

L'Amant. Paris: Minuit, 1984. (Trans. by Barbara Bray as *The Lover*, London: Jonathan Cape, 1985).

Durgnat, Raymond. *The Strange Case of Alfred Hitchcock*. London: Faber and Faber, 1974.

Eliot, George. *Daniel Deronda*. Harmondsworth: Penguin, 1967.

Eliot, T. S. *Collected Poems 1909–1962*. London: Faber and Faber, 1963.

Felman, Shoshana (ed.). *Literature and Psychoanalysis*. Baltimore: John Hopkins University Press, 1977.

Felstiner, John. 'Langue maternelle, langue éternelle'. In *Etudes sur Paul Celan*, ed. Martine Broda, pp. 65–84.

Ferraris, Maurizio and Daniela de Agostini. 'Proust, Deleuze et la répétition: notes sur les niveaux narratifs d'*A la recherche du temps perdu*'. In *Littérature*, 32 (1978), 66–85.

Fisch, Harold. *A Remembered Future: A Study in Literary Mythology*. Bloomington: Indiana University Press, 1984.

Fraser, Ronald. *In Search of a Past*. London: Verso, 1984.

Freccero, John. 'Dante's Pilgrim in a Gyre'. In *PMLA*, 76 (1961), 168–204.

Freud, Sigmund. 'Analysis of a Phobia in a Five-Year-Old Boy'. In *The Standard Edition of the Complete Psychological Works of Sigmund Freud*, trans. James Strachey, London: The Hogarth Press and the Institute of Psychoanalysis, 1961, x, 151–249.

'Notes upon a Case of Obsessional Neurosis'. In *Standard Edition*, x, 151–249.

'Psychoanalytic Notes upon an Autobiographical Account of a Case of Paranoia (Dementia Paranoides)'. In *Standard Edition*, xii, 1–82.

'The Dynamics of Transference'. In *Standard Edition*, xii, 97–108.

'Remembering, Repeating and Working Through'. In *Standard Edition*, xii, 146–56.

'Observations on Transference-Love'. In *Standard Edition*, xii, 157–71.

'On Narcissism: An Introduction'. In *Standard Edition*, xiv, 68–102.

Introductory Lectures on Psychoanalysis. *Standard Edition*, xv and xvi.

List of works cited

'"A Child is Being Beaten": A Contribution to the Study of the Origin of Sexual Perversity'. In *Standard Edition*, XVII, 175–204.

'The Uncanny'. In *Standard Edition*, XVII, 217–56.

Beyond the Pleasure Principle. In *Standard Edition*, XVIII, 3–64.

'Inhibitions, Symptoms and Anxiety'. In *Standard Edition*, XX, 75–175.

Frye, Northrop. *Anatomy of Criticism: Four Essays*. Princeton: Princeton University Press, 1957.

A Natural Perspective: The Development of Shakespearean Comedy and Romance. Columbia: Columbia University Press, 1965.

Fuller, Peter. *Art and Psychoanalysis*. London: Writers and Readers, 1980.

Robert Natkin. New York: Henry Abrams Inc., 1981.

'D. W. Winnicott'. In *The Naked Artist: Art and Biology and Other Essays*. London: Writers and Readers, 1983, pp. 233–40.

Gaillard, Françoise. 'Le discours médical pris au piège du récit'. In *Etudes Françaises*, 19 no. 2 (1983), 81–95.

Gallop, Jane. *Reading Lacan*. Ithaca and London: Cornell University Press, 1985.

Genette, Gérard. 'Proust Palimpsest'. In *Figures of Literary Discourse*, trans. Alan Sheridan, Oxford: Basil Blackwell, 1982, pp. 203–28.

'Proust and Indirect Language'. In *Figures of Literary Discourse*, pp. 229–86.

Narrative Discourse. Trans. Jane E. Lewin, Oxford: Basil Blackwell, 1980.

Gori, Roland. 'Ce que parler peut être ou de l'allégeance du texte au corps'. In *L'Evolution psychiatrique*, 2 (1974), 293–313.

Greenson, Ralph. 'The Mother Tongue and the Mother'. In *International Journal of Psychoanalysis*, 31, part 1–2 (1950), 18–23.

Guyomard, Patrick. 'Jacques Lacan'. In *Encyclopaedia Universalis* (1984), corpus 10, pp. 910–13.

'Le temps de l'acte: l'analyste entre la technique et le style'. In Maud Mannoni, *Un savoir qui ne se sait pas*, Paris: Denoël, 1985, pp. 139–87.

Handwerk, Gary J. *Irony and Ethics in Narrative: From Schlegel to Lacan*. New Haven and London: Yale University Press, 1985.

Harrison, Bernard. 'Parable and Transcendence'. In *Ways of Reading the Bible*, ed. Michael Wadsworth, Brighton: Harvester Press, 1981, pp. 190–212.

Hartman, Geoffrey. *Criticism in the Wilderness: The Study of Literature Today*. New Haven and London: Yale University Press, 1980.

Heath, Stephen. *Questions of Cinema*. London: Macmillan, 1981.

Holland, Norman. 'Unity Identity Text Self'. In *PMLA*, 90 (1975), 813–22.

Homer. *The Iliad*. Trans. Richmond Lattimore, Chicago: University of Chicago Press, 1951.

The Odyssey. Trans. Richmond Lattimore, New York: Harper and Row, 1965.

Janvier, Ludovic. *Beckett*. Paris: Seuil, 1969.

Jones, Ernest. *Sigmund Freud: Life and Work*. 3 vols., London: The Hogarth Press, 1954.

Hamlet and Oedipus. New York: Anchor, 1954.

Josipovici, Gabriel. *The Echo Chamber*. Brighton: Harvester Press, 1980.

Writing and the Body. Brighton: Harvester Press, 1982.

Juliet, Charles. *Rencontre avec Samuel Beckett*. Paris: Fata Morgana, 1986.

Kafka, Franz. *America*. Trans. Willa and Edwin Muir, Harmondsworth: Penguin, 1967.

Metamorphosis. Trans. Willa and Edwin Muir, in *The Penguin Complete Short*

List of works cited

Stories of Franz Kafka, Harmondsworth: Penguin, 1983, pp. 89–139.
'The Trees'. Trans. Willa and Edwin Muir, in *Complete Stories*, 1983, p. 382.
'The Judgement'. Trans. Willa and Edwin Muir, in *Complete Stories*, pp. 77–88.
The Trial. Trans. Willa and Edwin Muir, Harmondsworth: Penguin, 1953.
'In the Penal Colony'. Trans. Willa and Edwin Muir, in *Complete Stories*, pp. 140–67.
'Letter to his Father'. In *Wedding Preparations in the Country and Other Stories*. Trans. various, Harmondsworth: Penguin, 1978, pp. 30–76.
'Investigations of a Dog'. Trans. Willa and Edwin Muir, in *Complete Stories*, pp. 278–316.
The Castle. Trans. Willa and Edwin Muir with Eithne Wilkins and Ernst Kaiser, Harmondsworth: Penguin, 1957.
Letters to Felice. Trans. James Stern and Elisabeth Duckworth, ed. Erich Heller and Jürgen Born, Harmondsworth: Penguin, 1978.
The Diaries of Franz Kafka. Trans. Joseph Kresh and Martin Greenberg, ed. Max Brod, Harmondsworth: Penguin, 1972.
Letters to Friends, Family, and Editors. Trans. Richard and Clara Winston, ed. Max Brod, New York: Schocken, 1977.
Kawin, Bruce. *Telling it Again and Again: Repetition in Literature and Film*. Ithaca and London: Cornell University Press, 1972.
Khan, M. Masud R. 'The Concept of the Cumulative Trauma'. In *The Privacy of the Self*, London: The Hogarth Press and the Institute of Psychoanalysis, 1974, pp. 42–58.
'On Symbiotic Omnipotence'. In *The Privacy of the Self*, pp. 82–92.
'Montaigne, Rousseau and Freud'. In *The Privacy of the Self*, pp. 99–111.
'The Becoming of a Psychoanalyst'. In *The Privacy of the Self*, pp. 112–28.
'"To Hear with Eyes": Clinical Notes on Body as Subject and Object'. In *The Privacy of the Self*, pp. 234–50.
Kristeva, Julia. *Histoires d'amour*. Paris: Denoël, 1983.
Lacan, Jacques. 'Les complexes familiaux dans la formation de l'individu'. In *La Vie mentale*, tome VIII, *Encyclopédie Française*, ed. Henri Wallon, Paris: Larousse, 1938, 8.40–8.42–8.
'Le stade du miroir comme formateur de la fonction du Je'. In *Ecrits*, Paris: Seuil, 1966, pp. 93–100. (Trans. by Alan Sheridan as 'The Mirror Stage as Formative of the Function of the I', in *Ecrits: A Selection*, London: Tavistock Publications, 1977. pp. 1–7.)
'La signification du phallus'. In *Ecrits*, pp. 685–95.
Le Séminaire, ed. Jacques-Alain Miller, Paris: Seuil. Livre I: *Les Ecrits techniques de Freud* (1975); livre II: *Le Moi dans la théorie de Freud et dans la technique de la psychanalyse* (1978); livre III: *Les Psychoses* (1981); *Le Désir et son interprétation* (extracts published in *Ornicar?*, 24, autumn 1981, 5–31; 25, spring 1982, 11–36; 26/27, summer 1983, 5–44 – trans. by James Hulbert in *Literature and Psychoanalysis* (ed. Shoshana Feldman)); livre VII: *L'Éthique de la psychanalyse* (1986); livre VIII: *Sur le transfert* (unpublished); livre XI *Les Quatre concepts fondamentaux de la psychanalyse* (1973) (trans. by Alan Sheridan as *The Four Fundamental Concepts of Psychoanalysis*, London: The Hogarth Press and the Institute of Psychoanalysis, 1973).

List of works cited

Lacoue-Labarthe, Philippe. *La Poésie comme expérience*. Paris: Christian Bourgeois, 1986.

Laing, R. D. *The Voice of Experience*. London: Allen Lane, 1982.

Laplanche, J. *Vie et mort en psychanalyse*. Paris: Flammarion, 1970. (Trans. by Jeffrey Mehlman as *Life and Death in Psychoanalysis*, Baltimore and London: Johns Hopkins University Press, 1976.)

Laplanche, J. and J.-B. Pontalis. 'Fantasme originaire, fantasmes des origines, origine du fantasme'. In *Les Temps Modernes*, 21 (1964), 1833–68.

The Language of Psychoanalysis. Trans. D. Nicholson-Smith, London: The Hogarth Press and the Institute of Psychoanalysis, 1980.

Leavy, Stanley A. 'The Recovery of the Past in Psychoanalysis'. In *The Psychoanalytic Dialogue*, New Haven and London: Yale University Press, 1980, pp. 86–117.

Leclaire, Serge. *Démasquer le réel*. Paris: Seuil, 1971.

On tue un enfant: un essai sur le narcissisme primaire et la pulsion de mort. Paris: Seuil ('Points' collection), 1975.

'Le psychanalyste à l'envers'. In *Rompre les charmes: recueil pour des enchantés de la psychanalyse*, Paris: InterEditions, 1981, pp. 9–13.

'Fragments de langue d'avant Babel'. In *Rompre les charmes*, pp. 77–90.

L'inconscient: une autre logique'. In *Rompre les charmes*, pp. 62–76.

Loewald, Hans W. 'Some Considerations on Repetition and Repetition Compulsion'. In *International Journal of Psychoanalysis*, 52 (1971), 59–66.

Lord, James. *A Giacometti Portrait*. London: Faber and Faber, 1980.

Luria, A. R. *The Mind of a Mnemonist*. Trans. Lynn Solotaroff, London: Jonathan Cape, 1969.

Malcolm, Janet. *Psychoanalysis: The Impossible Profession*. London: Pan/Picador, 1982.

In the Freud Archives. London: Jonathan Cape, 1984.

Mallarmé, Stéphane. *Œuvres complètes*. Paris: Gallimard (Bibliothèque de la Pléiade) 1945.

Mannoni, Maud. *L'Enfant arriéré et sa mère*. Paris: Seuil ('Points' collection), 1964.

Le Premier rendez-vous avec le psychanalyste. Paris: Denoël/Gonthier, 1965.

L'Enfant, sa 'maladie' et les autres. Paris: Seuil ('Points' collection), 1967. (Trans. by unacknowledged as *The Child, his 'Illness', and the Others*, Harmondsworth: Penguin University Books, 1973a.)

Le Psychiatre, son 'fou' et la psychanalyse. Paris: Seuil ('Points' collection), 1970.

Education impossible. Paris: Seuil, 1973b.

Un lieu pour vivre. Paris: Seuil, 1976.

La Théorie comme fiction. Paris: Seuil, 1979.

D'un impossible à l'autre. Paris: Seuil, 1982.

Le Symptôme et le savoir (soutenance). Paris: Seuil, 1983.

Un savoir qui ne se sait pas. Paris: Denoël, 1985.

Mannoni, Maud (ed.). *Enfance aliénée*. Paris: Denoël, 1984.

Bonneuil, seize ans après. Paris: Denoël, 1986.

Mannoni, Maud and Guy Seligmann. *Secrète enfance*. Paris: EPT, 1979.

Mannoni, Octave. 'L'amour de transfert et le réel'. In *Etudes Freudiennes*, 19–20 (1982), 7–13.

List of works cited

Masson, Jeffrey. *Freud: The Assault on Truth: Freud's Suppression of the Seduction Theory.* London: Faber and Faber, 1984.

Michalski, Elaine and Maurice Cagnon. 'Marguerite Duras: vers un roman de l'ambivalence'. In *French Review: Journal of the American Association of Teachers of French*, 51, no. 3 (1978), 368–76.

Miller, Jacques-Alain. 'Suture: Elements of the Logic of the Signifier'. Trans. Jacqueline Rose, in *Screen*, 18, no. 4 (1977–8), 24–34.

Miller, J. Hillis. *Fiction and Repetition: Seven English Novels.* Oxford: Basil Blackwell, 1982.

Miller, Milton. *Nostalgia: A Psychoanalytic Study of Marcel Proust.* Boston: Houghton Mifflin Company, 1956.

Mitchell, Juliet and Jacqueline Rose (eds.). *Feminine Sexuality, Jacques Lacan and the 'Ecole freudienne'.* London: Macmillan, 1982.

M'Uzan, Michel de and J.-B. Pontalis. 'Ecrire, psychanalyser, écrire: échange de vues'. In *Nouvelle revue de psychanalyse*, 16 (1977), 5–26.

Olivier, Christiane. *Les Enfants de Jocaste.* Paris: Denoël/Gonthier, 1980.

Pingaud, Bernard. 'Les contrebandiers de l'écriture'. In *Nouvelle revue de psychanalyse*, 20 (1979), 141–62.

Pinter, Harold. *The Proust Screenplay.* London: Eyre Methuen, 1978.

Pontalis, J.-B. *Frontiers in Psychoanalysis: Between the Dream and Psychic Pain.* Trans. Catherine Cullen and Philip Cullen, London: The Hogarth Press and the Institute of Psychoanalysis, 1981.

Poulet, Georges. 'Proust et la répétition'. In *L'Arc*, 47, (1972), 5–13.

Proust, Marcel. *Jean Santeuil*, with *Les Plaisirs et les jours.* Ed. Pierre Clarac, Paris: Gallimard (Bibliothèque de la Pléiade), 1971.

Pleasures and Regrets. Trans. Louise Varese, London: Dennis Dobson Limited, 1950.

Jean Santeuil. Trans. Gerard Hopkins, London: Weidenfeld and Nicolson, 1955.

Contre Sainte-Beuve, with *Pastiches et mélanges* and *Essais et articles.* Ed. Pierre Clarac, Paris: Gallimard (Bibliothèque de la Pléiade), 1971.

A la recherche du temps perdu. 3 vols., ed. Pierre Clarac and André Ferré, Paris: Gallimard (Bibliothèque de la Pléiade), 1954.

Remembrance of Things Past. 3 vols., trans. C. K. Scott Moncrieff and Terence Kilmartin, London: Chatto and Windus, 1981.

Quignard, Pascal. *Le Lecteur.* Paris: Gallimard, 1976.

Rabaté, Etienne. 'Watt à l'ombre de Plume – l'écriture du désoeuvrement'. In *Beckett avant Beckett*, ed. Jean-Michel Rabaté, Paris: Presses de l'Ecole Normale Supérieure, 1984, pp. 175–83.

Richard, Jean-Pierre. *Proust et le monde sensible.* Paris: Seuil, 1974.

Robert, Marthe. *Franz Kafka's Loneliness.* Trans. Ralph Manheim, London: Faber and Faber, 1982.

Rohmer, Eric and Claude Chabrol. *Hitchcock: The First Forty-Four Films.* New York: Ungar, 1979.

Ross, Juhn Munder. 'Oedipus Revisited: Laius and the "Laius Complex"'. In *The Psychoanalytic Study of the Child*, 37 (1982), 169–200.

Rossner, Judith. *August.* London: Jonathan Cape, 1983.

Roudinesco, Elisabeth. *La Bataille de cent ans: histoire de la psychanalyse en France, vol. 2, 1925–1985.* Paris: Seuil, 1986.

List of works cited

Roustang, François. 'Du chapitre VII'. In *Nouvelle revue de psychanalyse*, 16 (1977), 65–95.

Sacks, Oliver. *Awakenings*. London: Duckworth, 1973.

Said, Edward. 'On Repetition'. In *The Literature of Fact: Selected Papers from the English Institute*, ed. Angus Fletcher, New York: Columbia University Press, 1976, pp. 135–58.

Sartre, Jean-Paul. *Words*. Trans. Irene Clephane, London: Hamish Hamilton, 1964.

Schafer, Roy. 'Narration in the Psychoanalytic Dialogue'. In *Critical Inquiry*, 7, no. 1 (1980), 29–55.

Segres, Elisabeth Bregman. 'Style in Beckett's Prose: Repetition and the Transformation of the Functions of Language'. Dissertation, University of California (Berkeley), 1976.

Shakespeare, William. *The Comedy of Errors*. Ed. R. A. Foakes ('The Arden Shakespeare'), London: Methuen, 1958.

A Midsummer Night's Dream. Ed. Harold F. Brooks ('The Arden Shakespeare'), London: Methuen, 1979.

As You Like It. Ed. Agnes Latham ('The Arden Shakespeare'), London: Methuen, 1975.

Hamlet. Ed. Harold Jenkins ('The Arden Shakespeare'), London: Methuen, 1982.

The Tempest. Ed. Frank Kermode ('The Arden Shakespeare'), London: Methuen, 1962.

King Lear. Ed. Kenneth Muir ('The Arden Shakespeare'), London: Methuen, 1972.

Shattuck, Roger. *Proust*. Glasgow: Collins/Fontana, 1974.

Shelley, Mary. *Frankenstein: Or the Modern Prometheus*. London: Oxford University Press, 1969.

Sollers, Philippe. *Paradis*. Paris: Seuil, 1981.

Sophocles. *King Oedipus*. In *The Theban Plays*, trans. E. F. Watling, Harmondsworth: Penguin, 1947.

Electra. In *Three Tragedies*, trans. H. D. F. Kitto, Oxford: Oxford University Press, 1962.

Spivak, Gayatri Chakravorty. Translator's Preface, in Jacques Derrida, *Of Grammatology*, Baltimore: Johns Hopkins University Press, 1974, pp. ix–xc.

Splitter, Randolph. *Proust's 'Recherche': A Psychoanalytic Interpretation*. London: Routledge and Kegan Paul, 1981.

Stanton, Martin. *Outside the Dream: Lacan and French Styles of Psychoanalysis*. London: Routledge and Kegan Paul, 1983.

Starobinski, Jean. 'Hamlet et Oedipe'. In *La Relation critique*, Paris: Gallimard, 1970, pp. 286–319.

Sterne, Laurence. *The Life and Opinions of Tristram Shandy*. Harmondsworth: Penguin, 1967.

Stevens, Wallace. *The Collected Poems of Wallace Stevens*. New York: Vintage, 1982.

Thomas, D. M. *The White Hotel*. Harmondsworth: Penguin, 1981.

Turkle, Sherry. *Psychoanalytic Politics: Freud's French Revolution*. London: Burnett Books and André Deutsch, 1979.

Wilden, Anthony. 'Lacan and the Discourse of the Other'. In *The Language of the Self*, trans. and ed. Anthony Wilden, New York: Delta, 1968, pp. 157–311.

List of works cited

'The Symbolic, the Imaginary and the Real'. In *System and Structure*, London: Tavistock Publications, 1972, pp. 1–30.

Winnicott, D. W. *Playing and Reality*. Harmondsworth: Penguin, 1974.

'The Theory of the Parent–Infant Relationship'. In *The Maturational Process and the Facilitating Environment*, London: The Hogarth Press and the Institute of Psychoanalysis, 1965, pp. 37–55.

Winton, Alison. *Proust's Additions: The Making of 'A la recherche du temps perdu'*. Cambridge: Cambridge University Press, 1977.

Wolfson, Louis. *Le Schizo et les langues, ou la phonétique chez le psychotique*. Paris: Gallimard, 1970.

Index of names (with principal works) and concepts

Index

Index

Index

Index